Rangers and Outlaws

Rangers and Outlaws
Two accounts of the Old Texas Frontier

ILLUSTRATED

Six Years With the Texas Rangers, 1875 to 1881
James B. Gillett

Life and Adventures of Sam Bass the Notorious
Union Pacific and Texas Train Robber
Sam Bass

Rangers and Outlaws
Two accounts of the Old Texas Frontier
Six Years With the Texas Rangers, 1875 to 1881
by James B. Gillett
Life and Adventures of Sam Bass the Notorious Union Pacific and Texas Train Robber
by Sam Bass

ILLUSTRATED

FIRST EDITION

Leonaur is an imprint of Oakpast Ltd
Copyright in this form © 2022 Oakpast Ltd

ISBN: 978-1-915234-02-5 (hardcover)
ISBN: 978-1-915234-03-2 (softcover)

http://www.leonaur.com

Publisher's Notes

The views expressed in this book are not necessarily those of the publisher.

Contents

Six Years With the Texas Rangers, 1875 to 1881 7

Life and Adventures of Sam Bass the Notorious Union Pacific and Texas Train Robber 195

SERGEANT J. B. GILLETT, TEXAS RANGER
IN 1879

Six Years With the Texas Rangers,
1875 to 1881

Contents

Foreword	13
The Making of a Ranger	15
The Texas Rangers	25
I Join the Rangers	34
My First Brush With Indians	43
The Mason County War	52
Major Jones and His Escort	57
The Horrell-Higgins Feud	70
Service With Reynolds, the Intrepid	79
Sam Bass and His Train Robber Gang	98
A Winter of Quiet and a Transfer	114
The Salt Lake War and a Long Trek	119
Our First Fight With Apaches	129
Scouting in Mexico	136
Treacherous Braves, a Faithful Dog, and a Murder	142
Victorio Becomes a Good Indian	149
Some Undesirable Recruits	156
Last Fight Between Rangers and Apaches	163
An International Episode	171
Last Scoutings	180
Fruits of Ranger Service	187

To My Old Ranger Comrades
Wherever They May Be

James B. Gillett. From a photograph taken in 1925.

Foreword

To write a true and complete history of the Texas Rangers as a state organisation would require much time and an able historian. I am not a historian and could not undertake such an exhaustive treatise, which would fill several volumes the size of this, and it is only at the earnest solicitation of my children, frontier friends, and old comrades that I have undertaken to write a short history of the rangers during the years I served with them. This little volume, then, has only the modest aim of picturing the life of the Texas Rangers during the years 1875-1881. I cannot, at this late date, recount in detail all the scouts that were made while I was in the service. I have, therefore, confined myself principally to the description of those in which I was a participant. Naturally, I remember those the best.

It has been said that truth never makes very interesting reading. Of the accuracy of this *dictum* I leave my readers to judge, for I have told my story just as I remember it, to the very best of my ability and without any effort to embroider it with imagination. If I can interest any of my old ranger comrades or even just one little boy that loves to read about a real frontier, I will feel amply repaid for all the time, trouble and expense expended in presenting this work.

I wish sincerely to thank Miss Mary Baylor for placing at my disposal all the books and papers of her distinguished father, Captain G. W. Baylor. And I would be an ingrate, indeed, did I fail here to record my obligation to my wife without whose inspiration and sympathetic encouragement this book had never been written.

That I might show the training of the typical Texas Ranger, I have ventured to include a short biography of my own life up to the time I became a ranger, June 1, 1875.

Friendly Enemies: Meeting of Sergeant Gillett and Herman Lehman at San Antonio in 1924.

Chapter 1

The Making of a Ranger

The greatest shaping force in human life is heredity, and from my father I inherited my love of the open frontier and its life of danger and excitement. This inheritance was further strengthened by environment and training, and finally led me to embrace the life of the Texas Ranger. My father, James S. Gillett, was himself a frontiersman, though born in the quieter, more settled east. At a very early age his parents emigrated from his birthplace in Kentucky and moved to Missouri. Here, after a short time, they died and the young orphan lived with a brother-in-law. When still quite a youth my father, with three other adventurous Missourians, set out on an expedition to Santa Fe, New Mexico. While passing through Indian Territory, now the State of Oklahoma, the little party was captured by the Osage Indians. Fortunately for the youngsters, their captors did them no harm, but turned them loose after two weeks' imprisonment in the redskin camp.

Despite this first setback my father persevered and reached Santa Fe. Here he lived several years and mastered the Spanish language. Not long afterward the emigrating fever again caught him up and he journeyed to Van Buren, Arkansas. While living there he studied law and was admitted to the bar. Shortly thereafter he removed to Paris, Texas, from which he was elected to the Texas Legislature as representative for Lamar and adjoining counties.

When Texas entered the Union and brought on the Mexican War with the United States, my father enlisted in 1846, and rose to the rank of major. In 1854, he was Adjutant-General of Texas. Between 1859, and 1860, during the governorship of Sam Houston, my father was quartermaster of a battalion of rangers, thus making it natural that I should also feel drawn toward this famous organisation.

At the beginning of the Civil War my father was beyond military age—he was born in 1810—but as the South became hard pressed for men he enlisted in the spring of 1864, and served in Captain Carington's company until the end of the war.

In 1850, a few years before he became adjutant-general, my father married Miss Bettie Harper, then a resident of Washington County, Texas. My mother's father, Captain Harper, was a southern planter who emigrated from North Carolina between 1846, and 1848, and, settling in Washington County, established a Dixie plantation with a hundred slaves. My mother was a highly cultivated and refined woman. On her marriage she brought several negro servants with her to her new home in Austin. Of her union with my father five children were born. The first two, both boys, died in infancy. I was the fourth child born to my parents, and first saw the light of day in Austin, Texas, on November 4, 1856. An older sister, Mary, and a younger, Eva, survived to adulthood.

At the close of the Civil War my father returned to his family pretty well broken in health and probably also in spirit. His slaves were all freed and his land holdings, about two hundred acres of cedar land, some five or six miles from Austin, and a tract of pine land in Grimes County, Texas, were not very productive. There was not much law practice in Austin in the early post-war days, but my father set to work resolutely to provide for his family. Though I did not realise it then, I now know that he had a hard struggle. I was only eight and a half years old when father returned to us from the Confederate Army, but I remember he used to amuse himself by relating to us vivid accounts of his Indian fighting and frontier adventures. What heredity gave me a predilection for was strengthened by these narratives, and I early conceived a passionate desire to become a frontiersman and live a life of adventure.

In those early days in Texas there were no free schools in Austin, so my father sent the three of us, Mary, Eva, and myself, to the pay schools. None of these was very good, and I lost nearly two years at a German school, trying to mix German and English. I have never been of a studious nature—the great out of doors always called to me, and I found the desk's dead wood particularly irksome. When school closed in the early summer of 1868, like some of Christ's disciples, I went fishing and never attended school an hour thereafter. For books I substituted the wide-open volume of nature and began the life of sport and freedom that was to prepare me later for service with the rangers.

As poor as he was my father always kept a pony, and I learned to ride almost before I could walk. Raised on the banks of the Colorado River, I learned to swim and fish so long ago that I cannot now remember when I was unable to do either. I fished along the river with a few hand lines and used to catch quantities of *gaspergou* or drums. These were fine fish and sold readily on the streets of Austin, so I soon saved money enough to buy a small skiff or fishing boat. I now bought a trot line with a hundred hooks and began fishing in real earnest. About five or six miles below Austin on the Colorado was Mathews' mill. Just below the dam of this mill the fishing was always good, and here I made my fishing grounds. I had a large dry goods box with inch auger holes bored in it. This box, sunk in the river and secured by a rope tied to a stob, made a capital trap, and into it I dropped my fish as they were caught. In this way I kept them alive and fresh until I had enough to take into town.

Many free negroes were farming along the banks of the Colorado, and I would hire a pony of them for twenty-five cents a trip when I was ready to take my catch into town. Many times, I have left the river by starlight and reached the Old Market House at Austin at dawn, spread out a gunny sack, bunch my fish and be ready for the first early marketers. I kept up my fishing until the fish stopped biting in the fall of 1868.

Confederate soldiers returning home from the war brought with them many old Enfield muskets. These were smooth bore and chambered one large ball and three buckshot. These old guns, loaded with small shot, were fine on birds and squirrels, but they had one serious objection—they would kick like a mule. As the boys used to say, they "would get meat at both ends!" A day's shooting with one of these muskets would leave one's shoulder and arm black and blue for a week.

When fishing failed, I decided to become a hunter, and bought one of these old guns for $3.50. It was as long as a fence rail, and at my age I could not begin to hold it out and shoot off hand, so I had to use a rest. The Enfield musket had the longest barrel I ever saw on a gun, and the hammer was as long as a man's hand. I could cock my gun with both hands, but if I failed to get a shot, I was not strong enough to let the hammer down without letting it get away, so I had to carry it cocked to keep from losing the cap. I would take it off the tube and put it in my pocket until I had a chance for another shot. I remember once when I cocked my musket, I could see no cap on the tube and, thinking it had fallen off, I pulled the trigger. The cap had stuck up in the old hammer and the gun roared like a cannon. I was always sure to look for the cap after this. I did not make much headway using this kind of weapon, but it taught me the use and danger of firearms—a knowledge I was to find very useful in later years.

When fishing opened up in the spring of 1869, I returned to my fishing lines, and in the fall of the same year I bought a double-barrelled shotgun for $12. With it I killed quail, ducks and other small game, all of which I sold on the streets of Austin. By the fall of 1870, I was fourteen years old and could handle a gun rather well for one of my age.

Early that winter wild geese came south by the hundreds. I used to hunt them down the Colorado River, ten or twelve miles below Austin. The birds would feed in the cornfields in the early morning, then flock to the sand bars in the river during the middle of the day. There was nothing silly about those geese, for they were smart enough to frequent only the big islands, three or four hundred yards from any cover.

It was impossible to reach them with any kind of a shotgun. I used to slip up to them as close as I could and watch them for hours, trying to think of some plan to get within gun shot of them. I saw as many as a thousand geese on those bars at a single time. I have thought regretfully of those birds many times since, and have wished I could have shot into one of those flocks with a modern rifle—I could have killed a dozen geese at a shot.

In the spring of 1871, I had my first trip to the frontier of Texas. My father traded some of his Grimes County pine land for a bunch of cattle in Brown County, and took me with him when he went to receive the herd. This was the first time I had ever been twenty-five miles from Austin. I was delighted with the trip, the people, and the country. Those big, fine frontiersmen, each wearing a pair of six-shooters and most of them carrying a Winchester, fired my boyish imagination. Their accounts of frontier life and their Indian tales fascinated me. I wanted to stay right there with them and lost all interest in ever living in town again. During the same year my father drove several bunches of cattle to Austin and I helped him on those drives. Thus I began to be a cowboy—my first step toward the life of the open, upon which I had set my heart.

In the summer of 1872, my mother's health began to fail and my father took her to Lampasas Springs. The water seemed to help her so much that he decided to make Lampasas our home. At that time Lampasas County was strictly a cattle country, but there was not much cow hunting during the winter in those days. The cattlemen and the cowboys spent a good deal of time in town just having a good time. During this period, I became well acquainted with them. In the spring of 1873, my father made a trip back to Austin on some business. The frontier had been calling to me ever since my first visit there, and I now took advantage of my father's absence to slip out to Coleman County, at that time on the frontier of Texas.

Monroe Cooksey and Jack Clayton had bought a bunch of cattle in Coleman County and I saw the outfit when it left Lampasas. I was slightly acquainted with most of the men in this outfit, so I decided to follow it and try to get work. It was an Indian country every step of the way, and I was afraid to make the trip alone. In a day or two I met a man named Bob McCollum. He was hauling a load of flour to Camp Colorado and let me travel with him. I bade my mother and sisters goodbye and did not see them again until the next December.

We reached old Camp Colorado without mishap in about five days. Clayton and Cooksey's outfit was there loading up supplies for the spring work. I stood around watching the cowboys making their preparations, but lacked the courage to ask them for work. Finally, the outfit started down on Jim Ned Creek to camp for dinner. I went with the men and at last got up spunk enough to ask Mr. Monroe Cooksey for a job. He looked at me for a minute and then asked, "What kind of work can a boy of your size do?"

I told him I was willing to do anything a boy of my age could do. He made no reply and we went on and camped for dinner. After dinner the men made ready to go over on Hoard's Creek to camp for the night. The boys made a rope corral and began to catch their mounts. I just stood there like an orphan watching them. Presently Mr. Cooksey dashed his rope on a heavy-set bay horse. The animal showed the whites of his eyes, made a rattling noise in his nose and struggled so violently that it took three men on the rope to hold him. Mr. Cooksey then turned to me and said, "Here, boy, if you can ride this —— (giving an unmentionable name to the horse) you have a job cinched."

I turned, grabbed my saddle, bridle and blanket and started to the animal. An elderly man in the outfit headed me off.

"Young man," he said, "this is an old spoiled horse, and unless you are a mighty good rider you had better not get on him."

I brushed him aside.

"Pshaw, I'm hunting work, and while I'm not a broncho buster, I will make a stab at riding him if he kills me."

By this time one of the boys had caught the horse by both ears and was holding him fast. They threw my saddle on him, tightened up the cinch, and finally, after much trouble, got the bridle on him and lifted me into the saddle. When I had fixed myself as best I could they let the animal go. He made two or three revolting leaps forward and fell with his feet all doubled up under him.

Mr. Cooksey seemed to realise the danger I was in, and shouted to me to jump off. Before I could shake myself loose the old horse had scrambled to his feet and dashed off in a run. I circled him around to the remuda and rode him until night without further trouble. I had won my job, but it was a dirty trick for a lot of men to play on a boy, and a small boy at that. However, to their credit, I wish to say they never put me on a bad horse again but gave me the best of gentle ponies to ride.

Our first work was to gather and deliver a herd of cattle to the Horrell boys, then camped on Home Creek. We worked down to the Colorado River, and when we were near old Flat Top ranch the men with the outfit left me to drive the remuda down the road after the mess wagon while they tried to find a beef. I had gone only a mile or two when I saw a man approaching me from the rear. As he came up, I thought he was the finest specimen of a frontiersman I had ever seen. He was probably six feet tall, with dark hair and beard. He was heavily armed, wearing two six-shooters and carrying a Winchester in front of him and was riding a splendid horse with a wonderful California saddle. He rode up to me and asked whose outfit it was I was driving. I told him Cooksey and Clayton's. He then inquired my name. When I told him he said, "Oh, yes; I saw your father in Lampasas a few days ago and he told me to tell you to come home and go to school."

I made no reply, but just kept my horses moving. The stranger then told me his name was Sam Gholston. He said it was dangerous for one so young to be in a bad Indian country and unarmed, that the outfit should not have left me alone, and counselled me to go back to my parents. I would not talk to him, so he finally bade me goodbye and galloped off. His advice was good, but I had not the least idea of going home—I had embraced the frontier life.

The Cooksey and Clayton outfit did not stay in the cow business long. After filling their contract with the Horrell boys they sold out to Joe Franks. I suppose I was sold along with the outfit, at least I continued to work for Mr. Franks. A kinder heart than that of Joe Franks never beat in a human breast. He was big of stature and big of soul.

He seemed to take an interest in his youthful cowpuncher, and asked me where I was raised and how I came to be away out on the frontier. As cold weather came on that fall, he gave me one of his top coats. It made a pretty good overcoat for me and came down quite to my knees. The sleeves were so long I could double them up and hold my bridle reins, and in one garment I had both coat and gloves.

During the summer of 1873, John Hitsons, Sam Gholston and Joe Franks were all delivering cattle to old John Chislom, whose outfit was camped on the south side of the Concho River, about where the town of Paint Rock now stands. The other outfits were scattered along down the river about half a mile apart. There were probably seventy-five or a hundred men in the four camps and at least five hundred horses. One evening just after dark the Indians ran into Gholston's outfit, captured about sixty head of horses and got away with them. The redskins and the cowboys had a regular pitched battle for a few moments, probably firing two hundred shots.

This fight was in plain view of our camp and I saw the flash of every gun and heard the Indians and the cowboys yelling. One of Mr. Gholston's men received a flesh wound in the leg and several horses were killed. Two nights later the Indians ran upon Franks' outfit and tried to take our horses. Bob Whitehead and Pete Peck were on guard and stood the redskins off. We saved our horses by keeping them in a pen for the remainder of the night. I was beginning to get a taste of frontier life early in the game.

For years cattle had drifted south into Menard and Kimble Counties, and Joe Franks was one of the first of the Coleman County outfits to go south into the San Saba and Llano country. He worked the Big and Little Saline Creeks, the Llano and San Saba Rivers and found many of his cattle down there. By the last of November, he had about finished work for the year, and, gathering three hundred fat cows to drive to Calvert, Texas, he left John Banister down on the Big Saline to winter the horses.

I passed through Lampasas with these cows, and saw my mother and sisters for the first time in nine months. When we reached Bell County a cow buyer met us and bought the cows at $10 per head. He just got down off his horse, lifted a pair of saddle bags off and counted out three thousand dollars in twenty-dollar gold pieces, and hired some of the boys to help him drive the cattle into Calvert. Mr. Franks, with most of the outfit, turned back to Lampasas. When he settled with me Mr. Franks owed me just $200, and he handed me ten twenty-dollar gold pieces. It was the most money I had ever earned and almost the greatest amount I had seen in my life.

I spent December and January at home, and early in February, 1874, I started back to Menard County with Mr. Franks, as he was anxious to begin work as early in the spring as possible. When we reached Parsons Ranch on the Big Saline, we learned that the Indians had stolen all his horses—seventy-five or eighty head, and he had left only eight or ten old ponies. Mr. Franks sent Will Banister and myself back to Coleman County to pick up ten or twelve horses he had left there the year before, while he himself returned to Lampasas and Williamson Counties to buy horses.

This trip from Menard County to Coleman County, a distance of about one hundred and fifty miles, was rather a hazardous trip for two boys to make alone. However, we were both armed with new Winchesters and would have been able to put up a stiff fight if cornered. Our ponies were poor and weak, so that it would have been impossible for us to have escaped had we met a band of Indians. And this is what we came very near doing.

There was no road from Menard to Coleman at that time, so we just travelled north. I had cow hunted over most of that country the year before and knew by landmarks pretty well how to go. We reached the head of Big Brady Creek one evening while a cold north wind was blowing. We camped for the night right down in the bed of a dry creek to get out of the wind. We saddled up next morning and had not gone more than a hundred and fifty yards from camp before we discovered where sixteen or seventeen Indians had just gone along—at least there was that number of pony tracks. These redskins had hopped a skunk, gotten down and killed it with a chunk of wood. When we found the body, it had scarcely quit bleeding. We saw *moccasin* tracks as if the savages had all gotten off their ponies for a few moments. Banister and I made the trip safely, and returned to Menard County early in March. Mr. Franks soon came with a new bunch of horses, and we went right to work gathering and delivering cattle.

About the first of June, Bee Clayton came to the outfit from Lampasas County and told me my father had been dead more than a month. Mr. Franks settled with me and I started for home the next day. Upon reaching Lampasas I began work with Barrett and Nicholls' outfit. They were the biggest cattle owners in that country and ran three large outfits, one in Llano County, one in San Saba County, and another in Lampasas. I worked with the last mentioned outfit that I might be near my mother and sisters.

I had now become familiar with most aspects of frontier life. I had cow punched and seen Indian raids, but I had not yet met the Texas "bad man"—the murderer and the bandit. My education was not long neglected, for it was while working with Barrett and Nicholls that I made my acquaintance with gentry of that ilk. One day five or six of our boys were sitting down in a circle eating on a side of calf ribs. One of the men, Jack Perkins, suddenly became involved in an altercation with Levi Dunbar, and, without warning, jerked out his six-shooter and shot him to death. In rising to my feet, I had my right shoulder powder burned.

I stayed with Barrett and Nicholls until they quit work about December 1, 1874. In those days' cattle were not worked much in the winter months, so I spent the winter at home. By spring I had become as restless as a bear and longed to get back to the frontier. Finally, I could stand the idleness no longer and told my mother I was going back to Menard County to work for Mr. Franks. I reached the town of Menardville early in March, 1875. There I learned that Joe Franks was then at work on South Llano in Kimble County, about sixty miles from Menard. Wess Ellis had just bought the Rufe Winn stock of cattle and was ready to start on a cow hunt. He wanted me to work for him, declaring he could pay me as much as Joe Franks or anybody else, so I hired to him for $30 a month—the top wages for a cowboy at that time.

During the year I was at home a company of Texas Rangers commanded by Captain Dan W. Roberts had been stationed over on Little Saline. This company received its mail at Menardville, and I became acquainted with this famous organisation. Their free, open life along the frontier had fired me with longing to become one of them and join in their adventurous lives. In the spring of 1875, the Governor of Texas authorised Captain Roberts to increase his command to fifty men. Almost immediately Captain Roberts announced in Menardville and vicinity that he would enlist twenty good men on June 1st to bring his company to full strength. Here was my opportunity, and I decided I would be one of those twenty recruits.

General John B. Jones.

Chapter 2

The Texas Rangers

The Texas Rangers, as an organisation, dates from the spring of 1836. When the Alamo had fallen before the onslaught of the Mexican troops and the frightful massacre had occurred, General Sam Houston organised among the Texan settlers in the territory a troop of 1,600 mounted riflemen. This company, formed for the defence of the Texan borders, was the original Texas Ranger unit, and it is interesting to note that the organisation from its very inception to the present moment has never swerved from that purpose—the protection of Texan borders, whether such protection be against the Indian, the bandit or marauding Mexicans from beyond the Rio Grande. This little troop of rangers won everlasting laurels in its stand against Santa Anna at the Battle of San Jacinto.

When the Republic of Texas was organised in December, 1837, the new state found herself with an enormous frontier to protect. To the south was the hostile Mexico while to the west and northwest roved the Indian and the bandit. To furnish protection against such enemies and to form the nucleus of a national standing army the ranger troop was retained. During the seven years that Texas had to maintain her own independence before she was admitted into the American Union, her rangers repelled hordes of Mexicans, fought the murderous Apaches, Comanches, and Kiowas, and administered justice on a wholesale plan to a great number of outlaws and ruffians that had flocked pell-mell into the new Republic from the less attractive parts of the United States.

So vital was the service rendered by the rangers in protecting the lives and property of the settlers along the frontiers of the state that Texas retained twelve hundred rangers as mounted police for patrol of the Mexican border and as a safeguard against the savage redskins of the southwest. When the Civil War broke out between the North and the South, Texas was drawn into the conflict on the side of the Confederacy. General Con Terry, an old ranger, organised the famous body of men known as Terry's Texas Rangers. This command was composed almost exclusively of ex-rangers and frontiersmen. From Bull Run to Appomattox this ranger troop rendered gallant service, and lost seventy-five *per cent* of its original muster roll. General Sherman, in his *Memoirs*, speaks admiringly of the bravery of the rangers at the Battle of Shiloh.

Return to peace and the days of reconstruction did not do away with the necessity for the service that could only be rendered by the ranger. Banditry, Indian uprisings and massacres, cattle thievery, all flourished, for the bad man confidently expected the post-war turmoil would protect him from punishment for his misdeeds. He was to be undeceived, for the rangers effectively taught him that they were in the state for the purpose of protecting lives and property, and right royally did they perform that duty. From 1868, to 1873, the ranger companies were gradually reduced from one thousand to about three hundred men.

The Federal Government adopted a most unfortunate policy toward the Indians after the war. The tribes were removed to reservations and rationed as public charges. Unscrupulous dealers, in their desire for gain, illegally sold firearms to the Indians, and whenever a redskin massacred a frontiersman, he was sure to capture good weapons, so that they soon became well armed and very expert in handling their new weapons. As no attempt was made to confine them to the reservation limits, the redskins, under their native chiefs, were always sneaking off and raiding West Texas. These marauders stole thousands of horses and cattle, and did not hesitate to murder and scalp the defenceless people along the frontier. Numbers of women and children were carried off as captives, a very small proportion of which were subsequently ransomed. Repeated complaints to Washington brought no redress. Indeed, some of the government officials calmly declared that the Indians were doing no harm—it was white men disguised as redskins that caused the trouble!

In 1874, conditions along the frontier had become so acute that the need for an organised mounted police for the protection of the settlers against the continued Indian raids became apparent. As in the past the state looked again to her rangers. Early in 1874, during the administration of Governor Richard Coke, the first Democratic governor since secession, the Legislature appropriated $300,000 for frontier defence, thus authorising the formation of the Texas Rangers as now constituted. The governor immediately issued a call for four hundred and fifty volunteers. These were formed into six companies of seventy-five men each.

Each of these units was officered by a captain and a first and second lieutenant. The companies were designated A, B, C, D, E, and F, and received the official name of the Frontier Battalion of Texas Rangers. Major John R. Jones of Corsicana, Texas, was commissioned major of the command. At this time the captains received a salary of $100 per month, lieutenants $75, sergeants $50, and corporals and privates $40. Subsequently, as the Legislature continually sliced into the ranger appropriation, the pay of the private was reduced to only $30 a month, a mere pittance for the hazardous service demanded of them.

Early in 1874, the force took the field, and each company was assigned a definite territory along the frontier. Company "A," being the northernmost company, was camped on the main fork of the Brazos River; Company "F," the southernmost, was stationed on the Nueces River. The remaining four companies were posted along the line between the two commands mentioned about one hundred and twenty-five miles apart, so that the battalion of four hundred and fifty men was required to cover a frontier of between five and six hundred miles.

Major Jones was a very able commander, and quickly won the confidence of his men and of the people along the border he was sent to protect. The frontiersmen cooperated with him in every way possible, sending runners to the various ranger camps whenever an Indian trail was found or a bunch of horses stolen. During the very first six months of its existence nearly every company in the battalion had had an Indian fight and some of them two or three. This command finally cleared the Texas frontier of the redskins and then turned its attention to the other pests of the state—thieves, bandits, and fugitives from justice. In this work the ranger rendered service second to none, and became in an incredibly short time the most famous and the most efficient body of mounted police in the world.

Between 1865, and 1883, the Texas Rangers followed one hundred and twenty-eight Indian raiding parties, and fought the redskins in eighty-four pitched battles. During this same period, they recovered six thousand stolen horses and cattle and rescued three citizens carried off by Indians. In this period twelve rangers were killed. Despite this record of service, the Legislature at Austin could not always be made

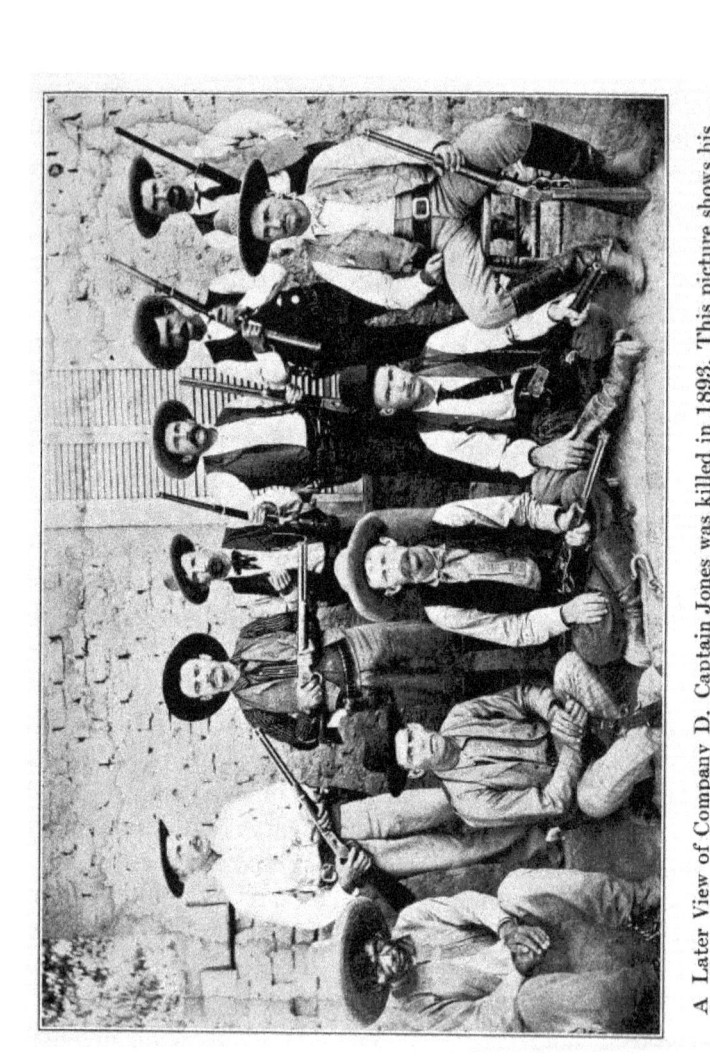

A Later View of Company D. Captain Jones was killed in 1893. This picture shows his successor in command, Captain John R. Hughes (seated on chair in right foreground), a group of his men, and a captive bandit.

to see the advantages—nay, the necessity—for a ranger force, and it was continually tinkering with the appropriations for the support of the force. When the appropriation was small the command was reduced to keep within the expenditure doled out by the parsimonious solons, and recruited to full strength whenever the lawmakers could be prevailed upon to increase the annual ranger budget.

By 1885, conditions had changed. Texas was no longer endangered by Indians, for the rangers had done much to convert the red devils into good Indians—that is, into dead ones. Although the Indians had utterly disappeared from the state, the activities of the rangers did not cease. The white "bad man" who had stirred up the first Indian troubles now began to plunder and murder his own race and indulge in every form of lawlessness. From hunting the murderous redskins, the rangers became now stalkers of the man-killers and those who despoiled their neighbours of their property.

The local legal authorities could not or would not handle this task themselves, so the rangers were made peace officers and given the right of arrest without warrant in any part of the state. They then became mounted constables to quell disorder, prevent crime and bring criminals to justice and assist the duly constituted authorities in every way possible. This new work was less romantic than the old Indian warfare, but it was every bit as dangerous and as necessary in the building up of the fast-developing state. As in every other task assigned him the ranger did his duty fearlessly and well.

Between 1889, and 1890, the rangers made five hundred and seventy-nine arrests, among them seventy-six murderers. With the coming of the railroads the rangers began to use them, as they permitted speed and the covering of greater distances than were possible on horseback. Moreover, commands could be dispatched from one part of the state to another as occasion demanded. This greater mobility led to larger usefulness and increasing number of arrests by the ranger forces.

The outbreak of the Spanish-American War found the ranger ready and anxious for service in the defence of the Union. Large numbers of them were enlisted in the world-famous Rough Riders.

General Miles, in speaking of the ranger service in Cuba, declared:

I have heard from the lips of reliable rangers, tales of daring that are incomparable. It is indeed too bad that the world knows so little about those marvellous men. There have been hosts of men among the Texas Rangers who were just as nervy as Davy Crockett, Travis, or Bowie at the Alamo.

Thanks to her rangers, Texas is now one of the most law-abiding, most orderly states in the Union. And, today, more than forty-six years since the organisation of the battalion, the state still maintains a tiny force of rangers numbering sixty-three officers and men. In 1920-21, the battalion was composed of a headquarters company and Companies A, C, D, E, and F. As in the beginning of its history, the force is stationed along the frontier.

The headquarters company, under command of Captain J. P. Brooks, was stationed at Austin and used for emergency calls. Company "A," stationed at Presidio, and commanded by Captain Jerry Gray, patrols the border between El Paso, Presidio, and Jeff Davis Counties and the back country southward. Company "E," Captain J. L. Anders, patrols the line of Presidio and Brewster Counties to the line of Terrell and Val Verde Counties and eastward. Company "F," under Captain W. W. Davis, was stationed at Del Rio and covered the line from Terrell and Val Verde Counties down the river to the line between Maverick, Dimmit and Webb Counties and the back country. Under the command of Captain William Ryan, Company "C" was located at Laredo and patrolled the line of Maverick, Dimmit and Webb Counties to the line of Zapata and Starr Counties and the back country, while Company "D," stationed at Brownsville, under Captain W. L. Wright, patrols from the line of Zapata and Starr Counties down the Rio Grande to its mouth and the adjacent back country.

Sketchy as has been this history, it will show a ranger record of continuous duty throughout the forty-six years of its existence in guarding the lives, the liberty and the property of Texas citizens. And the ranger has been content to perform his duty unheralded and almost unsung. Performance of duty, it matters not where it may lead him, into whatever desperate situation or howsoever dangerous the thing demanded, has always been the slogan of the organisation. For courage, patriotic devotion, instant obedience and efficiency, the record of the Texas Ranger has been equalled by no body of constabulary ever mustered.

Though formed into military units and officered as a soldier, the ranger is not a military man, for scant attention is paid to military law and precedent. The state furnished food for the men, forage for their horses, ammunition and medical attendance. The ranger himself must furnish his horse, his accoutrements and his arms. There is, then, no uniformity in the matter of dress, for each ranger is free to dress as he pleases and, in the garb, experience has taught him most convenient for utility and comfort.

A ranger, as any other frontiersman or cowboy, usually wears good heavy woollen clothes of any colour that strikes his fancy. Some are partial to corduroy suits, while others prefer buckskin. A felt hat of any make and colour completes his uniform. While riding, a ranger always wore spurs and very high-heeled boots to prevent his foot from slipping through the stirrup, for both the ranger and the cowboy ride with the stirrup in the middle of the foot. This is safer and less fatiguing on a long ride. For arms, the ranger after 1877, carried a Winchester rifle or carbine, a Colt's .45 revolver, and a Bowie knife. Two cartridge belts, one for Winchester and one for revolver ammunition, completed his equipment, and so armed he was ready to mount and ride.

"We live in the saddle and the sky is our roof," say the old rangers, and this is literally true. The rangers are perfect centaurs and almost live in the saddle. They take horse where they will and may arrest or search in any part of the state. There is very little of what a West Point graduate would call drill. A ranger is expected simply to be a good rider and a quick and accurate shot. Every one of them are skilled horsemen and crack shots. No crack cavalryman in any army can mount a horse more quickly or more expertly than a ranger, and he can keep a constant stream of fire pouring from his carbine when his horse is going at top speed and hit the mark nine times out of ten! Should a ranger drop anything on the ground that he wants he does not even check the speed of his horse, but, bending from the saddle as if he were made of India rubber, he picks up the object in full gallop.

While not on active duty the rangers amuse themselves in various ways. Some play cards, others hunt, while the studious spend their time over books and good literature. Horse racing is popular, and the fastest horse in the company is soon spotted, for the rangers match their mounts one against the other. At night around their camp fires the men are constantly telling stories of their own or some comrade's adventures that put to shame all the inventions of the imaginative fiction writers. But when on duty all this is changed. No pace is too quick, no task too difficult or too hazardous for him.

Night and day will the ranger trail his prey, through rain and shine, until the criminal is located and put behind the bars where he will not

Ready to Take the Field. From a photograph of Company D, Captain Frank Jones, taken in 1889. Captain Jones (seen at right of picture) and one-third of his men were subsequently killed in action.

again molest or disturb peaceful citizens. For bravery and endurance and steadfast adherence to duty at all times the ranger is in a class all to himself. Such was the old ranger, and such is the ranger of today. Is it surprising, then, that I was early attracted to the force and wished to join them in their open, joyous and adventurous life?

CHAPTER 3

I Join the Rangers

The fame of the Texas Rangers had, of course, become common knowledge among all Texans. Their deeds of adventure and their open, attractive life along the frontier, had always appealed to me, and I had long cherished the desire to enlist in the battalion. But the enlistment, as announced by Captain Roberts, would not be made until June 1, 1875, and I reached Menardville early in March. I had intended going on to join Mr. Franks' outfit, but, as explained in a previous chapter, I hired out to Mr. Ellis until I could enlist in Captain Roberts' company.

About the middle of May, 1875, Joe Franks had worked back over into Menard County. I wished to see my old friends in his outfit, and so went over to meet them. While there I mentioned that I was going to join the rangers. A cowboy named Norman Rodgers, who was working for Mr. Franks, said he would also like to join, so we decided we would go over to Captain Roberts together and see if we couldn't get him to recruit us into his company.

Rodgers and I rode over to the ranger camp beyond Menardville. Neither of us had ever been in such a camp before nor did we know anyone in the company. Of the first ranger we met we inquired where we could find the captain. His tent was pointed out to us and we went toward it.

"Jim," said Norman as we approached the tent, "you will have to do the talking."

Captain Roberts met us as we came up and invited us to be seated. I told him at once that we had come to enlist as rangers. He asked us our names, where we were working, and finally inquired if we had anyone that would recommend us. We had not thought of references, but told him that probably Mr. Franks or Mr. Ellis would stand for us, as they were well known and prominent cattlemen for whom we had worked.

Captain Roberts looked straight at me and said, "Did you say your name was Gillett?"

"Yes, Jim Gillett," I replied.

He then asked me where I was born, and I told him at Austin, Texas.

"Are you a son of James S. Gillett who was Adjutant-General under Governor Sam Houston?"

I told him I was.

"I have often heard my father, Buck Roberts, speak of your father," he said in a friendly tone.

Captain Roberts then asked us what kind of horses we had, telling us that a ranger was required to have a good a mount, for each man was allowed to have only one horse, which had to be a good one, that could be ridden every day for a month if necessary. I told the captain I had two good pony mares. He burst out laughing, and said a mare was not allowed in the service. He then told us to go and see what kind of a mount we could get, come back and let him inspect the animals. The captain never once said he would enlist us, but, as the interview was now over and he had not refused us, we went back to camp feeling very hopeful we would soon be rangers.

I secured a big black pony and Norman a grey one, not so large as mine but a much prettier horse. We returned to the ranger camp a few days later mounted on these ponies. The captain looked them over, said they were rather small but that he would accept them, and told us to be at his camp by May 31st to be sworn into the service. We left camp that evening all puffed up at the prospect of being Texas Rangers.

The last day of May arrived. Norman Rodgers and myself with many other recruits we had never seen before were at the ranger camp. On June 1, 1875, at 10 o'clock, we were formed in line, mounted, and the oath of allegiance to the State of Texas was read to us by Captain Roberts. When we had all signed this oath, we were pronounced Texas Rangers. This was probably the happiest day of my life, for I had realised one of my greatest ambitions and was now a member of the most famous and efficient body of mounted police in the world.

Immediately upon being sworn in the men were divided into messes, ten men to the mess, and issued ten days' rations by the orderly sergeant. These rations consisted of flour, bacon, coffee, sugar, beans, rice, pepper, salt and soda. No potatoes, syrup or lard was furnished, and each man had to supply his own cooking utensils. To shorten our bread, we used bacon grease. Beef was sometimes supplied the men, but wild game was so plentiful that but little other meat was required. Furthermore, each recruit was furnished a Sharps carbine, .50 calibre, and one .45 Colt's pistol. These arms were charged to each ranger, their cost to be deducted from our first pay. Our salary of $40 per month was paid in quarterly instalments. The state also supplied provender for the horses.

Though a ranger was forced to supply his own mount, the state undertook to pay for the animal if it were killed or lost in an Indian fight. To establish the impartial value of our animals, Captain Roberts marched us into Menardville and asked three citizens of the town to place a value on each man's mount. This was done, and I was highly gratified when old Coley, my mount, was appraised at $125. This formality over, the company was moved from Little Saline to Camp Los Moris, five miles southwest of Menardville, Texas. We were now ready to begin scouting for Indians.

As is usual under the same circumstances the new recruits came in for their share of pranks and mishaps. One raw rooky in my mess, fired with love of economy, undertook to cook ten days' rations for the whole mess at one time. He put a quantity of rice on the fire. Soon it began to boil and swell, and that surprised ranger found his rice increasing in unheard of proportions. He filled every cooking vessel in the mess with half-cooked rice, and still the kettle continued to overflow. In desperation he finally began to pour it on the ground. Even then he had enough rice cooked to supply the entire company.

Another recruit, anxious to test his new weapons, obtained Captain Roberts' permission to go hunting. He had not gone far from camp before he began firing at some squirrels. One of his bullets struck the limb of a tree and whizzed close to camp. This gave an old ranger an idea. He hastened after the hunter and gravely arrested him, declaring that the glancing bullet had struck a man in camp and that Captain Roberts had ordered the careless hunter's arrest. The veteran brought in a pale and badly scared recruit.

One of the favourite diversions of the old rangers was to make a newcomer believe that the state furnished the rangers with socks and start him off to the captain's tent to demand his share of free hosiery. The captain took these pranks in good part and assured the crestfallen applicant that the rangers were only playing a joke on him, while his tormentors enjoyed his discomfiture from a safe distance.

The Rangers at Home. From a photograph, taken in 1890, showing Captain Frank Jones at his mess, some visitors, and the cook.

When they had run out of jokes the rangers settled down to the regular routine of camp. Each morning the orderly sergeant had roll call, at which time he always detailed six or eight men with a non-commissioned officer to take charge of the rangers' horses and the pack mules until relieved the following morning by a new guard. The guard was mounted and armed and drove the loose stock out to graze. The horses were never taken far from camp for fear of being attacked by Indians, and also to keep them near at hand in case they were needed quickly.

The rangers not on guard spent their time as they wished when not on duty, but no man could leave the camp without the captain's permission. The boys played such games as appealed to them, horseshoe pitching and cards being the favourite diversions. As long as it did not interfere with a man's duty as a ranger, Captain Roberts permitted pony racing, and some exciting contests took place between rival horse owners. And hunting and fishing were always available, for woods and streams were stocked with game and fish.

I soon had cause to congratulate myself on my enlistment in Company "D," for I found Captain D. W. Roberts the best of company commanders. At the time I joined his command he was just thirty-five years of age, very slender and perhaps a little over six feet tall. His beard and hair were dark auburn. He was always neatly dressed and was kind and affable in manner—looking more like the dean of an Eastern college than the great captain he was.

Captain Roberts was a fine horseman and a good shot with both pistol and rifle. He was also a fine violinist and often played for the boys. He had been raised on the frontier and had such a great reputation as an Indian fighter that the Fourteenth Legislature of Texas presented him with a fine Winchester rifle for his gallantry in fighting the redskins. The captain had made a close study of the habits and actions of the Indians and had become such an authority that their life was an open book to him. This, of course, gave him a great advantage in following and fighting them, and under his able leadership Company "D" became famous. There was not a man in the company that did not consider it a compliment to be detailed on a scout with Captain Roberts.

In the latter part of the summer or early fall of 1875, Captain Roberts visited Colorado County, Texas, and returned with a bride, a Miss Lou Conway. Mrs. Roberts was a very refined and elegant lady, and soon adapted herself to the customs of the camp. She was with her husband on the San Saba River during the winter of 1875-76 and soon became as popular with the company as Captain Roberts himself.

Most people consider the life of the Texas Ranger hard and dangerous, but I never found it so. In the first place, the ranger was always with a body of well-armed men, more than a match for any enemy that might be met. Then, there was an element of danger about it that appealed to any red-blooded American. All of western Texas was a real frontier then, and for one who loved nature and God's own creation, it was a paradise on earth. The hills and valleys were teeming with deer and turkey, thousands of buffalo and antelope were on the plains, and the streams all over Texas were full of fish. Bee caves and bee trees abounded. In the spring time one could travel for hundreds of miles on a bed of flowers. Oh, how I wish I had the power to describe the wonderful country as I saw it then. How happy I am now in my old age that I am a native Texan and saw the grand frontier before it was marred by the hand of man.

The Lipans, Kickapoos, Comanches, and Kiowa Indians used to time their raids so as to reach the Texas settlements during the light of the moon so they would have moonlight nights in which to steal horses and make their getaway before they could be discovered. By morning, when their thefts became known, they would have a long lead ahead and be well out on their way into the plains and mountains. The captains of the ranger companies knew of this Indian habit, and accordingly kept scouts constantly in the field during the period of the raids. The redskins coming in from the plains where water was scarce, generally took the near cut to the headwaters of the Colorado, Concho, San Saba, Llanos, Guadalupe, and Nueces Rivers. By maintaining scouts at or near the heads of these streams the rangers frequently caught parties of Indians going in or coming out from the settlements, and destroyed them or recaptured the stolen stock.

The first light moon in June Captain Roberts ordered a detail of fifteen men in command of Sergeant James B. Hawkins to make a ten days' scout toward the head waters of the North Llano River. He was to select a secluded spot near old abandoned Fort Territ and make camp there. Each morning a scout of one or two men would be sent out ten or fifteen miles south and another party a like distance toward the north to hunt for Indian trails. The main body of rangers, keeping carefully concealed, was in readiness to take up an Indian trail at a moment's notice should one be found by the scouts.

Rangers on a Scout in the Big Bend Country, western Texas.

One morning Sergeant Hawkins ordered me to travel south from camp to the head draws of the South Llano and watch for pony tracks.

"Suppose the Indians get me?" I asked laughingly as I mounted my pony.

"It's your business to keep a sharp lookout and not let them catch you," he replied.

However, though I watched very carefully I could find no pony tracks or Indian trails.

We had with us on this scout Mike Lynch, a pure Irishman. Though he was old and grey-headed, he was a good ranger, and had much native wit. One morning it was Uncle Mike's turn to go on scout duty, but in a few hours, he was seen coming into camp with his horse, Possum, on the jump. He reported a fresh Indian trail about ten miles north of our camp. When asked how many pony tracks, he had counted, Lynch at once declared he had counted seventeen and thought there were more. As the Indians usually came in on foot or with as few ponies as they could get by on until they could steal others, Sergeant Hawkins suspected the tracks Lynch had seen were those of mustangs. The excited scout declared vehemently that the tracks were not those of wild horses but of Indians. The sergeant was just as positive that no Indian party was responsible for the trail, and the two had quite a heated argument over the tracks.

"But how do you know it is an Indian trail?" demanded Hawkins.

"Because I know I know," cried out Lynch in a loud voice.

That settled it. Horses were saddled and mules packed as quickly as possible, and the rangers marched over to the suspicious trail. When Sergeant Hawkins examined the trail, he soon discovered that the sign had been made by mustangs but could not convince the hard-headed Irishman until he followed the trail two or three miles and showed him the mustang herd quietly grazing under some shade trees. Uncle Mike did not mention Indian trail any more on that scout.

Though we did not find any trails or Indians the scouting party killed two black bear, several deer and about fifteen wild turkey.

Early in September, 1875, Captain Roberts again ordered Sergeant Hawkins to take fifteen men and make a ten days' scout on the Brady Mountains. To my great joy I was detailed on this expedition. When near the head of Scalp Creek, Menard County, on our return trip, the sergeant told the boys to keep a sharp lookout for a deer, as we would reach the San Saba by noon and would camp on that stream for the night. We had not travelled far before Ed Seiker killed a nice little spiked buck. We strapped him on one of the pack mules, and when we arrived at the river we came upon a flock of half-grown wild turkeys. Bill Clements leaped from his horse and killed six of them.

We then camped, hobbled and side-lined our horses and put a strong guard with them. While some of the boys were gathering wood for our fire, they found an old elm stump ten to twelve feet high with bees going in at the top. One of the rangers rode over to Rufe Winn's ranch and borrowed an axe and a bucket. When he returned, we cut the tree and got more honey than sixteen men could eat, besides filling the bucket with nice sealed honey, which we gave to Mrs. Winn in return for the use of her axe. Then, after dinner, out came fishing tackle and, using venison for bait, we caught more catfish than the entire crowd could eat.

Hunting conditions in those days were ideal. I have known a single scout to kill three or four bears on a single trip. The companies to the north of us were never out of buffalo meat in season. Then, in the fall, one could gather enough pecans, as fine as ever grew, in half a day to last the company a month. I have seen hundreds of bushels of the nuts go to waste because there was no one to gather them—besides they sold on the market for fifty cents per bushel. No wonder that a boy that loved the woods and nature was charmed and fascinated with the life of the Texas Ranger. It was a picnic for me from start to finish, and the six years I was with the battalion were the happiest and most interesting of my life.

But hunting and fishing and vacation scouts were not the sole duties of a ranger. Pleasure was abundant, but there were times when all these were laid aside. For the game guns and the fishing rod we exchanged our carbines and our six-shooters and engaged in hazardous expeditions after marauding redskins. I was soon to see this latter aspect of ranger life, for in the latter part of August, 1875, I became a real ranger and entered upon the real work of our battalion—that of protecting the frontier against the roving Indians and engaging them in regular pitched battles.

CHAPTER 4

My First Brush With Indians

The latter part of August, 1875, Private L. P. Seiker was sent on detached service to Fort Mason, about fifty miles due east of our camp. While there a runner came in from Honey Creek with the report that a band of fifteen Indians had raided the John Gamble ranch and stolen some horses within twenty-five steps of the ranch house. The redskins appeared on their raid late in the evening and the runner reached Mason just at dark.

Lam Seiker had just eaten his supper and was sitting in the lobby of the Frontier Hotel when the message came. He hurried to the livery stable, saddled his horse, Old Pete, and started on an all-night ride for the company. The nights in August are short, but Seiker rode into our camp about 8 o'clock the following morning and reported the presence of the Indians.

The company horses were out under herd for the day, but Captain Roberts sent out hurry orders for them. Sergeant Plunk Murray was ordered to detail fifteen men, issue them ten days' rations and one hundred rounds of ammunition each. Second Sergeant Jim Hawkins, Privates Paul Durham, Nick Donnelly, Tom Gillespie, Mike Lynch, Andy Wilson, Henry Maltimore, Jim Trout, William Kimbrough, Silas B. Crump, Ed Seiker, Jim Day, John Cupps and myself, under command of Captain Roberts, were selected as the personnel of the scout. As can be imagined I was delighted with my good fortune in getting on the party and looked forward with intense satisfaction to my first brush with Indians.

The mules were soon packed and by the time the horses reached camp the scout was ready. Sergeant Hawkins, as soon as the men had saddled their horses, walked over to the captain, saluted and told him the scout was ready. Before leaving camp Captain Roberts called to

Sergeant Murray and told him that he believed the Indians had about as many horses as they could well get away with, and that they would probably cross the San Saba River near the mouth of Scalp Creek and follow the high divide between the two streams on their westward march back into the plains.

If the redskins did not travel that way the captain thought they would go out up the Big Saline, follow the divide between the North Llano and San Saba Rivers westward and escape, but he was confident the band would travel up the divide north of Menardville. He determined to scout that way himself, and instructed Murray to send two rangers south over to the head waters of Bear Creek to keep a sharp lookout for the trail. These two scouts were to repeat their operations the next day, and if they discovered the Indian trail Murray was to make up a second scout and follow the redskins vigorously.

His plan outlined, Captain Roberts gave the order to mount, and we rode toward Menardville, making inquiry about the Indians. All was quiet at this little frontier village, so we crossed the San Saba River just below the town, and after passing the ruins of the Spanish Fort, Captain Roberts halted his men and prepared to send out trailers. Two of the best trailers in the command were ordered to proceed about four hundred yards ahead of the party and keep a close watch for pony tracks while they travelled due north at a good saddle horse gait. The main body of men, under the captain himself, would follow directly behind the outposts.

Our party had travelled about eight or nine miles when Captain Roberts' keen eyes discovered a lone pony standing with his head down straight ahead of us. He sighted the animal before the trailers did, and remarked to us that there the trail was. The outposts halted when they saw the pony and waited for us to come up. Sure enough, here was the Indian trail probably twenty yards wide. Captain Roberts dismounted and walked over the sign, scrutinising every pony track, bunch of grass and fallen leaf. He then examined the old pony. The animal was cut with a lance, with his back sore and his feet all worn out. It was then between 12 and 1 o'clock, and the captain thought the Indians had passed that way about sunrise, for the blood and sweat on the horse was now dry. The trail showed the raiders were driving rather fast and were probably thirty-five or forty miles ahead of us. The captain decided it would be a long chase and that we would just have to walk them down if we caught them at all.

There was no water on this divide so we took the trail without stopping for dinner. Captain Roberts had a fine saddle horse, Old Rock, and we followed the trail at a steady gait of five or six miles an hour. At sundown we reached the old government road that runs from Fort McKavett to Fort Concho. We were then about twelve or fifteen miles south of Kickapoo Springs, so we turned up the road, reaching the springs late at night. The horses had not had a drop of water since leaving the San Saba that morning, and, facing a hot August sun all day, the men were pretty well tired out when they reached camp, had supper and gotten to bed. We estimated we had ridden about sixty miles since leaving camp. During the day Captain Roberts' horse cast a shoe, so Tom Gillespie shod him by firelight, as it was the captain's intention to resume the trail at daylight.

The following morning Captain Roberts took a southwest course from Kickapoo Springs and paralleled the Indian trail we had left the evening before. It was late in the day before we picked the trail up again, and many of the boys were afraid we had lost it altogether, but the captain laughed at their fears and never doubted that we should find it again. The Indians, as their trail showed, were now travelling over a tolerably rough country, which made our progress slow. About noon we found some rainwater, and, as it was fearfully hot, we camped for dinner and to give the horses a short rest.

When the boys went out to catch their mounts, we found that we had camped right in a bed of rattlesnakes. Two of our horses had been bitten. Jim Day's Checo had a head on him as big as a barrel, while the captain's horse, Old Rock, had been bitten on his front leg just above the ankle, and it had swollen up to his body. Neither of the animals was able to walk. Jim Day could not be left alone in that Indian country, so Captain Roberts detailed Private Cupps to stay with Day until the horses died or were able to travel—in either case they were then to return to camp. The animals soon recovered and Day and Cupps beat us back to camp.

The pack loads were now doubled on one mule so Captain Roberts could ride the other. Reduced to thirteen men, we followed the Indians until night. It was a hard day on both men and beasts, so we camped where we found a little water in a draw that drained into the South Concho River. Considering the way, we had come, the captain thought we had covered sixty miles during the day's ride. We had two rather old men on the scout, Mike Lynch and Andy Wilson, and they were nearly all in. I awoke Andy at 2 a. m. to go on guard. The poor fellow was so stiff he could hardly stand, and I tried to get him to go back to bed, telling him I would stand his guard, but he was game, and in a few minutes hobbled out to the horses and relieved me.

Early in the morning we were up and travelling. The mule Captain Roberts was riding did not step out as fast as Old Rock had done, and the boys had an easier time keeping up. We camped at noon on just enough rain water to do us and took up the trail again after dinner. The trailers stopped suddenly, and as we rode up Captain Roberts asked what was the matter. They said it seemed as though the Indians at this point had rounded up the horses and held them for some cause or other.

The captain dismounted and swept the country with his field glasses. He circled around where the horses had been standing and found where a lone Indian had walked straight away from the animals. He followed the tracks to an old live oak tree that had been blown down. Then the reason for the stop became apparent: the Indians had sighted a herd of mustangs grazing just beyond this tree and the redskin had slipped up on them and killed a big brown mare. Captain Roberts picked up the cartridge shell the old brave had used and found it to be from a .50 calibre buffalo gun. We also found the mustang, from which the Indians had cut both sides of ribs and one hindquarter.

Captain Roberts was much elated, he said with a smile:—

Boys, we now have ninety-five chances out of a hundred to catch those Indians. They will not carry this raw meat long before stopping to cook some. We have followed them now over one hundred and fifty miles, and they have never stopped to build a fire. They are tired and hungry and probably know where there is water not far away.

He spoke with such confidence that I marvelled at his knowledge of the Indian habits.

We were now on the extreme western draw of the South Concho River, far above the point at which the water breaks out into a running stream. Finally, the trail led out on that level and vast tract of country between the head of South Concho and the Pecos on the west. These Indians turned a little north from the general direction they had been travelling, and all of a sudden, we came to some rock water holes.

Here the redskins had built three fires, cooked both sides of the mustang ribs and had picked them clean. From this high tableland, they could look back over their trail for fifteen miles. The captain thought they had been there early in the morning, as the fires were out and the ashes cold. We did not lose any time at this camp, but hurried on, following the trail until late in the evening, when the trailers again halted. When we came up, we found that the trail that had been going west for nearly two hundred miles had suddenly turned straight north.

Captain Roberts seemed to be puzzled for a time, and said he did not understand this move. About one mile north there was a small motte of *mesquite* timber. This he examined through his glasses, seeming to me to examine each tree separately. The trail led straight into these trees, and we followed it. In the *mesquite* timber we found the Indians had hacked some bushes partly down, bent them over, cut up the horse meat they had been carrying with them into tiny strips, strung it on the bushes and, building a fire beneath them, had barbecued their flesh. The redskins had made the prettiest *scafelo* for meat cooking I ever saw. We found plenty of fire here, and the captain was sure we would have an Indian fight on the morrow.

From the trees the trail swung west again. The redskins were travelling slowly now, as they evidently thought they were out of danger. Just before sundown the scout halted, and we were ordered not to let any smoke go up lest the band we were trailing should spot it and take alarm. As soon as we had cooked our supper Captain Roberts had the fires carefully extinguished. It had been a good season on the table lands and there were many ponds filled with water, some of them one hundred yards wide. We camped right on the edge of one of these big holes and where the Indians had waded into it the water was still muddy. The boys were cautioned not to strike a match that night as we were certain the Indians were not far ahead of us. We covered between forty and fifty miles that day.

Camp was called at daybreak. We dared not build a fire, so we could have no breakfast. We saddled our horses and again took the trail. Old Jennie, the pack mule, was packed for the last time on earth, for she was killed in the fight that shortly followed. As soon as it was light enough to see a pony track two of the boys traced it on foot and led their horses, the remainder of our party coming along slowly on horseback. By sunrise we were all riding and following the trail rapidly, eager to sight the marauding thieves. We had travelled some five or six miles when Paul Durham called Captain Roberts' attention to a dark object ahead that looked as if it were moving. The captain brought his field glasses to bear on the object specified and exclaimed it was the Indians.

He ordered the boys to dismount at once, tighten their cinches, leave their coats and slickers and make ready to fight. As we carried out this order a distressing stillness came over the men. Captain Roberts and Sergeant Hawkins were the only ones of our party that had ever been in an Indian fight, and I suppose the hearts of all of us green, unseasoned warriors beat a little more rapidly than usual at the prospect of soon smelling powder. Captain Roberts called out to us in positive tones not to leave him until he told us to go, and not to draw a gun or pistol until ordered, declaring that he wanted no mistake on the eve of battle. He ordered the pack mule caught and led until we went into the fight, when she was to be turned loose.

The Indians were out on an open prairie dotted here and there with small skirts of *mesquite* timber. The captain thought our only chance was to ride double file straight at them in the hope they would not look back and discover us. We moved forward briskly, and as luck would have it, we got within four or five hundred yards of the redskins before they sighted us.

At once there was a terrible commotion. The Indians rounded up their stock and caught fresh mounts almost in the twinkling of an eye. Then, led by their old chief, they took positions on a little elevated ground some two hundred yards beyond the loose horses. The redskins stationed themselves about fifteen or twenty feet apart, their battle line when formed being about one hundred yards wide. As each warrior took his station he dismounted, stood behind his horse and prepared to fire when given the signal.

The captain with a smile turned to us and said, "Boys, they are going to fight us. See how beautifully the old chief forms his line of battle."

From a little boy I had longed to be a ranger and fight the Indians. At last, at last, I was up against the real thing and with not so much as an umbrella behind which to hide. I was nervous. I was awfully nervous.

We were now within one hundred steps of the redskins. Then came the order to dismount, shoot low and kill as many horses as possible. The captain said as we came up that every time, we got an Indian on foot in that country we were sure to kill him. With the first shot everybody, Indian and ranger, began firing and yelling.

In a minute we had killed two horses and one Indian was seen to be badly wounded. In another minute the redskins had mounted their horses and were fleeing in every direction. Captain Roberts now ordered us to mount and follow them. The roar of the guns greatly excited my pony and he turned round and round. I lost a little time in mounting, but when I did get settled in the saddle, I saw an Indian running on foot. He carried a Winchester in his hand and waved to another Indian who was riding. The latter turned and took the one on foot up behind him.

As they started away for a race, I thought to myself that no grass pony on earth could carry two men and get away from me and Old Coley. The Indians had a good animal, but I gradually closed on them. The redskin riding behind would point his gun back and fire at me, holding it in one hand. I retaliated by firing at him every time I could get a cartridge in my old Sharps carbine. I looked back and saw Ed Seiker coming to my aid as fast as old Dixie would run. He waved encouragement to me.

Finally, the old brave ceased shooting, and as I drew a little closer, he held out his gun at arm's length and let it drop, probably thinking I would stop to get it. I just gave it a passing glance as I galloped by. He then held out what looked to be a fine rawhide rope and dropped that, but I never took the bait. I just kept closing in on him. He now strung his bow and began using his arrows pretty freely. Finally, he saw I was going to catch him, and turned quickly into a little grove of *mesquite* timber. I was considered a fairly good brush rider, and as we went in among the trees, I drew right up within twenty steps of the brave, jumped from my mount and made a sort of random shot at the horse, Indian and all. The big .50 calibre bullet struck the Indian pony just where its head couples on its neck, passed through the head and came out over the left eye. It killed the horse at once and it fell forward twenty feet.

The old warrior hit the ground running, but I jumped my horse and ran after him. As I passed the dead horse, I saw the front rider struggling to get from under it. To my surprise I saw he was a white boy between fifteen and sixteen years old with long bright red hair.

By this time Ed Seiker had arrived and was dismounting. The fugitive warrior now peeped from behind a tree and I got a fine shot at his face but overshot him six inches, cutting off a limb just over his head. He broke to run again, and as he came into view Ed placed a bullet between his shoulders. He was dead in a minute. As Ed and I walked up to the dead Indian we found he had also been shot in one ankle and his bow had been partly shot in two. In his quiver he had left only three arrows.

Seiker and I hurried back to the dead horse to help the white boy, but he had extricated himself and disappeared. We then returned to the dead warrior and Seiker scalped him. We took the Indian's bow shield and a fine pair of *moccasins*. I also found a fine lance near where the horse fell, and I presume it was carried by the white boy. We found the redskin had no Winchester cartridges, and this was why he dropped the gun—he could not carry it and use his bow. We went back over the trail but were unable to find the gun the brave had dropped as a bait.

By noon that day the boys had all returned to where the fight had begun and the Indian horses had been left. Jim Hawkins and Paul Durham captured a Mexican boy about fifteen years old. He looked just like an Indian, had long plaited hair down his back, was bare headed, wore *moccasins* and a breech-clout. Had he been in front of me I would surely have killed him for a redskin. Captain Roberts spoke Spanish fluently, and from this boy he learned that the Indians were Lipans that lived in Old Mexico. He was taken back to our camp and finally his uncle came and took him home. He had been captured while herding oxen near old Fort Clark, Texas, and an elder brother, who was with him at the time, had been killed.

The boys were then sent back by Captain Roberts to find the white lad that had been with the Indian Seiker had killed. Though we searched carefully we could find no trace of the mysterious youngster. Some years later I learned that this boy's name was Fischer and that his parents went into Old Mexico and ransomed him. He was from Llano County, and after his return he wrote, or had written, a small pamphlet that contained an account of his life with the Indians. He told of being with old Chief Magoosh in this fight. He declared he hid in the grass within sight of the rangers while they were hunting him, but was afraid to show himself for fear of being killed.

When the rangers had all gathered after the fight our pack mule, Jennie, was missing. We supposed in the run that she had followed the Indians off. Six months later Ed Seiker was detailed to pilot a body of United States soldiers over that same country to pick out a road to the Pecos River. He visited our old battlefield and found Jennie's carcass. She had a bullet hole in the centre of her forehead. The Indians in shooting back at their attackers probably hit her with a chance shot. The pack saddle was still strapped to her body, but wolves had eaten all the supplies. Five hundred rounds of ammunition were still with her, showing that no one had seen her since the day of her death.

Lacking Jennie's supplies, we did not have a blooming thing to eat but the barbecued horse meat we had captured from the Indians. This had no salt on it, and I just could not swallow it. In the fight we killed three horses and one Indian and captured the Mexican lad. At least two redskins were badly wounded, and as victors we captured fifty-eight head of horses and mules, several Indian saddles and bridles and many native trinkets. Not a man or a horse of our party was hurt, the pack mule being our only fatality. All voted Captain Roberts the best man in the world.

We turned our faces homeward, hungry and tired but highly elated over our success. The second day after the fight we reached Wash Delong's ranch on the head waters of the South Concho River. Mr. Delong, a fine frontiersman, killed a beef for us and furnished us with flour and coffee without cost. Three days later we were back at our camp at Los Moris. The stolen stock was returned to their owners, and thus ended my first campaign against the Indians.

CHAPTER 5

The Mason County War

Soon after our return from our first brush with Indians we were introduced to yet another phase of ranger activity—the quieting of feuds, for not only were the rangers employed in protecting the frontiers against the Indians, but they were also frequently called upon to preserve law and order within the towns and cities of the state. In those early days men's passions were high and easily aroused. In a country where all men went armed, recourse to fire arms was frequent, and these feuds sometimes led to active warfare between the adherents of each party to the great discomfort of the citizens among whom such a miniature war was staged.

Mason and the adjoining county, Gillespie, had been settled by Germans in the early history of the state. These settlers were quiet, peaceful and made most excellent citizens, loyal to their adopted country and government when undisturbed. Most of these Germans engaged in stock raising and were sorely tried by the rustlers and Indians that committed many depredations upon their cattle.

In the latter part of September, 1875, Tim Williamson, a prominent cattleman living in Mason County, was arrested on a charge of cattle theft by John Worley, a deputy sheriff of that county. Previous to that time there had been a number of complaints about loss of cattle, and the Germans charged that many of their cattle had been stolen and the brands burned. Much indignation had been aroused among the stockmen of the county and threats of violence against the thieves were common.

As soon as the news of Williamson's arrest on charge of cattle thieving became known a large mob formed and set out in pursuit of the deputy sheriff and his prisoner. On his way to Mason, Worley was overtaken by this posse. When he saw the pursuing men Williamson divined their purpose and begged the sheriff to let him run in an effort to save his life. Worley refused and, it is said, drew his pistol and deliberately shot Williamson's horse through the loin, causing it to fall. Unarmed and unmounted Williamson was killed without a chance to protect himself and without any pretence of a trial. After the murder Worley and the mob disappeared.

Whether or not Williamson was guilty of the charge against him, he had friends who bitterly resented the deputy sheriff's refusal to allow the murdered man a chance for his life and his death caused a great deal of excitement and bitter comment in the county. A man named Scott Cooley, an ex-ranger of Captain Perry's Company "D," was a particular friend of Williamson and his family. Cooley had quit the ranger service at the time of his friend's murder and was cultivating a farm near Menardville. He had worked for the dead man and had made two trips up the trail with him. While working with the murdered cattleman Cooley had contracted a bad case of typhoid fever and had been nursed back to health by Mrs. Williamson's own hands.

When the news of Tim Williamson's murder reached Scott Cooley, he was much incensed, and vowed vengeance against the murderers of his friend. He left his farm at once and, saddling his pony, rode into the town of Mason heavily armed. He had worked out a careful plan of his own and proceeded to put it into execution immediately on his arrival. Stabling his horse in a livery stable, he registered at the hotel. As he was entirely unknown in Mason, Cooley remained in town several days without creating any suspicion. He proved himself a good detective, and soon discovered that the sheriff and his deputy were the leaders in the mob that had killed his friend. Biding his time and pursuing his investigations he soon learned the names of every man in the posse that murdered Williamson.

His information complete, Cooley decided upon action. He mounted his pony and rode out to the home of John Worley, the deputy sheriff that had refused Williamson a chance to flee for his life. Cooley found Worley engaged in cleaning out a well. The avenger dismounted, asked for a drink of water and entered into conversation with the unsuspecting man. Finally, as Worley was drawing his assistant out of the well, Cooley asked him if his name was John Worley. The deputy sheriff replied that it was. Cooley then declared his mission and shot the sheriff to death.

At the first crack of Cooley's pistol Worley let the windlass go, and the man he was drawing up out of the well fell back about twenty-five feet into it. Cooley deliberately stooped down, cut off both of Worley's ears, put them in his pocket, and galloped off. Victim number one was chalked up to Williamson's credit. Making a quick ride across Mason County to the western edge of Llano County, Cooley waylaid and killed Pete Brader, the second on his list of mob members.

These two murders struck terror into the hearts of nearly every citizen of Mason County. No one could tell who would be the next victim of the unerring aim of Scott Cooley's rifle. The whole county rose up in arms to protect themselves. Terrified lest he be the next victim of the avenger, Cooley, the sheriff of Mason County promptly left Mason and never returned. Tim Williamson had other friends anxious to avenge him, and the killing of Brader was their rallying signal. John and Mose Beard, George Gladden, and John Ringgold immediately joined Cooley in his work of vengeance. The gang rode into the town of Mason, and in a fight with a posse of citizens, killed another man.

Fearing the outbreak of a real feud war in Mason, the Governor of Texas ordered Major Jones to the relief of the frightened citizens. The order reached Major Jones while he was on his way down the fine near the head of the Guadalupe River. He at once turned his company back, and with a detachment of ten men from Company "D" he marched to Mason. Company "A," Major Jones' escort, was then commanded by Captain Ira Long, and the thirty men in that company and the ten boys of Company "D" gave the major forty men for his relief expedition.

Before the rangers could reach Mason, the sheriff's party had a fight with Cooley's gang down on the Llano River and killed Mose Beard. On his arrival in Mason, Major Jones sent scouts in every direction to hunt Cooley. He kept this up for nearly two weeks but without result. He finally learned that nearly the whole of his command, especially the Company "D" boys that had ranged with Cooley, was in sympathy with the outlaw and was making no serious attempt to locate or imperil him, It was even charged that some of the Company "D" rangers met Cooley at night on the outskirts of Mason and told him they did not care if he killed every d—d Dutchman in Mason County that formed part of the mob that had murdered Williamson.

Major Jones saw he would have to take drastic steps at once. He drew up his whole force of forty men and made them an eloquent speech. He said he had a special pride in the Frontier Battalion and was making it his life's study and that he personally had a kindly feeling for every man in the service. He then reminded the men in the most feeling manner of the oath they had taken to protect the State of Texas against all her enemies whatsoever—an oath every true man was bound to honour. He declared he knew many of the command had a friendly feeling for Scott Cooley, especially those boys who had shared the life of a ranger with him, and that he, himself, felt keenly the position in which they were placed. While Tim Williamson had met a horrible death at the hands of a relentless mob, that did not justify Cooley in killing people in a private war of vengeance in defiance of the law and the rangers.

As the climax of his speech the major said:—

Men, I now have a proposition to make to you. If every man here who is in sympathy with Scott Cooley and his gang and who does not wish to pursue him to the bitter end will step out of ranks, I will issue him an honourable discharge and let him quit the service clean.

The major paused and about fifteen men stepped to the front. Major Jones continued:—

Gentlemen, those who do not avail themselves of this opportunity I shall expect to use all diligence and strength in helping me to break up or capture these violators of the law.

After the discharge of the Cooley sympathisers, the rangers went to work with a new vigour, and finally captured George Gladden and John Ringgold. Gladden was sent to the state penitentiary for twenty-five years, while Ringgold received a life sentence. Probably Scott Cooley was informed of Major Jones' appeal to the rangers, for he became less active around Mason after this. John Beard, it was reported, skipped Texas and went to Arizona.

Soon after Cooley killed John Worley, Norman Rodgers got permission from Captain Roberts to ride over to Joe Franks' cow outfit to exchange his horse for a better one. When Rodgers rode into the cowboy camp, he noticed a man resting under a tree near the fire. The stranger called one of the cowboys and asked him who Norman was. As Rodgers left camp this man followed him and asked if he were one of Roberts' rangers and if he knew "Major" Reynolds. Rodgers replied that he knew Reynolds very well.

The man then declared he was Scott Cooley and, reaching into his pocket, he pulled out John Worley's ears.

"You take these ears to 'Major' Reynolds with my compliments, but don't you tell anybody you saw me."

Rodgers duly delivered the ears and Reynolds cautioned him to say nothing about them. Forty years afterward, at an old settler's reunion in Sweetwater, Norman Rodgers mentioned this incident in a speech—he had kept his promise to Cooley and Reynolds all those years.

Having lost his friends and his sympathisers in the rangers, Cooley returned to Blanco County, where he had formerly lived. Here he was stricken with brain fever, and though tenderly nursed, shielded by his friends, he died without ever being brought to trial for his killings. This ended the Mason County War, but before the feud died some ten or twelve men were killed and a race war narrowly averted.

Chapter 6

Major Jones and His Escort

Despite their usefulness in protecting the frontiers and in maintaining law and order, the Texas Rangers have always had to fight more or less strenuously to obtain the necessary appropriation for their annual maintenance from the State Legislature. Whenever the appropriation is small there is but one remedy—reduce the personnel of each company to the lowest limits possible. In the fall of 1875, the adjutant-general notified the captains all along the line to reduce their companies to twenty men each for the winter at the end of the current quarter. As the day for reduction arrived there were some anxious moments among the men of Company "D" as no one knew just who was to be retained in the service.

On December 1st Captain Roberts formed the command in line and explained it was his sad duty to reduce the company to twenty men, and announced that the orderly sergeant would read the names of those to be retained in the company. The sergeant then stepped forward and began to read. First Sergeant Plunk Murray, Second Sergeant James Hawkins, First Corporal Lam Seiker, Second Corporal Tom Griffin, and Privates Charles Nevill, Tom Gillespie, Nick Donley, Jim Trout, Henry Maltimore, Bat Maltimore, Jack Martin, W. T. Clements, Ed Seiker, Andy Wilson, J. W. Bell, Norman Rodgers, Dock Long, Tom Mead, Frank Hill, and Jim Gillett were the lucky ones to be retained in the command. The remainder of the company was thereupon discharged. My relief may be imagined when my name was read out, for I had learned to love the ranger life and was loth to quit it.

After reduction we went into winter camp in a bend of the San Saba River about three miles east of Menardville. In the river bottom was plenty of good timber, so each mess of five men built a log cabin, sixteen to eighteen feet square, for their occupancy. These cabins, each with a chimney and a fireplace, formed the western side of our horse corral and made most comfortable winter abodes. During the winter the boys played many tricks upon each other, for there were no Indian raids during the time we were in this winter camp.

One of the favourite stunts was to extract the bullet from a cartridge, take out the powder and wrap it in a rag, and then, while the inmates of a given cabin would be quietly smoking or reading or talking around their fire, climb upon the roof and drop the rag down the chimney. When the powder exploded in the fire the surprised rangers would fall backward off their benches—to the huge glee of the prank player. At other times a couple of rangers would post themselves outside a neighbour's cabin and begin to yell, "Fire! Fire!!" at the top of their lungs. If the cabin owners did not stand in the doorway to protect it all the rangers in camp would rush up and throw bedding, cooking utensils, saddles and bridles, guns and pistols outside as quickly as they could. In a jiffy the cabin would be cleaned out and the victims of the joke would have to lug all their belongings back in again.

But not all our time was spent in practical joking. There were many rangers of a studious mind, and during the long winter evenings they pored over their books. Several of our boys, by their study here and at other leisure hours, qualified themselves for doctors, lawyers, and professional callings. And there were several writers in camp that contributed more or less regularly to the magazines and newspapers.

One of the rangers, Nick Donley, was a baker by trade, and he soon built a Dutch oven and made bread for the rangers. We pooled our flour and had fresh, warm bread every morning. This was so good and we ate so much of it that our allowance of flour would not last for the period issued, and Captain Roberts was compelled to order the bake oven torn down. Thereafter the boys baked their own bread and the flour lasted.

Some of the rangers had captured young bear cubs, and we had them in camp with us as pets. They grew rapidly and were soon big fellows and immensely popular with the boys. Sometimes a bear would break loose from its chain, and then all of us would turn out to hunt the escaped pet. Most often we would soon find him seated in a tree which he had climbed as soon as he had broken his shackles. And I cannot here forbear mentioning the useful little pack mules that served the rangers so long and so well.

When the battalion was formed in 1874, a number of little bronco mules were secured for packing. They soon learned what was expected of them and followed the rangers like dogs. Carrying a weight of one hundred and fifty to two hundred pounds, they would follow a scout of rangers on the dead run right into the midst of the hottest fight with Indians or *desperadoes*. They seemed to take as much interest in such an engagement as the rangers themselves.

These little pack animals had as much curiosity as a child or a pet coon. In travelling along a road, they sometimes met a bunch of horses or several campers along the highway. Immediately they would run over for a brief visit with the strangers and when the rangers had gone on a thousand yards or more would scamper up to us as fast as they could run. Later, when the rangers drew in from the frontier and scouted in a more thickly settled country the mules with their packs would march right up to strange horses and frighten them out of their wits. Once, in Austin, one of our mules calmly trotted up to a mule that was pulling a street car. As the pack *burro* would not give right of way the street car mule shied to one side and pulled its conveyance completely off the track to the surprise of its driver. The tiny animals pulled off several stunts like this and caused so much complaint that Adjutant-General Jones issued an order for all rangers to catch and lead their pack mules when passing through a town.

As soon as we were located in the new camp, Privates Nevill, Bell and Seiker obtained permission from Captain Roberts to visit Austin to buy a case of ten Winchesters. Up to this time the company was armed with a .50 calibre Sharps carbine. These guns would heat easily and thus were very inaccurate shooters. The state furnished this weapon to its rangers at a cost of $17.50, and at that time furnished no other class of gun. The new centre fire, 1873, model, Winchester had just appeared on the market and sold at $50 for the rifle and $40 for the carbine. A ranger who wanted a Winchester had to pay for it out of his own pocket and supply his own ammunition as well, for the State of Texas only furnished cartridges for the Sharps gun.

However, ten men in Company "D," myself included, were willing to pay the price to have a superior arm. I got carbine number 13,401, and for the next six years of my ranger career I never used any other weapon. I have killed almost every kind of game that is found in Texas, from the biggest old bull buffalo to a fox squirrel with this little .44 Winchester. Today I still preserve it as a prized memento of the past.

The boys were all anxious to try their new guns, and as Christmas approached, we decided to have a real Yule-tide dinner. Ed Seiker and myself visited a big turkey roost on the head of Elm Creek and

A Typical Ranger Encampment. Company D in camp at Fort Inge in 1884. Several of these men were subsequently killed in action.

killed seven big wild turkeys, and on our return Seiker bagged a fine buck deer. J. W. Bell hunted on the San Saba and brought in six or eight wild geese and about a dozen mallard ducks. Donley, the baker, cooked up the pies, while Mrs. Roberts, wife of the captain, furnished the fruitcake. Some of the boys made eggnog, and altogether we had the finest Christmas dinner that ever graced the boards of a ranger camp. The little frontier village of Menardville was not far away, and most of the rangers visited it during Christmas week for the dancing. Jack Martin once remarked to Mrs. Roberts that there was very little society about a ranger camp. She told the joke on him and thereafter as long as he lived, he was known as "Society Jack."

During the winter we laid out a race course and had much sport with our horses. But there was work as well as play that winter. Though Captain Roberts kept scouts in the field during the entire winter they never discovered any Indian trails. The rangers had not yet turned their attention to outlaws, so we were not burdened with chained prisoners as we were in after years. This winter camp on the San Saba was the most pleasant time in my service with the rangers.

The first week in April, 1876, we moved out of our winter quarters to a camp some six or seven miles above Menardville and located in a pecan grove on the banks of the San Saba. We were all glad to get into our tents again after four months spent in log cabins. I remember our first night at the new camp. The boys set out some hooks and caught four or five big yellow catfish weighing twenty-five or thirty pounds each—enough fish to last the twenty men several days.

As the spring opened, Captain Roberts began sending out scouts to cut signs for Indians. I remember I was detailed on a scout that was commanded by a non-commissioned officer. We were ordered to scout as far north as the union of the Concho and Colorado Rivers. After crossing the Brady Mountains, we struck a trail of Indians going out. The redskins had probably been raiding in San Saba or McCulloch Counties. Their trail led west as straight to San Angelo as a bird could fly. Though the Indians were not numerous and had only a few horses, the trail was easily followed.

As well as we could judge the redskins had passed on a few days before we discovered their sign. We found where they had stolen some horses, for we picked up several pairs of hobbles that had been cut in two and left where they got the horses. At that time there were several big cattle ranches in the Fort Concho country, and in going to and from water the cattle entirely obliterated the trail. We worked hard two days trying to find it and then gave up the hunt. We needed the genius of Captain Roberts to help us out that time.

On June 1, 1876, the company was increased to forty men. Some of the boys that had quit at Mason the fall before now re-entered the service. Especially do I remember that "Mage" Reynolds enlisted with Company "D" once more.

During the summer of 1876, Major Jones planned a big scout out on the Pecos to strike the Lipans and Kickapoos a blow before they began raiding the white settlements. This scout started from Company "D" in July. The major drafted about twenty men from my company, his whole escort Company "A" of thirty men and marched into Kerr County. Here he drafted part of Captain Coldwell's Company "F," making his force total about seventy men with three wagons and about twenty pack mules.

The column travelled down the Nueces, then by Fort Clark up the Devil's River to Beaver Lake. Here Captain Ira Long with twenty men and the wagon train was sent up the San Antonio and El Paso road to old Fort Lancaster on the Pecos, where he was to await the arrival of Major Jones with the main force.

From Beaver Lake, the major with fifty men and the twenty pack mules turned southwest and travelled down Johnston's Run to the Shafer Crossing on the Pecos. From this crossing we scouted up the Pecos to the mouth of Independence Creek. The country through this section was very rough but very beautiful. We saw several old abandoned Indian camps, especially at the mouth of the creek. Here we found the pits and the scaffolds upon which the redskins had dried their meat, also evidence that many deer hide had been dressed and made into buckskin. Bows and arrows had also been manufactured in these camps. From this section the Indians had been gone probably a month or more.

After ten days of scouting we joined Captain Long at Fort Lancaster and marched up Live Oak Creek to its head. Here we prepared to cross that big stretch of table land between the Pecos and the head waters of the South Concho. We filled what barrels we had with water, topped out from the creek—and made about ten miles into the plains by night and made a dry camp. We got an early start next day and travelled until night without finding water. The stock suffered greatly from thirst and the men had only a little water in their canteens. All the land ponds had been dry two weeks or more, and I saw twelve head of buffalo that had bogged and died in one of them. Here we found an old abandoned Indian camp, where the redskins had dressed many antelope hides. At one old bent *mesquite* tree the antelope hair was a foot deep, with thirty or forty skulls scattered about.

By the second morning both men and horses were suffering a great deal from thirst, and Major Jones gave orders to begin march at 4 a. m. We got away on time and reached water on the South Concho at 2 p. m., the third day out from Live Oak Creek. As soon as we got near the water, we found a number of straggling buffalo, and killed two, thus securing a supply of fresh meat. We camped two days at this water and then marched back to Company "D" by easy stages. Here Major Jones turned back up the line with his escort after being out on this scout about a month.

On his return toward the Rio Grande, Major Jones reached Company "D" the last week in August and camped with us until September 1st, the end of the fiscal year for the rangers. On this date many men would quit service to retire to private life, while some would join other companies and new recruits be sworn into the service. This reorganisation usually required two or three days.

Nearly every ranger in the battalion was anxious to be at some time a member of Major Jones' escort company. The escort company was not assigned a stationary post nor did it endeavour to cover a given strip of territory. Its most important duty was to escort the major on his periodic journeys of inspection to the other companies along the line.

The escort always wintered in the south and made about four yearly tours of the frontier from company to company, taking part in such scouts as the major might select and being assigned to such extraordinary duty as might arise. In 1874, when the Frontier Battalion was first formed, Major Jones recruited his escort from a detail of five men from each of the other companies. However, in practice, this led to some confusion and envy in the commands, so Major Jones found it expedient to have a regular escort company, so he selected Company "A" for that purpose. This remained his escort until he was promoted to adjutant-general.

In September, 1876, there were several vacancies in Major Jones' escort, and several old Company "D" boys, among them "Mage" Reynolds, Charles Nevill, Jack Martin, Bill Clements, and Tom Gillespie, wished to enlist in Company "A." They wanted me to go with them, but I hesitated to leave Captain Roberts. My friends then explained that we could see a lot more country on the escort than we could in a stationary company; that we would probably be stationed down on the Rio Grande that winter, and going up the line in the spring would see thousands of buffalo. This buffalo proposition caught me, and I went with the boys. After fifteen months' ranging with Captain Roberts I now joined Company "A."

Early in September Major Jones marched his escort down to within five or six miles of San Antonio and camped us on the Salado while he went in to Austin. By the first of October he was back in camp and started up the line on his last visit to the different companies before winter set in.

At that time Major John B. Jones was a small man, probably not more than five feet seven inches tall and weighed about one hundred and twenty-five pounds. He had very dark hair and eyes and a heavy dark moustache. He was quick in action, though small in stature, and was an excellent horseman, riding very erect in the saddle.

The major was born in Fairfield District, South Carolina, in 1834, but emigrated to Texas with his father when he was only four years old. He was prominent in Texas state affairs from a very early age and served gallantly with the Confederate Army during the Civil War. On the accession of Governor Coke in 1874, he was appointed to command the Frontier Battalion of six companies of Texas Rangers. From his appointment until his death in Austin in 1881, Major Jones was constantly engaged in repulsing bloody raids of Indians, rounding up outlaws and making Texas secure and safe for the industrious and peaceful citizen. In this work his wonderful tact, judgment, coolness and courage found ample scope.

From the organisation of the battalion in 1874 until Major Jones was made adjutant-general, Dr. Nicholson was always with him. The doctor was a quaint old bachelor who loved his toddy. The boys would sometimes get him as full as a goose, and the major would give the doctor some vicious looks at such times. Dr. Nicholson was a great favourite with all the men, and it is said he knew every good place for buttermilk, butter, milk, and eggs from Rio Grande City to Red River, a trifling distance of eight hundred miles. The doctor always messed with Major Jones, and, mounted on a fine horse, travelled by his side. I don't think Dr. Nicholson ever issued a handful of pills to the boys during the year— he was just with us in case he was needed. When the escort was disbanded, he retired to private life at Del Rio, Texas, and finally died there.

This inspection tour was a wonderful experience for me. The

weather was cool and bracing, and the horses had had a month's rest. We had with us a quartet of musicians, among them a violinist, a guitar player and a banjo picker, and after the day's march the players would often gather around the camp fire and give us a concert. The major would frequently walk down and listen to the music. Nor was music our only amusement. Major Jones had provided his escort with a fish seine, and when we were camped on a big creek or river the boys would unroll the net, make a haul and sometimes catch enough fish to supply the thirty men several days.

When recruited to its full strength Company "A" consisted of a captain, orderly sergeant, second sergeant, first and second corporals, and twenty-six privates. Two four-mule wagons hauled the camp equipage, rations for the men and grain for the horses. One light wagon drawn by two mules and driven by George, the negro cook, carried the mess outfit, bedding, tent, etc., of Major Jones and Dr. Nicholson.

Each morning at roll call the orderly sergeant detailed a guard of nine men and one non-commissioned officer to guard for twenty-four hours. When ready to begin our day's journey the company was formed in line and the men counted off by fours. On the march Major Jones and Dr. Nicholson rode in front, followed by the captain of the company, the orderly sergeant and the men in double file. Following these came the wagons. An advance guard of two men preceded the column about one-half mile. Four men, known as flankers, two on each side of the company, paralleled the column at a distance of one-half to one mile, depending on the nature of the country. In a rough, wooded section the flankers travelled close in, but in an open country they sometimes spread out quite a distance. The non-commissioned officer with the remaining guard covered the rear and brought up the pack mules. Thus, protected it was almost impossible for the command to be surprised by Indians.

At one time Major Jones had with him two Tonkawa Indians as guides. For protection this tribe lived near Fort Griffin, a large military post. One of these old braves known as Jim had been given an old worn out army coat with the shoulder straps of a general upon it. Jim wore this coat tightly buttoned up and marched at the head of the column with as much dignity and importance as a general-in-chief. His companion wore a high crowned beaver stove-pipe hat with the top gone, and carried an old umbrella that someone had given him. Fitted out in this ridiculous and unique manner he marched for days with the umbrella over him. Think of an Indian shading himself from the sun.

Captain D. W. Roberts.

Lieutenant N. O. Reynolds.

Captain Neal Coldwell.

Captain George W. Baylor.

Four Great Ranger Leaders

Major Jones never paid much attention to these Indians unless he wished to inquire the lay of the country or the distance to some water hole. They did pretty much as they pleased, sometimes riding in front with the major, sometimes with the guard and at others with the men. These old redskins were a constant source of amusement to the boys. Jim and his pal were good hunters but as lazy as could be. They got into the habit of killing a buffalo late in the evening when they knew it was almost time to pitch camp, cutting out just enough meat for themselves and letting the remainder go to waste. The major told these lazy-bones when they killed a buffalo, he wanted to know of it so he could secure the meat for the company. The Tonks paid no attention to this request and late one evening came into camp with five or six pounds of buffalo meat.

The orderly sergeant spied them, so he walked over to Major Jones and said, "Major, those two old Tonkawas are back in camp with just enough meat for themselves."

"Sergeant, you get a pack mule, take a file of men with you and make those Indians saddle their horses and go with you to get that buffalo," the major commanded, determined that his order should be obeyed by the Indians.

The sergeant went to the Indians, who were busy about the fire roasting their meat, and told them what the major had said. Jim declared that he was tired and did not wish to go. The non-commissioned officer replied that that made no difference and commanded him and his pal to get their ponies and lead the way to the dead buffalo.

"Maybe so ten miles to buffalo," protested Jim, trying to avoid going.

The sergeant knew they were lying, for of all the Indians that ever inhabited Texas the Tonkawas were the biggest cowards. Just mention the Comanches or Kiowas to them and they would have a chill. It was well known that the Tonks would not venture very far away from the protection of the rangers for fear of being killed by their enemies. As soon as they knew they had to do as ordered, they mounted their ponies and led the sergeant over a little hill, and in a valley not more than half a mile from camp, was the fine, fat buffalo the Indians had killed. The animal was soon skinned and brought into camp, where all had plenty of fresh meat.

These Tonks were as simple as children and as suspicious. The weather had been hot and dry for several days. Old Jim thereupon killed some hawks with his bow and arrows, plaited the long tail and wing feathers into his pony's mane and tail, and said it would make "heap rain." Sure enough, in three or four days a hard thunder shower came up and thoroughly wet everybody on the march. Jim, with only his old officer's coat for protection, was drenched to the skin, and his pony looked like a drowned rat. The wood, grass, everything was wet. Jim stood by, shivering with the cold and watched the boys use up almost their last match trying to make a fire. Suddenly, with a look of disgust, he ran up to his horse, which was standing near, and plucked every hawk feather out of the animal's tail and mane and, throwing them on the ground, stamped upon them violently as if that would stop the rain.

After the escort had crossed the Colorado River on its way northward, we found an advance guard of buffalo on its way south, and it was an easy matter to keep the company in fresh meat. We spent about one week with Company "B" on the upper Brazos, then turned south again to make our winter camp near Old Frio Town in Frio County. It was November now and freezing hard every night.

The last guard would call the camp early, so we generally had breakfast and were ready to move southward by daylight. We did not stop a single time for dinner on this return trip, just travelled at a steady gait all day long without dinner until nearly night. We all wondered why we marched the live-long day without dinner, but it was not until many years afterward when I became a Mason that I learned the reason for our forced marches. Major Jones was in line to be made Most Worshipful Grand Master of Masons in Texas and he had to be in Houston on the first Tuesday in December for the annual meeting of the Most Worshipful Grand Lodge of Texas. If there were other Masons in the company besides Major Jones, I never knew it.

At this time, we had for commander of the escort, Lieutenant Benton. He was in bad health and rode most of the way back in one of the wagons. On arriving at the end of the line he tendered his resignation and was succeeded by Captain Neal Coldwell. The company camped for the winter on Elm Creek, three miles southwest of Old Frio Town.

Captain Neal Coldwell was born in Dade County, Missouri, in May, 1844, and served gallantly throughout the Civil War in the Thirty-second Regiment, Texas Cavalry, commanded by Col. W. P. Woods. At the organisation of the Frontier Battalion in 1874, Neal Coldwell was commissioned captain of Company "F."

It is difficult, in a single sketch, to do Captain Coldwell justice or convey any correct idea of what he accomplished as a Texas Ranger.

The station of Company "F," the southernmost company of the line, was the most unfavourable that could well be given him. His scouting grounds were the head of the Guadalupe, Nueces, Llanos, and Devil's Rivers—the roughest and most difficult part of South Texas in which to pursue Indians, yet he held them in check and finally drove them out of that part of the state.

CHAPTER 7

The Horrell-Higgins Feud

By the end of the year 1876, the Indians had been pretty well pushed back off the frontier, so that there were very few fights with the redskins after 1877. From the spring of 1877, onward, the rangers were transformed into what might properly be called mounted state police, and accordingly turned their attention to ridding the frontier of the outlaws that infested nearly every part of Texas. During the winter of 1876-77, Captain Neal Coldwell broke up a band of thieves that was operating in the north-western part of Atascosa County. I remember helping him capture a man named Wolf. He was wanted for murder, and we made several scouts after him before we succeeded in landing him safely in irons.

In April, 1877, Major Jones reached Coldwell's company and at once made arrangements to march up the line on a visit of inspection. When the major reached the headwaters of the South Llano River, he halted his escort and detailed several small scouting parties of five or six men, each with orders to arrest every man that could not give a good account of himself. One scout was sent down the South Llano, a second down Johnson's Fork, while a third was ordered over the divide with instructions to hit the head of the North Llano and sweep down that river,—all three parties to rejoin Major Jones and the main escort near where Junction City now stands.

In these outlaw raids some fifty or sixty men were arrested and brought in. Many of the suspects were released upon examination, but I remember one scout brought in two escaped convicts who had been captured up on Copperas Creek. We bagged several men wanted for murder and some horse and cattle thieves. Old Kimble County never had such a clean-up of bandits in her history.

While these prisoners were being held in camp other scouts were

Mounted Rangers in Readiness for a Scout. From a photograph of Captain Hughes's Company taken in the middle nineties. Three of these men were later killed in action.

sent out in the northern part of the county with orders to sweep Bear Creek, Gentry, Red Creek, Big and Little Saline, to cross the San Saba River in Menard County and sweep up that stream from old Peg Leg Station to Menard. Many more suspects were caught in this haul.

With a party of scouts, I was detailed on a mission to Fort McKavett, at that time one of the big military posts on the frontier. Many hard characters and gamblers gathered about these posts to fleece the soldiers out of their easy-made money. We made several arrests here, and camped for noon one mile below the government post on the San Saba River. During the dinner hour my horse, a grey, in lying down to wallow, rolled on some broken beer bottles and cut his back so badly that he was unfit for use for some time. When the escort moved north, I was left with old Company "D" until the return of Company "A" on its return march some six weeks later. I thereby missed some of the exciting scouts that took place on the march north.

When Major Jones reached Coleman City, he found orders from Governor Coke to send a scout of rangers to Lampasas County to help the civil authorities suppress a war known as the Horrell-Higgins feud. Second Sergeant N. O. Reynolds was detached from Company "A" and with ten men ordered to proceed to Lampasas and report to the sheriff of that county.

After leaving Coleman, Major Jones visited the northernmost ranger company and began his return march. This was to be his last trip with his escort, for immediately upon his return to Austin he was commissioned Adjutant-General of Texas. As there was no longer a major of the battalion, there was no need of an escort, so old Company "A" took its place on the line as a stationary company. Captain Neal Coldwell was ultimately made quartermaster of the battalion, and I believe ranked as major.

I was picked up at Company "D" by the escort on their return march and was with Company "A" when it was made a stationary command and located in Frio County.

In the latter part of 1877—during the late summer—a party of filibusters under command of a Mexican general named Winkler assembled in Maverick County, near Eagle Pass, and prepared to invade Mexico. Captain Coldwell, then commanding Company "A," was ordered to the Rio Grande to break up the expedition. This he did by arresting more than fifty participants. I was with him on this expedition and saw much border service during this summer.

I remember a scout I was called upon to make with Captain Coldwell over in Bandera County. The captain took with him John Parker, Hawk Roberts, and myself. In one week's time we caught some ten or twelve fugitives from justice and literally filled the little old jail at Bandera. Captain Coldwell detailed Hawk Roberts and myself to capture an especially bad man wanted in Burnet County for murder. The captain warned us to take no chances with this man—that meant to kill him if he hesitated about surrendering. I can't remember this murderer's name at this late date, but I recall perfectly the details of his capture. Sheriff Jack Hamilton of Bandera County sent a guide to show us where this fugitive lived. The guide led us some fifteen miles northwest of Bandera and finally pointed out the house in which the murderer was supposed to be. He then refused to go any farther, saying he did not want any of this man's game, for the fellow had just stood off a deputy sheriff and made him hike it back to Bandera.

It was almost night when we reached the house, so Roberts and I decided to wait until morning before attempting the arrest. We staked our horses, lay down on our saddle blankets without supper, and slept soundly till dawn. As soon as it was daylight we rode over near the house, dismounted, slipped up, and, unannounced, stepped right inside the room. The man we wanted was sleeping on a pallet with a big white-handled .45 near his head. Hawk Roberts kicked the pistol out of the man's reach. The noise awakened the sleeper and he opened his eyes to find himself looking into the business ends of two Winchesters held within a foot of his head. Of course, he surrendered without fight.

His wife, who was sleeping in a bed in the same room, jumped out of it and heaped all kinds of abuse on us for entering her home without ceremony. She was especially bitter against Sheriff Hamilton, who, she said, had promised to notify her husband when he was wanted so he could come in and give himself up. She indignantly advised her husband to give old Sheriff Hamilton a d—d good whipping the first chance he had.

While Company "A" was rounding up outlaws along the border, Sergeant Reynolds was covering himself with glory in the north. Upon reaching Lampasas and reporting to the sheriff as ordered by Major Jones, the sergeant was told that the Horrell boys were living on the Sulphur Fork of the Lampasas River and were defying the authorities to arrest them.

The Horrells were native Texans and had been raised on the frontier. These brothers, of which five were involved in the feud (the sixth, John Horrell, had been killed at Las Cruces, New Mexico, previously) were expert riders, and, having grown up with firearms in their hands, were as quick as chained lightning with either Winchester or pistol. Sam Horrell, the eldest, was married and had a large family of children. He was a farmer and lived a quiet life over on the Lampasas River. The other four boys, Mart, Tom, Merritt, and Ben, were all cattlemen. They stood well in the community, but were considered dangerous when aroused.

At this time Lampasas was a frontier town and wide open as far as saloons and gambling were concerned. The Horrells, like most cattlemen of the period, loved to congregate in town, go to the saloons and have a good time, perhaps drink too much and sometimes at night shoot up the town for fun, as they termed it. Some of the more pious and more settled citizens of the town did not approve of these night brawls, and called upon Governor Edmund J. Davis, Provisional Governor in 1873, to give them protection. Governor Davis had formed in Texas a State Police. Naturally they were rank Republicans, and many of them were termed carpetbaggers. This body was never popular in Texas.

In answer to the call of the citizens, Governor Davis dispatched Captain Williams with three white men and one negro to Lampasas. On the way up Captain Williams met several freighters going to Austin and stopped one of them, Tedford Bean, to ask the distance to Lampasas. The captain had been drinking, and he told Mr. Bean he was going to town to clean up those damn Horrell boys.

The little squad of police reached Lampasas about 3 p. m., hitched its horses to some live oak trees on the public *plaza*, left the negro to guard them, and then made a bee line to Jerry Scott's saloon on the west side of the square. Mart, Tom, and Merritt Horrell, with some ten or fifteen cow men, were in the saloon drinking, playing billiards and having a good time generally. One man was picking a banjo and another playing a fiddle. Captain Williams, an exceedingly brave but unwise man, took in the situation at a glance as he walked up to the bar and called for drinks.

He turned to Bill Bowen, a brother-in-law to Merritt Horrell, and said, "I believe you have a six-shooter. I arrest you."

"Bill, you have done nothing and need not be arrested if you don't want to," interrupted Mart Horrell.

Like a flash of lightning Captain Williams pulled his pistol and fired on Mart Horrell, wounding him badly. The Horrell boys drew their guns and began to fight. Captain Williams and one of his men,

Dr. Daniels, were shot down in the saloon. William Cherry was killed just outside the door, and Andrew Melville was fatally wounded as he was trying to escape. He reached the old Huling Hotel, where he died later. At the first crack of a pistol the negro police mounted his horse and made a John Gilpin ride for Austin. Thus, within the twinkling of an eye, four state police were killed and only one of the Horrells wounded.

Tom and Merritt Horrell carried the wounded Mart to their mother's home, some two hundred yards from Scott's saloon, then mounted their horses and rode away. Great excitement prevailed in the town. The state militia was called out, and Governor Davis hurried other state police to Lampasas. They scoured the country for the Horrell boys, but to no avail.

Mart Horrell and Jerry Scott were arrested and carried to Georgetown, Williamson County, and placed in jail. Mart Horrell's wife went to the jail to nurse her husband and, of course, kept her brothers-in-law informed as to Mart's condition. As soon as he was well the Horrell boys made up a party and rode to Williamson County and assaulted the jail at night. The citizens and officers of Georgetown, taken unawares, put up a stiff fight, but the Horrells had ten or fifteen well organised and armed men with them. They took stations at all approaches to the jail and kept up a steady fire with their Winchesters at anyone who showed up to oppose them. Mr. A. S. Fisher, a prominent lawyer of the town, took an active hand in the fight and was badly wounded. Bill Bowen was slightly hurt while battering in the jail door with a sledge hammer. Mart Horrell and Jerry Scott were liberated and rode off with their rescuers.

By the next evening the Horrells were back on Lucies Creek. They at once made arrangements to leave the country and go to New Mexico. They had gathered about them Bill and Tom Bowen, John Dixon, Ben Turner, and six or eight other men as desperate and dangerous as themselves. They were so formidable that they no longer attempted to hide but openly and without hindrance gathered their cattle, sold the remnant to Cooksey and Clayton to be delivered to them in Coleman County. They even notified the sheriff of Lampasas County just what day they would pass with their herd through Russell Gap, but they were not molested.

As a cowboy I had worked for Cooksey and Clayton, and was with them when they delivered cattle to the Horrell boys on Home Creek, Coleman County. I had dinner in camp with the outlaws and they made no effort to hide from the authorities. I remember they sat about their camps with Winchesters across their laps.

When all was ready the Horrells moved slowly out of the country with their families and cattle and finally reached New Mexico, settling on the head of the Hondo River in Lincoln County. They had not been at their new home many months before Ben Horrell was shot and killed at a *fandango* near old Fort Stanton. Ben's brothers at once repaired to the dance hall and killed eight Mexicans and one woman.

This brought on a war between the Horrell boys and the Mexican population along the Hondo River, and it is said that in the fights that followed thirty or forty Mexicans were killed between Fort Stanton and Roswell. In one of those pitched battles Ben Turner was killed. Turner was prominent in all of the fights staged by the Horrells, was with them when Captain Williams was killed and was one of the assaulting party on the Georgetown jail. His death was keenly felt by his companions.

Having now outlawed themselves in New Mexico, the Horrells could no longer stay in that country. They turned back to Texas, and next year showed up at their old haunts in Lampasas County. The shock of the Civil War was beginning to subside and the State of Texas was then under civil government with a Democratic governor in office. The friends of the Horrells advised them to surrender to the authorities and be tried for the killing of Captain Williams and his men. They were assured a fair trial by the best citizens of Lampasas County. Accordingly, the Horrells gave up, and upon trial were acquitted of the charges against them.

The Horrells had not long been at ease before Merritt, the youngest of the brothers, was accused by Pink Higgins of unlawfully handling his cattle. Shortly afterward, while Merritt was seated unarmed in a chair in the old Jerry Scott saloon, Pink Higgins stepped to the back door of the place and shot him to death. Thus, Merritt met his death in the same saloon where four years before he had been a party to the killing of Captain Williams. At this time Mart and Tom Horrell were living down on Sulphur Fork of Lampasas River. The news of their brother's death was quickly carried to them. They armed themselves and started in a run for Lampasas.

This move had been anticipated by the Pink Higgins party. They waylaid the Horrell boys outside the town and at their first fire killed Tom Horrell's horse and badly wounded Mart. Tom advanced single handed on the attackers and put them to flight. He then partly supported and partly carried his brother to the home of Mr. Tinnins, a neighbour, where a doctor was hurried to the wounded man.

Thus, old Lampasas County was again the scene of war with Mart, Tom and Sam Horrell, Bill and Tom Bowen, John Dixon and Bill Crabtree on one side and Pink Higgins, Bob Mitchell and their friends on the other. These two factions met in the town of Lampasas and a furious battle followed. A man was killed on each side and the population greatly endangered. Hence the governor's order to Major Jones to send rangers to the aid of the officers at Lampasas.

When Sergeant N. O. Reynolds reported to the sheriff of Lampasas, he was informed that the Horrell boys were living ten miles east of Lampasas and had ten or twelve desperate men with them, so that it meant certain death to anyone making an attempt to capture them.

"But, Mr. Sheriff, I am sent here to effect the capture of all offenders against the law, and it is my duty to at least make the attempt," replied the brave Reynolds.

"These men have never been arrested," declared Sheriff Sweet, "and it is my honest opinion they cannot be."

Reynolds then asked if the sheriff would send a guide to show him where the Horrells lived. The rangers under the intrepid Reynolds left Lampasas late in the night and finally the guide pointed at a flickering light about a mile off.

"There is where the Horrell boys live. I am going back to town," he said.

When asked if he would not accompany the rangers to the house, the guide replied, "No, not for a million dollars!"

With that he turned his horse and rode away.

Reynolds thought it would be best to wait until daylight before attempting the arrest. He planned to surprise the outlaws, if such a thing were possible, but if the rangers were discovered and an engagement came on, they were to fight to the last man. As soon as dawn broke the rangers wended their way on foot to the Horrell brothers' ranch. It was a moment of great anxiety as they approached the house, but not a sound was heard, not a dog barked.

Sergeant Reynolds and his men tiptoed right into the room in which the Horrells were sleeping. Some of the men were on pallets on the floor, while others slept in beds in the one big room. Each ranger pointed a cocked Winchester at the head of a sleeper. Reynolds then spoke to Mart Horrell. At the sound of his voice every man sat up in bed and found himself looking into the muzzle of a gun. The sergeant quickly explained that he was a ranger and had come to arrest them. Mart replied they could not surrender, and Tom Horrell said it would be better to die fighting than to be mobbed.

This gave Reynolds his cue. He warned the outlaws that if anything was started there would be a dozen dead men in that house in one minute and advised them to listen to what he had to say. He then guaranteed the Horrells upon his honour that he would not turn them over to the sheriff to be put in jail and mobbed, but promised he would guard them in his camp until they could secure a preliminary examination and give bond.

"Boys, this seems reasonable," said Mart Horrell, rising to his feet. "I believe these rangers can be relied upon to protect us. Besides this fight has been thrust upon us. If we can get a hearing, we can give bond."

They all agreed finally to this proposition of Sergeant Reynolds and laid down their arms, mounted their horses and under guard of the rangers were marched into the town of Lampasas.

The news of the capture of the Horrells spread like wildfire through the town and county. Hundreds of people flocked to Lampasas to see Sergeant Reynolds, the man that had accomplished the impossible in rounding up the most desperate band of men that ever lived. The news was rushed to Austin, and General Jones himself hurried to the scene. This act of Sergeant Reynolds covered him with glory and brought to his name imperishable renown. He was at once commissioned First Lieutenant, commanding Company "E."

The Horrell boys were admitted to bond after a preliminary hearing. After their release Mart Horrell came to Lieutenant Reynolds and feelingly thanked him for carrying out his promise. With tears streaming down his face he grasped the lieutenant's hand and said, "You are undoubtedly the bravest man in the world today." These unfortunate men were later shot to death in the Meridian jail. The Higgins and Mitchell parties surrendered to the authorities. Pink Higgins was tried and acquitted of the murder of Merritt Horrell. This ended the feud, but it started Lieutenant Reynolds on a new and important phase of his career as a ranger.

CHAPTER 8

Service With Reynolds, the Intrepid

As soon as Sergeant Reynolds was commissioned first lieutenant he was placed in command of Company "E," then stationed in Coleman County, but immediately ordered to Lampasas. At this time Captain Sparks resigned the command of Company "C," and this company was also ordered to report to Lieutenant Reynolds at the same town. Late in August the two commands went into camp at Hancock Springs. Major Jones then authorised Lieutenant Reynolds to pick such men as he desired from these two companies for his own company and either discharge or transfer the remainder to other commands. No other officer in the battalion, I believe, was ever accorded this privilege.

Lieutenant Reynolds had a week or ten days in which to make his selection, so he studied the muster rolls of the companies carefully. He had ranged under such great captains as Perry, D. W. Roberts, Neal Coldwell, and with Major Jones himself. He knew what qualities were needed in a good ranger and made his selections accordingly. From old Company "A" Reynolds selected C. L. Nevill, Tom Gillespie, Shape Rodgers, Jack Martin, John Gibbs, W. T. Clements, and four others whose names I do not now remember. These were the scouts that had helped him capture the Horrells and naturally were his first choice.

From Company "E" came Dick Ware, who one year later killed the noted train robber, Sam Bass, then served Mitchell County as its first sheriff for many years, and finally became United States marshal for the Western District of Texas under President Cleveland's administration. Henry Thomas, Miller Mourland, George Arnett, and other Company "E" boys were selected. Henry Maltimore, Ben and Dock Carter, Bill Derrick, Chris Connor, Henry McGee, Abe Anglin, J. W. Warren, Dave Ligon, Lowe Hughes, George (Hog) Hughes, and others were picked from Company "C."

When he had exhausted the two companies Reynolds turned to General Jones and said, "There is a ranger down on the Rio Grande in Neal Coldwell's company that I want."

"Who is it?" asked the general.

"Private Jim Gillett."

"You shall have him," promised General Jones. "I will send an order to Captain Coldwell tonight to have Gillett report to you here."

It was late in the evening when Company "A's" mail came in from Frio Town, but Captain Coldwell sent for me as soon as General Jones' order arrived, and told me that I must leave the company next morning and report to the Adjutant-General at Austin. I was nonplussed, for I did not know what the order meant. Out on the frontier where we then were operating we seldom read newspapers or heard what the other companies were doing, so I did not even know that Reynolds had captured the Horrell boys and had been commissioned to command Company "E." The following morning I bade Captain Coldwell and the Company "A" boys goodbye and started on my long ride to Austin.

As I jogged along, I asked myself many hundred times why I was ordered to report at Austin, and, boy-like, it made me nervous and uneasy. It took me two days to reach San Antonio and three more to get to Austin. I arrived in the latter town just at nightfall, but I was at the adjutant-general's office as soon as it was opened next morning.

Presently General Jones entered with some officers of the State Militia. He shook hands with me and invited me to be seated, saying he had some business to attend to for the moment. It was probably an hour before the officers left and the general could turn to me. He very kindly inquired as to my trip and asked about Captain Coldwell and the company. He then told me about the arrest of the Horrell boys and Sergeant Reynolds' commission as first lieutenant commanding Company "E," vice Lieutenant Foster resigned. He explained Reynolds had requested that I be attached to his command, and ordered me to report to my new commander in Lampasas without delay.

I excused myself at once and lost no time in getting my horse out of the livery stable and resuming my way. A great load was lifted from my mind, and I was about as happy as a boy could be. I sang and whistled all the way to Liberty Hill, thirty miles from Austin. The following day about 2 p. m. I rode into Reynolds' camp at Hancock Springs.

I attracted some attention as I rode in, for I wore a big Mexican hat mounted with silver, a buckskin jacket fringed from shoulder to elbow with a bunch of flowers braided in highly coloured silk on its back. On my heels were enormous Mexican spurs. I never saw a ranger sent to the Rio Grande for the first time that did not rig himself out in some such outlandish attire, only to discard it a few weeks later, never to wear it again. I was no exception, and I think every man in camp tried on my hat.

Lieutenant Reynolds selected C. L. Nevill for first sergeant, Henry W. McGee as second sergeant, and J. W. Warren and L. W. Conner, first and second corporals, respectively. On September 1, 1877, the company was sworn in. The new command was the most formidable body of men I had ever seen. Our commander, Lieutenant Reynolds, was over six feet tall and weighed probably one hundred and seventy-five pounds. He was a very handsome man, a perfect blond, with steel blue eyes and a long, light moustache. At that time, he was about thirty years of age, vigorous in mind and body, and had a massive determination to succeed as a ranger. His mind was original, bold, profound and quick, with a will that no obstacle could daunt. He was the best ranger in the world—there was never another like him. The lieutenant was a native of Missouri, and was always known as "Major" or "Mage" Reynolds.

It was said that Reynolds, though a mere boy, had served with the Confederates in the latter part of the Civil War. He was one of a party that captured a troop of Federal cavalry, the major of which was well supplied with clothing. The captors, however, were very scantily clad and Reynolds appropriated the major's uniform, hence his nick-name "Mage." In later years when I had grown more intimate with him and was probably closer to him than any other, I mentioned this story. He neither affirmed nor denied it, declaring he was a Missourian by birth, a bootmaker by trade, and that his early history could interest no one.

First Sergeant Nevill was six feet and one inch in height and weighed one hundred and eighty-five pounds. All the non-commissioned officers were at least six feet tall and built in proportion, and many of the privates were from five feet eleven inches to six feet in height. I was probably the lightest man in the company, being only five feet nine inches and weighing but one hundred and forty pounds.

When the company's roster was complete Lieutenant Reynolds had but twenty-eight men—lacking two of his full complement of thirty. The company was then ordered to Austin, but before being assigned to its position on the frontier the lieutenant enlisted John and Will Bannister, two celebrated frontiersmen. They were old cowboys, splendid shots, and well acquainted with every part of Kimble, Menard, Mason, and Kerr Counties, in which Company "E" was destined to operate. In appearance and ability this company compared favourably with any thirty rangers ever sent to the Texas frontier. Nearly every member of the company had had more or less experience as an officer, and all were exceedingly fine marksmen. Sergeant Henry McGee had been marshal of Waco and had figured in several pistol duels in that city. Dave Ligon, the oldest man in the command, had been a Confederate soldier and had served with General Forrest's cavalry.

In the summer of 1877, Lieutenant Armstrong of Captain Hall's company, assisted by Detective Jack Duncan of Dallas, Texas, captured the notorious John Wesley Hardin. It has been said that Texas, the largest state in the Union, has never produced a real world's champion at anything. Surely, such critics overlooked Hardin, the champion *desperado* of the world. His life is too well known in Texas for me to go into detail, but, according to his own story, which I have before me, he killed no fewer than twenty-seven men, the last being Charley Webb, deputy sheriff of Brown County, Texas. So notorious had Hardin become that the State of Texas offered $4,000 reward for his capture. Hardin had left Texas and at the time of his capture was in Florida. His captors arrested and overpowered him while he was sitting in a passenger coach.

In September, 1877, Sheriff Wilson of Comanche County, in whose jurisdiction Hardin had killed Webb, came to Austin to convey the prisoner to Comanche for trial. Wilson requested the governor for an escort of rangers. Lieutenant Reynolds' company, being in Austin at the time, was ordered to accompany Wilson and protect Hardin from mob violence. This was the first work assigned Company "E" under its new commander.

The day we left Austin between one and two thousand people gathered about the Travis County jail to see this notorious *desperado*. The rangers were drawn up just outside the jail, and Henry Thomas and myself were ordered to enter the prison and escort Hardin out. Heavily shackled and handcuffed, the prisoner walked very slowly between us. The boy that had sold fish on the streets of Austin was now guarding the most desperate criminal in Texas; it was glory enough for me.

At his trial Hardin was convicted and sentenced to twenty-five years in the penitentiary. He appealed his case and was returned to Travis County for safekeeping. The verdict of the trial court was sustained, and one year later, in September, 1878, Lieutenant Reynolds' company was ordered to take Hardin back to Comanche County for sentence. There was no railroad at Comanche at that time, so a detachment of rangers, myself among them, escorted Hardin to the penitentiary. There were ten or twelve indictments still pending against him for murder in various counties, but they were never prosecuted.

Hardin served seventeen years on his sentence, and while in prison studied law. Governor Hogg pardoned him in 1894, and restored him to full citizenship.

In transmitting him the governor's pardon, Judge W. S. Fly, Associate Justice of the Court of Appeals, wrote Hardin as follows:

Dear Sir: Enclosed I send you a full pardon from the Governor of Texas. I congratulate you on its reception and trust that it is the day of dawn of a bright and peaceful future. There is time to retrieve a lost past. Turn your back upon it with all its suffering and sorrow and fix your eyes upon the future with the determination to make yourself an honourable and useful member of society. The hand of every true man will be extended to assist you in your upward course, and I trust that the name of Hardin will in the future be associated with the performance of deeds that will ennoble his family and be a blessing to humanity.

"Did you ever read Victor Hugo's masterpiece, *Les Miserables?* If not, you ought to read it. It paints in graphic words the life of one who had tasted the bitterest dregs of life's cup, but in his Christian manhood rose about it, almost like a god and left behind him a path luminous with good deeds.

With the best wishes for your welfare and happiness, I am,
Yours very truly,

W. S. Fly.

Despite all the kind advice given him by eminent lawyers and citizens, Hardin was unequal to the task of becoming a useful man. He practiced law for a time in Gonzales, then drifted away to El Paso, where he began drinking and gambling. On August 19, 1895, Hardin was standing at a bar shaking dice when John Selman, constable of Precinct No. 1, approached him from behind and, placing a pistol to the back of Hardin's head, blew his brains out. Though posing as an officer Selman was himself an outlaw and a murderer of the worst kind. He killed Hardin for the notoriety it would bring him and nothing more.

After delivering Hardin to the sheriff of Travis County in 1877,

Lieutenant Reynolds was ordered to Kimble County for duty. Of all the counties in Texas at that time Kimble was the most popular with outlaws and criminals, for it was situated south of Menard County on the North and South Llano Rivers, with cedar, pecan and *mesquite* timber in which to hide, while the streams and mountains furnished abundance of fish and game for subsistence.

Up on the South Llano lived old Jimmie Dublin. He had a large family of children, most of them grown. The eldest of his boys, Dick, or Richard, as he was known, and a friend, Ace Lankford, killed two men at a country store in Lankford's Cove, Coryell County, Texas. The state offered $500 for the arrest of Dublin and the County of Coryell an additional $200. To escape capture Dick and his companion fled west into Kimble County.

While I was working as cowboy with Joe Franks in the fall of 1873, I became acquainted with the two murderers, for they attached themselves to our outfit. They were always armed and constantly on the watch out for fear of arrest. Dublin was a large man, stout, dark complected, and looked more like the bully of a prize ring than the cowman he was. I often heard him say he would never surrender. While cow hunting with us he discovered that the naturally brushy and tangled county of Kimble would offer shelter for such as he, and persuaded his father to move out into that county.

Dublin had not lived long in Kimble County before another son, Dell Dublin, killed Jim Williams, a neighbour. Thus, two of the Dublin boys were on the dodge charged with murder. They were supposed to be hiding near their father's home. Bill Allison, Starke Reynolds and a number of bandits, horse and cattle thieves and murderers, were known to be in Kimble County, so Lieutenant Reynolds was sent with his company to clean them up.

It was late in October, 1877, before the company reached its destination and camped on the North Llano River below the mouth of Bear Creek. As soon as our horses had rested and camp was fully established for the winter we began scouting. Several men wanted on minor charges were captured. We then raided Luke Stone's ranch, which was about ten miles from our camp, and captured Dell Dublin. He was fearfully angry when he found escape impossible. He tore his shirt bosom open and dared the rangers to shoot him.

While he was being disarmed his elder brother, Dick, rode out of the brush and came within gun shot of the ranch before he discovered the presence of the rangers. He turned his horse quickly and made his escape, though the rangers pursued him some distance. When Dick learned that the Banister boys and myself were with Lieutenant Reynolds' company and hot on his trail, he declared he would whip us with a quirt as a man would a dog if he ever came upon us, for he remembered us as beardless boys with the Joe Franks' cow outfit. However, despite his threat, he never attempted to make it good, but took very good care to keep out of our way until the fatal January 18, 1878.

There was no jail in Kimble County, so with a detachment of rangers I took Dell Dublin and our other prisoners to Llano County lockup.

Shortly afterward Reynolds selected Sergeant McGee, Tom Gillespie, Dick Harrison, and Tim McCarthy and made a scout into Menard County. He also had with him his negro cook, George, to drive his light wagon. On the return toward Bear Creek the scout camped for the night at Fort McKavett. At that time each frontier post had its *chihuahua* or scab town, a little settlement with gambling halls, saloons, etc., to catch the soldiers' dollars. At Fort McKavett were many discharged soldiers, some of them negroes from the Tenth Cavalry. These men had associated with white gamblers and lewd women, and became mean and overbearing.

On this particular night these negro ex-soldiers gave a dance in scab town, and our negro, George, wanted to go. He was a light *mulatto*, almost white, but well thought of by all the boys in the company. He obtained Lieutenant Reynolds' permission to attend the dance, and borrowed Tim McCarthy's pistol to carry to it. When George arrived at the dance hall the ex-soldiers did not like his appearance, as he was allied with the rangers, whom they despised. They jumped on George, took his pistol and kicked him out of the place. The boys were all in bed when George returned and told McCarthy that the negroes at the dance hall had taken his pistol from him.

Lieutenant Reynolds was sleeping nearby and heard what George said. He raised up on his elbow and ordered Sergeant McGee to go with McCarthy and George and get the pistol. The negroes saw McGee coming and, closing the door, defied him to enter the dance hall.

McGee was cool and careful. He advised the negroes to return the pistol, but they refused, saying they would kill the first white-livered s— o— b— that attempted to enter the house. The sergeant then stationed himself at the front door, ordered McCarthy to guard the back entrance of the place, and sent George for the lieutenant. Reynolds hurried to the scene, taking with him Tom Gillespie and Dick

Harrison. The lieutenant knocked on the door and told the blacks he was the commander of the rangers and demanded their surrender. They replied with an oath that they would not do so. Reynolds then ordered the house cleared of women and gave the negroes just five minutes in which to surrender.

Up to this time the women had been quiet, but they now began to scream. This probably demoralised the negro men. One of them poked McCarthy's pistol, muzzle foremost, out of a window.

"Here, come get your d—n pistol," he said.

McCarthy, a new man in the service, stepped up and grasped it. The instant the negro felt the touch of McCarthy's hand on the weapon he pulled the trigger. The ball pierced McCarthy's body just above the heart, giving him a mortal wound.

At the crack of the pistol the rangers opened fire through the doors and windows on the negroes within the house. Reynolds and his men then charged the place, and when the smoke of battle cleared, they found four dead negro men and a little negro girl that had been killed by accident. Only one black escaped. He was hidden under a bed, and as the rangers came in, made a dash to safety under cover of darkness. McCarthy died the following day and was buried near old Fort McKavett. Negro George fought like a tiger and won the boys' praise.

A few days afterward the sheriff of Tom Green County, following the trail of a bunch of stolen cattle from San Angelo, came into our camp. Lieutenant Reynolds sent Sergeant Nevill and a scout of rangers with the sheriff. The trail led over to the South Llano, where the cattle were recovered. While scouting around the herd, Sergeant Nevill discovered a man riding down the trail toward him. He and his men secreted themselves and awaited the stranger's approach. It was getting quite dark, and when the newcomer had ridden almost over the concealed rangers without noticing their presence they rose up, presented their guns and ordered him to halt.

"Yes—like hell!" he exclaimed, and, turning his horse, dived into a cedar brake. A shower of bullets followed, but failed to strike the fugitive. This was the notorious Dick Dublin with a $700 reward on his head.

Sergeant Nevill returned to camp with about fifty head of burnt cattle, but let the most notorious criminal in the county escape. Lieutenant Reynolds was disappointed at this, and said he did not understand how four crack rangers could let a man ride right over them and then get away. He declared his negro cook could have killed Dublin had he been in their place. This mortified the boys a great deal.

The latter part of December, 1877, Lieutenant Reynolds sent a scout out on Little Saline, Menard County. On Christmas day this detail had a running fight with four men. John Collins, the man who stole a yoke of oxen at Fredericksburg and drove them up to within two miles of our camp, was captured, as was also John Gray, wanted for murder in one of the eastern counties. Jim Pope Mason, charged with the murder of Rance Moore, was in this skirmish, but escaped.

One cold morning about the middle of January Corporal Gillett, with Privates John and Will Banister, Tom Gillespie, Dave Ligon, and Ben Carter, was ordered on a five days' scout. We saddled our horses and packed two mules. When all was ready, I walked over to Lieutenant Reynolds. He was sitting on a camp stool before his tent and seemed in a brown study. I saluted and asked for orders.

"Well, Corporal," he said, after a moment's hesitation, "it is a scout after Dick Dublin again. That man seems to be a regular Jonah to this company. He lives only ten miles from here and I have been awfully disappointed at not being able to effect his capture. It is a reflection on all of Company 'E.' There is one thing sure if I can't capture him, I will make life miserable for him. I will keep a scout in the field after him constantly."

I then asked if he had any instructions as to the route I should travel.

"No, no," he replied. "I rely too much on your judgment to hamper you with orders. After you are once out of sight of camp you know these mountains and trails better than I do. Just go and do your best. If you come in contact with him don't let him get away."

After riding a half mile from camp the boys began inquiring where we were going and who we were after. I told them Dick Dublin. We quit the road and travelled south from our camp over to the head of Pack Saddle Creek. Here we turned down the creek and rounded up the Potter ranch, but no one was at home, so we passed on into the cedar brake without having been seen.

On the extreme headwaters of South Llano River some cattlemen had built a large stock pen and were using it to confine wild cattle. This was far out beyond any settlement and probably fifty or sixty miles from our camp. I thought it possible that Dick Dublin might be hanging around the place, so we travelled through the woods most of the way to it. Here I found that the cattlemen had moved.

The scout had now been out two days, so we began our return

journey. We travelled probably twenty-five miles on the third day. On the fourth day I timed myself to reach the Potter ranch about night. Old man Potter, a friend and neighbour of Dublin's, lived here with two grown sons. It was known that Dublin frequented the place, and I hoped to catch him here unawares. About sundown we were within a mile of the ranch. Here we unsaddled our horses and prepared to round up the house. If we met with no success we were to camp there for the night. I left John Banister and Ligon to guard camp while Gillespie, Will Banister, and Ben Carter, with myself, approached the ranch on foot. If I found no one there I intended to return to our camp unseen and round up the ranch again the following morning.

We had not travelled far before we discovered a lone man riding slowly down the trail to the Potter ranch. We remained hidden and were able to approach within fifty yards of the house without being seen. We now halted in the bed of a creek for a short consultation. The one-room cabin had only a single door, and before it was a small wagon. The Potters cooked out of doors between the house and the wagon. We could see a horse tied to the south side of the vehicle, but could not see the camp fire for the wagon and the horse. To our right and about twenty-five steps away old man Potter and one of his sons were unloading some hogs from a wagon into a pen.

We knew the moment we left the creek bed we would be in full view of the Potters and the ranch house. We decided, then, that we would advance on the house as fast as we could run and so be in good position to capture the man who had ridden into the camp. We rose from the creek running. Old man Potter discovered us as we came in view and yelled, "Run, Dick, run! Here comes the rangers!"

We then knew the man we wanted was at the camp. We were so close upon Dublin that he had no time to mount his horse or get his gun, so he made a run for the brush. I was within twenty-five yards of him when he came from behind the wagon, running as fast as a big man could. I ordered him to halt and surrender, but he had heard that call too many times and kept going. Holding my Winchester carbine in my right hand I fired a shot directly at him as I ran. In a moment he was out of sight.

I hurried to the place where he was last seen and spied him running up a little ravine. I stopped, drew a bead on him, and again ordered him to halt. As he ran, Dublin threw his hand back under his coat as though he were attempting to draw a pistol. I fired. My bullet struck the fugitive in the small of the back just over the right hip bone and passed out near his right collarbone. It killed him instantly. He was bending over as he ran, and this caused the unusual course of my ball.

The boys, whom I had outrun, now joined me, and Carter fired two shots at Dublin after he was down. I ordered him to desist as the man was dead. I examined the body to make sure it was Dublin, for I knew him intimately, as I had cow hunted with him before I became a ranger. We found him unarmed, but he had a belt of cartridges around his waist. He was so completely surprised by our sudden appearance he could do nothing but run. The $700 reward on him could never be collected, as it was offered for his arrest and conviction. Dublin's brothers, Role and Dell, swore vengeance against myself and the Banister boys, but nothing ever came of the oath.

In the month of February, 1878, Lieutenant Reynolds started to Austin with five prisoners we had captured in Kimble and Menard Counties. They were chained together in pairs, John Stephens, the odd man, was shackled by himself. As guard for these prisoners Reynolds had detailed Will and John Banister, Dave Ligon, Ben Carter, Dick Ware, and myself.

On the Junction City and Mason road, some ten miles east of our camp, was the small ranch of Starke Reynolds, a fugitive from justice, charged with horse stealing and assault to kill. Company "E" had scouted for him in Kimble County and had rounded up his ranch many times. We knew he was in the county, but he always managed to escape us. As we passed this ranch, Lieutenant Reynolds, Privates Ware, Carter, Ligon, and myself were marching in front, with a four-mule wagon following us, in which were the chained prisoners. Behind it came the Banisters, who were on guard that day and detailed to keep a constant watch on the captive outlaws.

We passed the Starke Reynolds' home about 10 o'clock in the morning, and Lieutenant Reynolds remarked that it was hardly worthwhile to round up the house as he had done so many times in the past without result, but that he would surely like to capture the fellow. We had not ridden more than half a mile beyond the ranch when we came face to face with Starke himself. He was a small man and riding an exceedingly good brown pony. We were about four hundred yards apart and discovered each other at the same instant. The outlaw was carrying a small sack of flour in front of him. He immediately threw this down, turned his horse quickly and made a lightning dash for the Llano bottoms, some three miles away.

At that point the Junction City and Mason road winds along a range of high mountains with the country sloping downward to the Llano River. This grade was studded with scrubby live oak and *mesquite* brush not thick enough to hide a man but sufficiently dense to retard his flight through it. We gave chase at once and for a mile and a half it was the fastest race I ever saw the rangers run. We were closely bunched the entire distance, with Lieutenant Reynolds—he was riding a fast race horse—always slightly in the lead. He finally got close enough to the fugitive to demand his surrender. Starke only waved his gun defiantly and redoubled his speed. Lieutenant Reynolds then drew his six-shooter and began firing at the outlaw. After emptying his pistol, he began using his Winchester.

The Llano bottoms were now looming right up in front of us. The race had been fast enough to run every horse into a big limber. Carter, Ware, and Ligon dropped out of the race. Up to this time I had contented myself by trying to keep up with Lieutenant Reynolds, for it is always easier to follow a man through the brush than to run in the lead. I had a good grip on my bridle reins and was trying to steady my pony as best I could. I now saw that the outlaw was beginning to gain on us. I ran up beside the lieutenant and said, "He is getting away from us. Must I go after him?"

Lieutenant Reynolds turned and looked at me with the wildest look on his face that I ever saw. His hat was gone, his face was badly scratched by the brush with the blood running down over his white shirt bosom.

"Yes, G— d—n him; stop or kill him!"

I changed the bridle reins to my left hand, drew my gun with my right and, digging my spurs deep into my pony's side, I was out of sight of the lieutenant in three hundred yards. The fugitive saw that I was alone and that I was going to overhaul him. He suddenly brought his pony to a standstill, jumped down, took shelter behind the animal and drew a bead on me with his gun.

"G— d—n you, stop, or I'll kill you!" he cried.

I tried to obey his order, but my pony was running down hill and ran straight at him for twenty-five yards more before I could stop. I jumped down from my horse and made ready to fight, but Starke broke for a thicket on foot. As soon as he ran out from behind his pony, I fired at him. The bullet must have come rather close to him, for he turned quickly and took shelter behind his mount again. As he peeped over his saddle at me, I attempted to draw a bead on his head, but I was tired, nervous and unsteady. Before I could shoot Dave

Ligon galloped right up to the outlaw, ordered him to surrender and drop his gun, which Starke did at once. The boys had heard me shoot and in five minutes were all upon the scene.

The captive was searched and ordered to remount his pony. With one of the boys leading Starke's mount we started back to the wagon, nearly three miles away. As soon as the outlaw was a prisoner and knew he would not be harmed no matter what he said, he began a tirade against the rangers. He declared the whole battalion was a set of d—d murderers, especially Company "E," and said it was kerbstone talk in Menard, Mason and Kimble Counties that Lieutenant Reynolds' men would kill a man and then yell for him to throw up his hands.

He kept up this running talk until he exhausted Lieutenant Reynolds' patience. The latter then ordered Starke to shut up, and declared the speaker was a d—d liar, for Company "E" never killed a man without first giving him a chance to surrender. Lieutenant Reynolds then said that with the last old brier-breaker captured he had accomplished the task set him and was now ready to go elsewhere.

As we rode along one of the boys remarked that my pony was limping badly.

"I wish his leg would come right off up to his shoulder," declared Starke in disgust. "If it hadn't been for him, I would have made it to the bottoms and escaped."

On approaching the wagon, the prisoner Stephens, a man of some intelligence and humour, stood up and called out to Starke, "By G—, old man, they got you! They rode too many corn fed horses and carried too many guns for you. I don't know who you are, but I'm sorry for you. While they were chasing you, I got down on my knees here in this wagon and with my face turned up to the skies I prayed to the Almighty God that you might get away."

Starke was chained to this good-natured liar, and now, for the first time, our prisoner seemed to realise his condition. He asked Lieutenant Reynolds to send word to his family that he had been captured. The lieutenant thereupon sent one of the boys to Starke's home to tell Mrs. Reynolds that the rangers would camp on Red Creek for dinner, and if she wished to see her husband, we would be there probably two hours.

Presently Starke's old grey-haired father came to our midday camp. When he saw his son chained, he burst out crying, saying, "My son, it is not my fault that you are in this condition. I did my best to give you good advice and tried to raise you right."

After dinner we resumed our march toward Austin. Starke Reynolds was finally turned over to the sheriff of Tarrant County. He was admitted to bail and gave bond, but before he came to trial, he was waylaid and killed, supposedly by relatives of the man he had previously attempted to murder.

Early in the spring of 1878, a ranchman living five miles above our camp saw a bunch of Indians on Bear Creek, Kimble County, and at once reported to Lieutenant Reynolds. The redskins had been seen late in the evening, and by the time a scout could be started after them it was almost night. The lieutenant, however, followed the trail until it entered a cedar brake. It was then too dark to work farther, so the scout returned to camp to make arrangements to resume the trail the following morning. On the march back to camp the rangers picked up a paint pony with an arrow sticking in its hip. The Indians had probably tried to catch the horse and, failing to do so, had shot it, as was their custom.

Just after dark a runner from Junction City came in and reported a bunch of redskins had been seen near the town stealing horses. It was a beautiful moonlight night and a close watch was kept on our horses. Just at midnight John Banister, an alert man on guard, noticed that one of our pack mules hitched at the end of our picket line was pulling back on its rope and looking over a brush fence that enclosed the camp. With Winchester in hand Banister passed through a gate, walked slowly down the fence and into some small underbrush near the mule.

Suddenly a man rose to his feet and fired on Banister at a distance of not more than ten steps, then broke and ran. Banister at once opened fire on the Indian. The very first report of a gun brought every man in camp out of his bed. We could see the flashes of Banister's gun and went to his aid in our night clothes and barefooted. I ran down by the picket line of horses and jumped the fence where the mule had seen the redskin. By moonlight I could glimpse the Indian running down the river bank. I shot at him nine times as he ran, but without effect. Some two hundred yards below our camp was a ford on the Llano and the fugitive was making for it.

Just as soon as the Indian reached the crossing and plunged into the river, eight or nine of the rangers that had followed Banister on the high ground were in a position to shell the swimmer as he crossed. There were probably a hundred shots fired at him, but he finally disappeared in the brush on the south side of the river. Investigation of the place where he crossed showed the timber cut all to pieces but, strange to say, not a shot hit the Indian as far as we ever knew. We found a blanket where the savage had risen and shot at Banister and, measuring the ground, found that the ranger was just twelve short steps from the Indian when fired upon by the redskin. It was a miracle that Banister was not killed; the bullet, a .45 calibre, buried itself in some sacks of corn in a tent just back of him.

The next morning, we found where ten or twelve Indians had waited under some large pecan trees while this scout slipped up to our camp to investigate and steal a horse. The trees were about four hundred yards from camp and on the opposite side of the river. Some of the rangers jokingly said those old braves must have thought this lone one stirred up hell at the ranger camp.

On account of the range cattle and horses along the Llano River, Lieutenant Reynolds lost some eight or ten hours the next morning before picking up the Indian trail. This gave the redskins ten or twelve hours start, as they were at our camp just at midnight. The trail passed out west between North and South Llano Rivers and followed a rough mountain country that made pursuit difficult and slow. We followed the savages five or six days and finally abandoned the trail near the head of Devil's River after a heavy rain.

While we had been active in rounding up the numerous outlaws and cattle thieves that infested Kimble County, we had not been able to clean up the mystery of the Peg Leg stage robbers, which had long baffled the best detectives, sheriffs, and rangers. Peg Leg was a small stage station on the San Saba in the midst of a rough and very mountainous country. Here the stage was repeatedly held up and as repeatedly the robbers escaped. The scene of the hold-up was many times examined and parties made determined efforts to trail the bandits but always without success, for the trail was quickly lost in the rough mountains.

One of the features that proved particularly puzzling was the constant recurrence of an exceedingly small footprint at each robbery. These marks were so very small they convinced many observers that a woman from Fort McKavett or Fort Concho was operating with the bandit gang. Naturally the rangers were anxious to round up this group of outlaws and put a stop to their depredations.

In May, 1878, Sergeant Nevill made a scout up on the South Llano and captured Bill Alison, a son-in-law of old Jimmie Dublin, father of the bandit, Dick Dublin. Alison was wanted on several charges of cattle theft, and was taken to Austin for safekeeping. After remaining in the Travis County jail for nearly a year without being able to give bond, Alison became discouraged. He believed his brothers-in-law, the Dublins, were not aiding him to get bond and became bitter and resentful toward them. This antagonism finally led to the unveiling of the Peg Leg mystery.

In the spring of 1879, Dick Ware and myself took some prisoners to the Austin jail. Bill Alison saw us and called out to me. He and I had been cowboys together long before I became a ranger.

"Jim," said Alison, "you know I have been cooped up here in this jail for nearly a year. People who ought to be my friends have evidently abandoned me and I am not going to stand it any longer. I can put the Peg Leg stage robbers behind the bars, and I am going to do it."

Ware, who was something of a diplomat, said, "Hold on, Bill. If you have anything to confess, we will get an order from the sheriff to take you to see General Jones so you can talk to him."

The general at once wrote a note to Dennis Corwin, sheriff of Travis County, and asked that he let Alison accompany us to his office. The sheriff turned his prisoner over to us and we took him to General Jones, who had a private interview with him for over an hour. What Alison confessed we did not know, but we returned him to the jail.

General Jones moved quickly, for the very next day a scout of rangers from Company "E" was sent back to Kimble County. I was just preparing to go west to El Paso with Colonel Baylor, so I missed this last and most important scout back into Kimble County. However, this final expedition was so successful I cannot omit it from a history of the rangers.

Arriving at Kimble County the Company "E" detail arrested Role and Dell Dublin, Mack Potter and Rube Boyce. In the running fight that resulted in their capture Role received a bad wound in the hip. The two Dublin brothers and Mack Potter when arraigned in Federal court plead guilty to stage robbery and were sentenced to fifteen years at hard labour. During their trial the mystery of the Peg Leg robberies was finally cleared up. The Dublin boys were the guiding spirits in the holdups and worked with great cleverness.

Old man Jimmie Dublin's ranch on the South Llano was their headquarters. From the ranch to Peg Leg Station on the San Saba was not more than sixty miles across a rough, mountainous country. As there were no wire fences in those days the robbers would ride over to the station, rob the stage and in one night's ride regain their home. Traveling at night they were never observed. Dick Dublin, whose death while resisting capture has already been described, was the leader of the bandit gang. Even the mystery of the tiny footprints was disclosed; they were made by Mack Potter, who had an unusually small foot for a man.

While Rube Boyce was confined in the Travis County jail, he made one of the most sensational jail escapes in the criminal annals of Texas. Mrs. Boyce called at the prison with a suit of clean underclothes for her husband. The basket in which she carried them was examined and she was admitted into the cell of her husband. However, she had hidden a big .45 Colt's revolver about her person and smuggled it in. Rube changed his underwear, put the soiled garments in the basket and hid the pistol under them.

At the end of her visit Mrs. Boyce started out and Rube accompanied her down the corridor to the door. Mr. Albert Nichols, the jailer, opened the door with his left hand to let the woman pass out, at the same time holding his pistol in his right hand. As the door swung open Rube reached into the basket he was carrying for his wife, whipped out the hidden pistol, thrust it into the jailer's face and ordered him to drop his .45 and step within the jail. Realising that a second's hesitation would mean his death, Nichols complied and was locked in by the outlaw.

Boyce then ran out of the back yard of the jail, mounted a pony that had been hitched there for him and galloped out of Austin, firing his pistol as he ran. He made a complete get-away. Three or four years later he was arrested at Socorro, New Mexico, and returned to Austin. At his trial for participation in the Peg Leg stage robberies he was acquitted, and perhaps justly so, for Bill Alison declared to me that Dick Dublin with his brothers Dell and Role and Mack Potter were the real robbers.

The arrest and conviction of the Dublins, together with the other men Lieutenant Reynolds had captured or killed completely cleaned out the stage robbers, cattle and horse thieves and murderers that had made Kimble County their rendezvous. Today Kimble County is one of the most prosperous and picturesque counties in the state. Its citizens are law-abiding and energetic. Junction City, the county seat, is a splendid little city of probably twenty-five hundred inhabitants.

Forty years ago, the time of which I write, there were no courthouses in Kimble County. The first district courts were held under the spreading boughs of a large oak tree. The rangers, of which I was frequently one, guarded the prisoners under another tree at a convenient distance from the judge and his attendants.

Late in the spring or early summer of 1878 at a session of the County Court of San Saba County, Billy Brown was being prosecuted by County Attorney Brooks for a violation of the prohibition laws. Brown took offense at a remark of the prosecuting attorney and attempted to draw his six-shooter on him. T. J. T. Kendall, a law partner of Brooks, saw Brown's move and quickly whipping out his own pistol, he killed Brown in the courtroom. Then, fearing a mob if captured, Kendall fortified himself in a second story of the courthouse and refused to surrender. He held the whole town at bay while his wife administered to his wants. Meantime, he sent a hurry call to the nearest rangers asking for protection against mob violence. Captain Arrington received the message and sent a detachment from Coleman to San Saba to preserve order.

General Jones was notified and ordered Lieutenant Reynolds at Junction City to march to San Saba with his company, take charge of Kendall and relieve Captain Arrington's men. It was probably two weeks after the killing before Company "E" reached San Saba, but Mr. Kendall was still holding fort in the upper storey of the courthouse.

On the arrival of Reynolds' company, Kendall asked the court for a preliminary examination. When court convened, the prisoner waived examination and asked for transference to the Travis County jail at Austin. The court, realising the feeling against Kendall, ordered his removal thither.

When the time came for Kendall's removal a hack was driven up to the courthouse door, where a great crowd had assembled to see the prisoner. Jim Brown, sheriff of Lee County, Texas, and brother of Bill Brown, heavily armed, had taken his station within ten feet of the prison door. Just before Mr. Kendall descended the courthouse steps Lieutenant Reynolds ordered the crowd to fall back fifty feet from the hack. The people immediately obeyed with the exception of Jim Brown, who sat perfectly still on his horse. The lieutenant looked at Brown for a minute, then turned to his rangers and ordered them to draw their guns and move everyone fifty yards from the courthouse. Like a flash every ranger drew his gun, dismounted and waved the crowd back.

Brown turned to Reynolds and said, "I am going to Austin with you."

"If you do, you will go in irons. Move back!"

Brown, who had killed several men, slowly turned his horse and rode away. He did not know the man with whom he was dealing. Lawyer Kendall was thereupon carried to Austin without incident.

When we reached Austin, Jim Brown met Lieutenant Reynolds on the street and apologised for the way he had acted at San Saba. He said he fully intended to kill Kendall as he approached the hack, but the presence of so many rangers caused him to change his mind. Lieutenant Reynolds declared he was anticipating just such a move and had instructed his men to shoot Brown into doll rags at his first move.

Soon after this Lieutenant Reynolds moved Company "E" down on the San Saba in a beautiful pecan grove, an ideal summer camp, about two miles from the town of San Saba. From this point we scouted all over Llano, Lampasas, Burnet and San Saba Counties at our favourite pursuit of rounding up bad men. It was from this camp that we made our sensational ride to Round Rock after Sam Bass, the notorious train robber.

CHAPTER 9

Sam Bass and His Train Robber Gang

Sam Bass, the noted train robber, was born in Indiana, July 21, 1851. He came to Texas while quite a youth and worked for Sheriff Everhart of Denton County until he reached manhood. While still an exemplary and honest young man, Bass came into possession of a small race pony, a little sorrel mare. On Saturday evenings, when most of the neighbourhood boys met in Denton, Bass raced his pony with much success. Mr. Everhart soon noticed that Sam was beginning to neglect his work because of his pony and, knowing only too well what this would lead to, he advised Sam to sell his mare. Bass hesitated, for he loved the animal. Finally matters came to such a point that Mr. Everhart told Sam he would have to get rid of the horse or give up his job. Thereupon Bass promptly quit, and this was probably the turning point in his life.

Bass left Denton County in the spring of 1877, and travelled to San Antonio. Here many cattlemen were gathered to arrange for the spring cattle drive to the north. Joel Collins, who was planning to drive a herd from Uvalde County to Deadwood, Dakota, hired Bass as a cowboy. After six months on the trail the herd reached Deadwood and was sold and all the cowboys paid off by Mr. Collins.

At that period Deadwood was a great, wide open mining town. Adventurers, gamblers, mining and cattlemen all mingled together. Though Joel Collins had bought his cattle on credit and owed the greater part of the money he had received for them to his friends in Texas, he gambled away all the money he had received for the herd. When he sobered up and realised all his money was gone, he did not have the moral courage to face his friends and creditors at home. He became desperate, and with a band of his cowboys held up and robbed several stage coaches in the Black Hills. These robberies brought Collins very little booty, but they started Sam Bass on his criminal career.

In the fall of 1877, Collins, accompanied by Bass, Jack Davis, Jim Berry, Bill Heffridge, and John Underwood, better known as Old Dad, left Deadwood and drifted down to Ogallala, Nebraska. Here he conceived, planned and carried into execution one of the boldest train robberies that ever occurred in the United States up to that time. When all was ready these six men, heavily armed and masked, held up the Union Pacific train at Big Springs, a small station a few miles beyond Ogallala. The bandits entered the express car and ordered the messenger to open the safe. The latter explained that the through safe had a time lock and could only be opened at the end of the route.

One of the robbers then began to beat the messenger over the head with a six-shooter, declaring he would kill him if the safe were not opened. Bass, always of a kindly nature, pleaded with the man to desist, declaring he believed the messenger was telling the truth. Just as the robbers were preparing to leave the car without a cent one of them noticed three stout little boxes piled near the big safe. The curious bandit seized a coal pick and knocked off the lid of the top box. To his great joy and delight he exposed $20,000 in shining gold coin! The three boxes each held a similar amount, all in $20 gold pieces of the mintage of 1877.

After looting these boxes, the robbers went through the train, and in a systematic manner robbed the passengers of about $5,000. By daylight the bandits had hidden their booty and returned to Ogallala. They hung around town several days while railroad officials, United States marshals and sheriffs' parties were scouring the country for the train robbers.

While in Ogallala before and after the robbery, Collins and his men frequented a large general merchandise store. In this store was a clerk who had once been an express messenger on the Union Pacific and who was well acquainted with the officials of that company. I have forgotten his name, but I will call him Moore for the sake of clearness in my narrative. Of course, the great train robbery was the talk of the town. Moore conversed with Collins and his gang about the hold-up, and the bandits declared they would help hunt the robbers if there was enough money in it.

Moore's suspicions were aroused and he became convinced that Collins and his band were the real hold-up men. However, he said nothing to anyone about this belief, but carefully watched the men. Finally, Collins came to the store and, after buying clothing and provisions, told Mr. Moore that he and his companions were going back to Texas and would be up the trail the following spring with another herd of cattle. When Collins had been gone a day's travel, Mr. Moore hired a horse and followed him. He soon found the route the suspects were travelling, and on the second day Moore came upon them suddenly while they were stopping at a roadside farmhouse to have some bread cooked. Moore passed by without being noticed and secreted himself near the highway. In a short time, Collins and his men passed on and Moore trailed them until they went into camp. When it was dark the amateur detective crept up to the bandits, but they had gone to sleep and he learned nothing.

The next day Moore resumed the trail. He watched the gang make their camp for the night and again crept up to within a few yards of his suspects. The bandits had built a big fire and were laughing and talking. Soon they spread out a blanket, and to Moore's great astonishment brought out some money bags and emptied upon the blanket sixty thousand dollars in gold. From his concealed position the trailer heard the robbers discuss the hold-up.

They declared they did not believe anyone had recognised or suspected them and decided it was now best for them to divide the money, separate in pairs and go their way. The coin was stacked in six piles and each man received $10,000 in $20 gold pieces. It was further decided that Collins and Bill Heffridge would travel back to San Antonio, Texas, together; Sam Bass and Jack Davis were to go to Denton County, Texas, while Jim Berry and Old Dad were to return to the Berry home in Mexico, Missouri.

As soon as Mr. Moore had seen the money and heard the robbers' plans he slipped back to his horse, mounted and rode day and night to reach Ogallala. He notified the railroad officials of what he had seen, gave the names and descriptions of the bandits and their destinations. This information was sent broadcast over southern Nebraska, Kansas, Indian Territory, and Texas. In the fugitive list sent to each of the companies of the Frontier Battalion of rangers Sam Bass was thus described:—

> Twenty-five to twenty-six years old, 5 feet 7 inches high, black hair, dark brown eyes, brown moustache, large white teeth, shows them when talking; has very little to say.

A few days after the separation of the robbers, Joel Collins and Bill Heffridge rode into a small place in Kansas called Buffalo Station. They led a pack pony. Dismounting from their tired horses and leaving them standing in the shade of the store building, the two men entered the store and made several purchases. The railroad agent at the place noticed the strangers ride up. He had, of course, been advised to be on the lookout for the train robbers. He entered the store and in a little while engaged Collins in conversation. While talking the robber pulled his handkerchief out of his coat pocket and exposed a letter with his name thereon. The agent was a shrewd man. He asked Collins if he had not driven a herd of cattle up the trail in the spring. Collins declared he had, and finally, in answer to a direct question, admitted that his name was Joel Collins.

Five or six hundred yards from Buffalo Station a lieutenant of the United States Army had camped a troop of ten men that was scouting for the train robbers. As soon as Collins and Heffridge remounted and resumed their way the agent ran quickly to the soldiers' camp, pointed out the bandits to the lieutenant and declared, "There go two of the Union Pacific train robbers!"

The army officer mounted his men and pursued Collins and Heffridge. When he overtook the two men, he told them their descriptions tallied with those of some train robbers that he was scouting for, and declared they would have to go back to the station and be identified. Collins laughed at the idea, and declared that he and his companion were cattlemen returning to their homes in Texas. They reluctantly turned and started back with the soldiers.

After riding a few hundred yards the two robbers held a whispered conversation. Suddenly the two pulled their pistols and attempted to stand off the lieutenant and his troop. The *desperadoes* were promptly shot and killed. On examining their packs, the soldiers found tied up in the legs of a pair of overalls $20,000 in gold, 1877, mintage. Not a dollar of the stolen money had been used and there was no doubt about the identity of the men.

Not long after the divide up in Nebraska Jim Berry appeared at his home in Mexico, Missouri. At once he deposited quite a lot of money in the local bank and exchanged $3,000 in gold for currency, explaining his possession of the gold by saying he had sold a mine in the Black Hills. In three or four days the sheriff of the county learned of Berry's deposits and called at the bank to see the new depositor's gold. His suspicion became a certainty when he found that Berry had deposited $20 gold pieces of 1877.

At night the sheriff with a posse rounded up Berry's house, but the suspect was not there. The home was well provisioned and the posse found many articles of newly purchased clothing. Just after daylight, while searching about the place the sheriff heard a horse whinny in some timber nearby. Upon investigating this he suddenly came upon Jim Berry sitting on a pallet. Berry discovered the officer at about the same time and attempted to escape by running. He was fired upon, one bullet striking him in the knee and badly shattering it. He was taken to his home and given the best of medical attention, but gangrene set in and he died in a few days. Most of his $10,000 was recovered. Old Dad evidently quit Berry somewhere *en route*, for he made good his escape with his ill-gotten gain and was never apprehended.

Sam Bass and Jack Davis, after the separation in Nebraska, sold their ponies, bought a light spring wagon and a pair of work horses. They placed their gold pieces in the bottom of the wagon, threw their bedding and clothes over it, and in this disguise travelled through Kansas and the Indian Territory to Denton County, Texas. During their trip through the Territory Bass afterward said he camped within one hundred yards of a detachment of cavalry. After supper he and Davis visited the soldiers' camp and chatted with them until bedtime. The soldiers said they were on the lookout for some train robbers that had held up the Union Pacific in Nebraska, never dreaming for a moment that they were conversing with two of them. The men also mentioned that two of the robbers had been reported killed in Kansas.

This rumour put Bass and Davis on their guard, and on reaching Denton County they hid in the elm bottoms until Bass could interview some of his friends. Upon meeting them he learned that the names and descriptions of every one of the Union Pacific train robbers were in the possession of the law officers; that Collins, Heffridge, and Berry had been killed; and that every sheriff in North Texas was on the watch for Davis and himself. Davis at once begged Bass to go with him to South America, but Bass refused, so Davis bade Sam goodbye and set out alone. He was never captured. On his deathbed Bass declared he had once received a letter from Jack Davis written from New Orleans, asking Bass to come there and go into the business of buying hides.

Bass had left Denton County early in the spring an honest, sincere and clean young man. By falling with evil associates, he had become within a few months one of the most daring outlaws and train robbers of his time. Before he had committed any crime in the state the officers of North Texas made repeated efforts to capture him for the big reward offered by the Union Pacific and the express company but owing to the nature of the country around Denton and the friends Bass had as long as his gold lasted, met with no success.

Bass's money soon attracted several desperate and daring men to him. Henry Underwood. Arkansas Johnson. Jim Murphy. Frank Jackson, Pipes Herndon, and Collins—the last one a cousin of Joel Collins—and two or three others joined him in the elm bottoms. Naturally Bass was selected as leader of the gang. It was not long before the outlaw chief planned and executed his first train robbery in Texas: that at Eagle Ford, a small station on the T. P. Railroad, a few miles out of Dallas. In quick succession the bandits held up two or three other trains, the last, I believe, being at Mesquite Station, ten or twelve miles east of Dallas. From this robbery they secured about $3,000. They met with opposition here, for the conductor, though armed with only a small pistol, fought the robbers to a fare-you-well and slightly wounded one of them.

The whole state was now aroused by the repeated train hold-ups. General Jones hurried to Dallas and Denton to look over the situation and, strange to say, he arranged to organise a company of rangers at Dallas. Captain June Peak, a very able officer, was given the command. No matter how brave a company of recruits, it takes time and training to get results from them, and when this raw company was thrown into the field against Bass and his gang the bandit leader played with it as a child plays with toys.

Counting the thirty rangers and the different sheriffs' parties, there were probably one hundred men in pursuit of the Bass gang. Sam played hide-and-seek with them all and, it is said, never ranged any farther west than Stephens County or farther north than Wise. He was generally in Dallas. Denton or Tarrant Counties. He would frequently visit Fort Worth or Dallas at night, ride up with his men to some outside saloon, get drinks all around and then vamoose.

Finally, in a fight at Salt Creek, Wise County, Captain June Peak and his rangers killed Arkansas Johnson, Bass's most trusted lieutenant. Either just before or soon after this battle the rangers captured Pipes Herndon and Jim Murphy and drove Bass and his two remaining companions out of North Texas. At that time the state had on the frontier of Texas six companies of veteran rangers. They were finely mounted, highly equipped, and were the best mounted police in the world. Any company on the line could have been marched to Denton in ten days, yet they were never moved one mile in that direction. Any one of those highly trained commands could have broken up the Sam Bass gang in half the time it took a command of new men.

After the fight on Salt Creek only Sam Bass, Sebe Barnes, and Frank Jackson were left of the once formidable gang. These men had gained nothing from their four train robberies in North Texas, and were so hard pressed by the officers of the law on all sides that Bass reluctantly decided to leave the country and try to make his way to Old Mexico. Through some pretended friends of Bass, General Jones learned of the contemplated move. He, with Captain Peak and other officers, approached Jim Murphy, one of Bass'ss gang captured about the time of the Salt Creek fight, who was awaiting trial by the Federal authorities for train robbery, and promised they would secure his release if he would betray Bass. Murphy hesitated and said his former chief had been kind to his family, had given them money and provisions, and that it would be ungrateful to betray his friend.

The general declared he understood Murphy's position fully, but Bass was an outlaw, a pest to the country, who was preparing to leave the state and so could no longer help him. General Jones warned Murphy that the evidence against him was overwhelming and was certain to send him to the Federal prison—probably for life—and exhorted him to remember his wife and his children. Murphy finally yielded and agreed to betray Bass and his gang at the first opportunity. According to the plan agreed upon Murphy was to give bond and when the Federal court convened at Tyler, Texas, a few weeks later he was not to show up. It would then be published all over the country that Murphy had skipped bond and rejoined Bass. This was carried out to the letter.

Murphy joined Bass in the elm bottoms of Denton County and agreed to rob a train or bank and get out of the country. Some of Bass's friends, suspicious of Murphy's bondsmen, wrote Sam that Murphy was playing a double game and advised him to kill the traitor at once. Bass immediately confronted Murphy with these reports and reminded him how freely he had handed out his gold to Murphy's family. Bass declared he had never advised or solicited Jim to join him, and said it was a low down, mean and ungrateful trick to betray him. He told Murphy plainly if he had anything to say to say it quickly. Barnes agreed with his chief and urged Murphy's death.

The plotter denied any intention of betraying Bass and offered to take the lead in any robbery Bass should plan and be the first to enter the express car or climb over the bank railing. Bass was mad and so was Barnes. They elected to kill the liar at once. Frank Jackson had taken no part in the conversation, but he now declared he had known Murphy since he was a little boy, and he was sure Murphy was sincere and meant to stand by them through thick and thin. Bass was not satisfied, and insisted that Murphy be murdered then and there. Jackson finally told Bass and Barnes that they could not kill Murphy without first killing him. Although the youngest of the party—Frank was only twenty-two years old—Jackson had great influence over his chief.

He was brave and daring, and Bass at that time could not very well get along without him, so his counsel prevailed and Murphy was spared. The bandits then determined to quit the country. Their plan was to rob a small bank somewhere *en route* to Old Mexico and thus secure the funds needed to facilitate their escape, for they were all broke.

Bass, Sebe Barnes, Frank Jackson, and Jim Murphy left Denton County early in July, 1878. With his usual boldness, Bass, after he had passed Dallas County, made no attempt at concealment, but travelled the public highway in broad daylight. Bass and Barnes were still suspicious of Murphy, and never let him out of their sight, though they refused to talk to or to associate with him in any way. When Bass reached Waco, the party camped on the outskirts of the town and remained there two or three days. They visited the town each day, looked over the situation, and in one bank saw much gold and currency. Jackson was enthusiastic and wanted to rob it at once. Bass, being more careful and experienced, thought it too hazardous an undertaking, for the run through crowded streets to the outskirts of the city was too far; and so, vetoed the attempt.

While in Waco the gang stepped into a saloon to get a drink. Bass laid a $20 gold piece on the bar and remarked, "There goes the last twenty of the Union Pacific money and d—n little good it has done me." On leaving Waco the robbers stole a fine mare from a farmer named Billy Mounds and travelled the main road to Belton. They were now out of money and planned to rob the bank at Round Rock, Williamson County.

General Jones was now getting anxious over the gang. Not a word had been heard from Jim Murphy since he had rejoined the band, for he had been so closely watched that he had had no opportunity to communicate with the authorities, and it seemed as if he would be forced to participate in the next robbery in spite of himself.

At Belton Sam sold an extra pony his party had after stealing the mare at Waco. The purchaser demanded a bill of sale as the vendors were strangers in the country. While Bass and Barnes were in a store writing out the required document, Murphy seized the opportunity to dash off a short note to General Jones, saying, "We are on our way to Round Rock to rob the bank. For God's sake be there to prevent it." As the post office adjoined the store the traitor succeeded in mailing his letter of betrayal just one minute before Bass came out on the street again. The gang continued their way to Round Rock and camped near the old town, which is situated about one mile north of New Round Rock. The bandits concluded to rest and feed their horses for three or four days before attempting their robbery. This delay was providential, for it gave General Jones time to assemble his rangers to repel the attack.

After Major Jones was made Adjutant-General of Texas he caused a small detachment of four or five rangers to camp on the Capitol grounds at Austin. He drew his units from different companies along the line. Each unit would be detailed to camp in Austin, and about every six weeks or two months the detail would be relieved by a squad from another company. It will readily be seen that this was a wise policy, as the detail was always on hand and could be sent in any direction by rail or on horseback at short notice. Besides, General Jones was devoted to his rangers and liked to have them around where he could see them daily. At the time of which I write four men from Company "E"—Corporal Vernon Wilson and Privates Dick Ware, Chris Connor, and Geo. Harold—were camped at Austin. The corporal helped General Jones as a clerk in his office, but was in charge of the squad on the Capitol grounds, slept in camp and had his meals with them.

When General Jones received Murphy's letter, he was astonished at Bass's audacity in approaching within fifteen or twenty miles of the state capital, the very headquarters of the Frontier Battalion, to rob a bank. The letter was written at Belton, Texas, and received at the Adjutant-General's office on the last mail in the afternoon. The company of rangers nearest Round Rock was Lieutenant Reynolds' Company "E," stationed at San Saba, one hundred and fifteen miles distant. There was no telegraph to San Saba then. General Jones reflected a few moments after receipt of the letter and then arranged his plan rapidly.

He turned to Corporal Wilson and told him that Sam Bass and his gang were, or soon would be, at Round Rock, Texas, to rob the bank there. He ordered:—

I want you to leave at once to carry an order to Lieutenant Reynolds. It is sixty-five miles to Lampasas and you can make that place early enough in the morning to catch the Lampasas and San Saba stage,. You must make that stage at all hazards, save neither yourself nor your horse, but get these orders to Lieutenant Reynolds as quickly as possible.

Corporal Wilson hurried to the livery stable, saddled his horse and got away from Austin on his wild ride just at nightfall. His horse was fresh and fat and in no condition to make such a run. However, Wilson reached Lampasas at daylight next morning and made the outgoing stage to San Saba, but killed his gallant little grey horse in the doing of it. From Lampasas to San Saba was fifty miles, and it took the stage all day to make the trip. As soon as he landed in town Corporal Wilson hired a horse and galloped three miles down to Lieutenant Reynolds' camp and delivered his orders.

After dispatching Corporal Wilson to Lieutenant Reynolds, General Jones hurried over to the ranger camp on the Capitol grounds and ordered the three rangers, Ware, Connor, and Harold, to proceed to Round Rock, put their horses in Highsmith's livery stable and keep themselves concealed until he could reach them himself by train next morning. The following morning General Jones went to Round Rock. He carried with him from Austin, Morris Moore, an ex-ranger but then deputy sheriff of Travis County. On reaching his destination the general called on Deputy Sheriff Grimes of Williamson County, who was stationed at Round Rock, told him Bass was expected in town to rob the bank, and that a scout of rangers would be in town as soon as possible. Jones advised Deputy Grimes to keep a sharp lookout for strangers but on no account to attempt an arrest until the rangers could arrive.

I well remember the hot July evening when Corporal Wilson arrived in our camp with his orders. The company had just had supper, the horses fed and tied up for the night. We knew the sudden appearance of the corporal meant something of unusual importance. Soon Sergeant Nevill came hurrying to us with orders to detail a party for an immediate scout. Lieutenant Reynolds' orders had been brief, but to the point:—

Bass is at Round Rock. We must be there as early as possible tomorrow. Make a detail of eight men and select those that have the horses best able to make a fast run. And you, with them, report to me here at my tent ready to ride in thirty minutes.

First Sergeant C. L. Nevill, Second Sergeant Henry McGee, Second Corporal J. B. Gillett, Privates Abe Anglin, Dave Ligon, Bill Derrick, and John R. and W. L. Banister were selected for the detail. Lieutenant Reynolds ordered two of our best little pack mules hitched to a light spring hack, for he had been sick and was not in condition to make the journey horseback. In thirty minutes from the time Corporal Wilson reached camp we were mounted, armed and ready to go. Lieutenant Reynolds took his seat in the hack, threw some blankets in, and Corporal Wilson, who had not had a minute's sleep for over thirty-six hours, lay down to get a little rest as we moved along. Say, boys, did you ever try to follow on horseback two fast travelling little mules hitched to an open-topped spring hack for one hundred miles? Well, it is some stunt. We left our camp on the San Saba River just at sunset and travelled in a fast trot and sometimes in a lope the entire night.

Our old friend and comrade, Jack Martin, then in the mercantile business at the little town of Senterfitt, heard us pass by in the night, and next morning said to some of his customers that hell was to pay somewhere as the rangers had passed his store during the night on a dead run.

The first rays of the rising sun shone on us at the crossing of North Gabriel, fifteen miles south of Lampasas. We had ridden sixty-five miles that short summer night—we had forty-five miles yet to go before reaching Round Rock. We halted on the Gabriel for breakfast of bread, broiled bacon and black coffee. The horses had a bundle of oats each. Lieutenant Reynolds held his watch on us and it took us just thirty minutes to breakfast and be off again. We were now facing a hot July sun and our horses were beginning to show the effects of the hard ride of the night before and slowed down perceptibly. We never halted again until we reached the vicinity of old Round Rock between 1 and 2 o'clock in the afternoon of Friday, July 19, 1878. The lieutenant camped us on the banks of Brushy Creek and drove into New Round Rock to report his arrival to General Jones.

Bass had decided to rob the bank at Round Rock on Saturday, the 20th. After his gang had eaten dinner in camp Friday evening, they saddled their ponies and started over to town to take a last look at the bank and select a route to follow in leaving the place after the robbery. As they left camp Jim Murphy, knowing that the bandits might be set upon at any time, suggested that he stop at May's store in Old

Round Rock and get a bushel of corn, as they were out of feed for their horses. Bass, Barnes and Jackson rode on into town, hitched their horses in an alley just back of the bank, passed that building and made a mental note of its situation. They then went up the main street of the town and entered Copprel's store to buy some tobacco. As the three bandits passed into the store, Deputy Sheriff Moore, who was standing on the sidewalk with Deputy Sheriff Grimes, said he thought one of the newcomers had a pistol.

"I will go in and see," replied Grimes.

"I believe you have a pistol," remarked Grimes, approaching Bass and trying to search him.

"Yes, of course I have a pistol," said Bass. At the words the robbers pulled their guns and killed Grimes as he backed away to the door. He fell dead on the sidewalk. They then turned on Moore and shot him through the lungs as he attempted to draw his weapon.

At the crack of the first pistol shot Dick Ware, who was seated in a barber shop only a few steps away, waiting his turn for a shave, rushed into the street and encountered the three bandits just as they were leaving the store. Seeing Ware rapidly advancing on them, Bass and his men fired on the ranger at close range, one of their bullets striking a hitching post within six inches of Ware's head and knocking splinters into his face. This assault never halted Ware for an instant. He was as brave as courage itself and never hesitated to take the most desperate chances when the occasion demanded it.

For a few minutes Dick fought the robbers single handed. General Jones, coming up town from the telegraph office, ran into the fight. He was armed with only a small Colt's double action pistol, but threw himself into the fray. Connor and Harold had now come up and joined in the fusillade. The general, seeing the robbers on foot and almost within his grasp, drew in close and urged his men to strain every nerve to capture or exterminate the *desperadoes*. By this time every man in the town that could secure a gun joined in the fight.

The bandits had now reached their horses, and realising their situation was critical fought with the energy of despair. If ever a train robber could be called a hero this boy, Frank Jackson, proved himself one. Barnes was shot down and killed at his feet, Bass was mortally wounded and unable to defend himself or even mount his horse while the bullets continued to pour in from every quarter. With heroic courage, Jackson held the rangers back with his pistol in his right hand while he unhitched Bass's horse with his left and assisted him into the saddle.

Then, mounting his own horse, Jackson and his chief galloped out of the jaws of hell itself. In their flight they passed through Old Round Rock, and Jim Murphy, standing in the door of May's store, saw Jackson and Bass go by on the dead run. The betrayer noticed that Jackson was holding Bass, pale and bleeding, in the saddle.

Lieutenant Reynolds, entering Round Rock, came within five minutes of meeting Bass and Jackson in the road. Before he reached town, he met posses of citizens and rangers in pursuit of the robbers.

When the fugitives reached the cemetery Jackson halted long enough to secure a Winchester they had hidden in the grass there, then left the road and were lost for a time. The fight was now over and the play spoiled by two over-zealous deputies in bringing on an immature fight after they had been warned to be careful. Naturally Moore and Grimes should have known that the three strangers were the Sam Bass gang.

Lieutenant Reynolds started Sergeant Nevill and his rangers early next morning in search of the flying bandits. After travelling in the direction, the robbers were last seen we came upon a man lying under a large oak tree. Seeing we were armed as we advanced upon him, he called out to us not to shoot, saying he was Sam Bass, the man we were hunting.

After entering the woods, the evening before, Bass became so sick and faint from loss of blood that he could go no farther. Jackson dismounted and wanted to stay with his chief, declaring he was a match for all their pursuers.

"No, Frank," replied Bass. "I am done for."

The wounded leader told his companion to tie his horse near at hand so he could get away if he felt better during the night. Jackson was finally prevailed upon to leave Bass and make his own escape.

When daylight came Saturday morning Bass got up and walked to a nearby house. As he approached the place a lady, seeing him coming holding his pants up and all covered with blood, left her house and started to run off, as she was alone with a small servant girl. Bass saw she was frightened and called to her to stop, saying he was perishing for a drink of water and would return to a tree not far away and lie down if she would only send him a drink. The lady sent him a quart cup of water, but the poor fellow was too far gone to drink it. We found him under this tree one hour later. He had a wound through the centre of his left hand, the bullet having pierced the middle finger.

Bass's death wound was given him by Dick Ware, who used a .45

calibre Colt's long barrelled six-shooter. The ball from Ware's pistol struck Bass's belt and cut two cartridges in pieces and entered his back just above the right hip bone. The bullet badly mushroomed and made a fearful wound that tore the victim's right kidney all to pieces. From the moment he was shot until his death three days later Bass suffered untold agonies. As he lay on the ground Friday night where Jackson had left him the wounded man tore his undershirt into more than one hundred pieces and wiped the blood from his body.

Bass was taken to Round Rock and given the best of medical attention, but died the following day, Sunday, July 21, 1878. While he was yet able to talk, General Jones appealed to Bass to reveal to the state authorities the names of the confederates he had had that they might be apprehended.

> Sam, you have done much evil in this world and have only a few hours to live. Now, while you have a chance to do the state some good, please tell me who your associates were in those violations of the laws of your country.

Sam replied that he could not betray his friends and that he might as well die with what he knew in him.

Sam Bass was buried in the cemetery at Old Round Rock. A small monument was erected over his grave by a sister. Its simple inscription reads:—

SAMUEL BASS

BORN JULY 21ST, 1851

DIED JULY 21ST, 1878

A BRAVE MAN REPOSES IN DEATH HERE.

WHY WAS HE NOT TRUE?

Frank Jackson made his way back into Denton County and hung around some time hoping to get an opportunity to murder the betrayer of his chief, an ingrate whose cause he himself had so ably championed. Jackson declared if he could meet Jim Murphy, he would kill him, cut off his head and carry it away in a gunny sack.

Murphy returned to Denton, but learned that Jackson was hiding in the elm bottoms awaiting a chance to slay him. He thereupon asked permission of the sheriff to remain about the jail for protection. While skulking about the prison one of his eyes became infected. A physician gave him some medicine to drop into the diseased eye, at the same

The End of the Trail for Sam Bass. From a photograph taken in March, 1925.

time cautioning him to be careful as the fluid was a deadly poison. Murphy drank the entire contents of the bottle and was dead in a few hours. Remorse, no doubt, caused him to end his life.

Of the four men that fought the Round Rock battle with Sam Bass and his gang all are dead: General J. B. Jones, and Rangers R. C. Ware, Chris Connor, and George Harold. Of the ten men that made the long ride from San Saba to Round Rock only two are now alive—Lieutenant N. O. Reynolds and myself.

CHAPTER 10

A Winter of Quiet and a Transfer

In the fall of 1878, a man named Dowdy moved from South Texas and settled on the headwaters of the Johnson Fork of the Guadalupe River in Kerr County. His family consisted of himself, wife, three grown daughters, a grown son, and a young son twelve or fourteen years old. Mr. Dowdy owned two or three thousand sheep and was grazing them on some fine upland pasture just above his home. He contracted for his winter supply of corn, and when the first load of grain arrived at the ranch the three girls walked out half a mile to where the sheep were grazing to stay with their younger brother while the elder returned to the ranch to measure and receive the corn.

When young Mr. Dowdy returned to the sheep an hour later he was horrified to find that his three sisters and his little brother had been massacred by a band of roving Indians. From the signs on a high bluff nearby the sheep and their herders had been under observation by the redskins for some time and, seeing the only man leave, the Indians descended upon the defenceless girls and boy and killed them. As there was no ranger company within one hundred miles of Kerr County at the time, a party of frontiersmen quickly gathered and followed the murderers, but after pursuing them for nearly two hundred miles the posse lost the trail in the rough Devil's River country.

Kerr County then called for rangers, and General Jones ordered Lieutenant Reynolds to proceed to that county and go into camp for the winter at the Dowdy ranch. This descent upon the Dowdy family was the last raid ever made by Indians in Kerr County, and was perhaps the most heartrending. We herded our horses that winter on the very ground where the unfortunate young Misses Dowdy and their brother were killed. At the time they were murdered the ground was soft and muddy from a recent rain, so one could see for months afterward where the poor girls had run on foot while the Indians charged on horseback.

I remember one of the young ladies ran nearly four hundred yards before she was overtaken and shot full of arrows by a heartless redskin. These murderers were probably Kickapoos and Lipans that lived in the Santa Rosa Mountains, Old Mexico, and frequently raided Southwest Texas, stole hundreds of horses and killed many people. While guarding their horses on the ground where the Dowdy family was killed the ranger boys built a rock monument eight or ten feet high to mark the spot where the victims fell.

Lieutenant Reynolds kept scouting parties in the field at intervals throughout the winter but, like lightning, Indians never strike twice in the same place. The winter of 1878-79, was the quietest one I ever spent as a ranger. Kerr County was pretty well cleaned of outlaws and we made fewer arrests that season than ever before.

The rangers encountered but one real bad man in Kerr County. His name was Eli Wixon, and he was wanted for murder in East Texas. It was known that Wixon would be at the polls of the county precincts to vote on election day, November, 1878, so Lieutenant Reynolds sent Corporal Warren and Privates Will Banister and Abe Anglin to arrest Wixon. Corporal Warren found his man at the polls and lost no time in telling Wixon what he was there for, and ordered him to unbuckle his belt and drop his pistol. Wixon hesitated and finally called on his friends to protect him from the rangers.

The crowd came to his relief, and for a time it looked as if there would be trouble. Wixon abused the rangers, called them a set of dirty dogs, and dared them to shoot him. Corporal Warren was brave and resolute. He told Wixon his abuse did not amount to anything; that the rangers were there to arrest him and were going to do it. The corporal warned the citizens to be careful how they broke the law and if they started anything, he declared Wixon would be the first man killed.

Then, while Banister and Anglin held the crowd back with their drawn Winchesters, Warren disarmed Wixon, grasped his bridle reins and led him away without further trouble. Lieutenant Reynolds took no chances with that sort of man, and as soon as Wixon was in camp he was promptly handcuffed and shackled. This usually took the slack out of all so-called bad men and it worked like a charm with our new prisoner.

As the winter wore on Lieutenant Reynolds, with but little to do, became restless. He once said of himself that he never had the patience to sit down in camp and wait for a band of Indians to raid the county so he might get a race. Action was what he wanted all the time, and he chaffed like a chained bear when compelled to sit idly in camp.

When the Legislature met early in 1879, it was known that it would be difficult to get an appropriation for frontier defence. From time immemorial there has been an element from East Texas in the Legislature that has fought the ranger appropriation, and in this instance that element fought the ranger bill harder than ever. The fund appropriated for frontier defence two years before was now running short and in order to make it hold out until it could be ascertained what the Legislature would do it became necessary for General Jones to order the various captains to discharge three men out of each company. In a week a similar order was promulgated, and this was kept up until the battalion was reduced to almost one-half its former strength. Lieutenant Reynolds was compelled to sit idly by and see his fine experienced rangers dwindle away before his eyes, and what he said about those short-sighted lawmakers would not look nice in print.

In March, 1879, Captain Pat Dolan, commander of Company "F," then stationed on the Nueces River, seventy-five miles southwest of Reynolds' company, wrote to Lieutenant Reynolds that a big band of horse and cattle thieves were reported operating in the vicinity of the head of Devil's River and along the Nueces. He wished to take a month's scout out in that country, but since the ranger companies had been so reduced, he did not feel strong enough to operate against them alone and leave a reserve in his own camp. He, therefore, asked Lieutenant Reynolds to send a detachment to cooperate with him.

I was then second sergeant, and with five men I was ordered to report to Captain Dolan for a three weeks' scout on Devil's River and the Pecos. I reported to the commander of Company "F" and we scouted up the Nueces River, then turned west to Beaver Lake on the head of Devil's River. From the lake we went over on Johnson's Run and covered the country thoroughly but without finding the reported outlaws.

One morning after starting out on our day's scout Captain Dolan halted the command and, taking with him Private Robb, went in search of water. A heavy fog came up after he left us and hung over the country the greater part of the day. The captain did not return to us, and Sergeant G. E. Chinn ordered his men to fire their guns to give the lost ones our position. We remained in the vicinity until night and then returned to Howard's Well, a watering place on Johnson's Run. The following morning, we scouted out to the point from which the captain had left us the day before.

It was now clear, the sun shining brightly, but the lost men could not be found. Dolan was an experienced frontiersman, and we concluded that, after finding himself lost in the fog, he would return to his headquarters on the Nueces, one hundred and twenty-five miles away. Sergeant Chinn, therefore, headed the command for this camp, and when we reached it we found Captain Dolan and Private Robb had preceded us. They had travelled through a bad Indian country with nothing to eat but what venison they had killed.

From Dolan's Company I marched my detail back to Company "E" by easy stages and reached our camp at Dowdy's ranch the last week in March with our horses ridden down. We had covered something like five hundred miles without accomplishing anything.

As soon as I arrived, I walked up to the lieutenant's tent to make my report. I was met by First Sergeant C. L. Nevill, who told me that Lieutenant Reynolds had resigned and left the company. At first, I thought the sergeant was only joking, but when I was convinced that the lieutenant had really gone, I was shocked beyond measure. The blow was too strong and sudden for me, and I am not ashamed now at sixty-five years of age to admit that I slipped out of camp, sat down on the bank of the Guadalupe River and cried like a baby. It seemed as if my best friend on earth had gone forever.

Reynolds had had me transferred from Coldwell's company to his own when I was just a stripling of a boy. As soon as I was old enough to be trusted with a scout of men and the vacancies occurred, I was made second corporal, first corporal and then second sergeant. I was given the best men in the company and sent against the most noted outlaws and hardened criminals in the State of Texas. Lieutenant Reynolds gave me every chance in the world to make a name for myself, and now he was gone. I felt the loss keenly. I feel sure the records now on file in Austin will bear me out when I say Reynolds was the greatest captain of his time—and perhaps of all time. The State of Texas lost a matchless officer when "Mage" Reynolds retired to private life. After leaving the ranger service he made Lampasas his home and served that county as its sheriff for several terms.

The Legislature finally made a small appropriation for frontier defence. Sergeant Nevill was ordered to report at Austin with Company "E" for the reorganisation of the command. Reynolds' resignation practically broke up the company, and though Sergeant Nevill was made Lieutenant of Company "E" and afterward raised to a captaincy and left behind him an enviable record, yet he was not a "Mage" Reynolds by a long shot.

On reaching Austin, R. C. Ware and the Banister boys secured their transfers to Captain Marshes' Company "R," while the Carter boys, Ren and Dock, C. R. Connor, and Rill Derrick resigned the service and retired to private life. Abe Anglin became a policeman at Austin, Texas. Henry Maltimore and myself, at our requests, were transferred to Lieutenant Baylor's Company "C" for duty in El Paso County. With my transfer to this command the winter of inaction was over, and I was soon to see some exciting times along the upper Rio Grande.

Chapter 11

The Salt Lake War and a Long Trek

At the foot of the Guadalupe Mountains, one hundred miles east of El Paso, Texas, are situated several large salt deposits known as the Salt Lakes. These deposits were on public state land. For a hundred years or more the residents along the Rio Grande in El Paso County and in northern Mexico had hauled salt from the lakes free of charge, for there was no one to pay, as the deposits were not claimed by any owner. All one had to do was to back his wagon to the edge of the lake and shovel it full of salt and drive off.

From San Elizario to the Salt Lakes was just ninety miles, and there was not a drop of water on the route. The road that had been travelled so long by big wagon trains was almost as straight as an arrow and in extra fine condition. The salt haulers would carry water in barrels to what was known as the Half-way Station, about forty-five miles from San Elizario. Here they would rest and water their horses and leave half their water for the return trip. The teamsters would then push on to the lakes, load their wagons, rest the teams a day or two, and on their return trip, stop at the Half-way Station, water their animals, throw the empty barrels on top of the salt and, without again halting, continue to San Elizario on the Rio Grande.

Charley Howard, after his election as judge of the El Paso District, made his home at the old town of Franklin, now known as El Paso. He saw the possibilities of these salt lakes as a money-making proposition and, knowing they were on public land, wrote his father-in-law, George Zimpleman, at Austin, to buy some land certificates and send them to him so he could locate the land covering the salt deposits. As soon as the land was located Judge Howard forbade anyone to haul salt from the lakes without first securing his permission. The Mexicans along both sides of the Rio Grande adjacent to El Paso became highly indignant at this order.

A sub-contractor on the overland mail route between El Paso and Fort Davis named Luis Cardis, supported the Mexicans and told them Howard had no right to stop them from hauling salt. Cardis was an Italian by birth, had come to El Paso County in 1860, married a Mexican wife, identified himself with the county, and become prominent as a political leader. He was a Republican, while Judge Howard was a Democrat. Cardis and Howard soon became bitter enemies, and in September, 1878, this conflict between them became so acute that Howard killed his opponent with a double-barrelled shotgun in S. Shultz and Brothers' store in Franklin. This at once precipitated the contest known as the Salt Lake War, for grave threats were made against Howard by the Mexicans.

After killing Cardis, Judge Howard fled to New Mexico, and from his seclusion in that state he called on the governor of Texas to send rangers to El Paso to protect him and the courts over which he presided. At that time not a company of the Frontier Battalion was within five hundred miles of that town. El Paso was seven hundred and fifty miles by stage from San Antonio or Austin and the journey required about seven days and nights' travel over a dangerous route—an unusually hard trip on any passenger attempting it.

The governor of Texas, therefore, sent Major John B. Jones from Austin to Topeka, Kansas, by rail and thence as far west into New Mexico as the Santa Fe Railroad ran at that time, and thence by stage down to El Paso. Major Jones dropped into the old town of Franklin (now El Paso) unheralded and unknown. He sat about the hotel and gained the information he needed, then made himself known to the authorities and proceeded at once to organise and equip a company of twenty rangers. John B. Tays, brother to the Episcopal minister of that district, was made lieutenant of the new command, which was known as a detachment of Company "C" and stationed in the old town of San Elizario, twenty-five miles southeast of El Paso.

Soon after this detachment of rangers had been authorised, Judge Howard appeared at San Elizario and sought protection with it. No sooner had it become known that Judge Howard was back in Texas than the ranger company was surrounded by a cordon of armed Mexicans, two or three hundred in number, who demanded the body of the jurist. Lieutenant Tays refused to surrender Howard, and the fighting began, and was kept up two or three days at intervals. Sergeant Maltimore, in passing through the court yard of the buildings in which the rangers were quartered was shot down and killed by Mexican snipers located on top of some *adobe* buildings within range of the quarters. Then an American citizen, a Mr. Ellis, was killed near Company "C's" camp.

After several days of desultory fighting, the leaders of the mob, under flag of truce, sought an interview with Lieutenant Tays. The lieutenant finally agreed to meet two of the leaders, and while the parley was in progress armed Mexicans one at a time approached the peace party until forty or fifty had quietly surrounded Lieutenant Tays and put him at their mercy. The mob then boldly demanded the surrender of the ranger company, Judge Howard, and two other Americans, Adkinson and McBride, friends of the judge, that had sought protection with them.

There is no doubt that the Mexicans intimidated Lieutenant Tays after he was in their hands and probably threatened him with death unless their demands were granted. The lieutenant returned to the ranger camp with the mob and said, "Boys, it is all settled. You are to give up your arms and horses and you will be allowed to go free."

The rangers were furious at this surrender, but were powerless to help themselves, for the mob had swarmed in upon them from all sides. Billie Marsh, one of the youngest men in the company, was so indignant that he cried out to his commander, "The only difference between you and a skunk is that the skunk has a white streak down his back!"

Judge Howard, seeing the handwriting on the wall, began shaking hands and bidding his ranger friends goodbye. As soon as the Mexicans had gotten possession of the rangers' arms, they threw ropes over the heads of Howard, McBride and Adkinson. Then, mounting fast running ponies, they dragged the unfortunate men to death in the streets of San Elizario and cast their mutilated bodies into *pososas* or shallow wells. The Mexicans then disappeared, most of them crossing the Rio Grande into Mexico.

Lieutenant Tays at once resigned as commander of the rangers, and Private Charles Ludwick was made first sergeant and placed in charge of the company until the governor of Texas could send a commissioned officer to take command of it. Had Lieutenant Tays held out twenty-four hours longer, a thing which he could easily have done, he would have escaped the disgrace and mortification of surrendering himself and his company to a mob of Mexicans, for within that time John Ford with a band of New Mexico cowboys swept into the Rio

Grande valley to relieve the besieged rangers. On learning of the fates of Howard, McBride, Adkinson, Ellis, and Sergeant Maltimore, the rescue party raided up and down the valley from San Elizario to El Paso and killed several armed Mexicans accused of being part of the mob that had murdered the Americans. The present battalion of Texas Rangers was organised May 1, 1874, and in all their forty-six years of service this surrender of Lieutenant Tays was the only black mark ever chalked up against it.

Afterward, when I arrived in El Paso with Lieutenant Baylor, I had many talks with Privates George Lloyd. Dr. Shivers, Bill Rutherford, and Santiago Cooper—all members of Tays' company—and most of them believed Lieutenant Tays had a streak of yellow in him, while a few thought he made a mistake in agreeing to an interview with the mob, thereby allowing himself to be caught napping and forced to surrender.

Conditions in El Paso County were now so bad that Lieutenant Baylor was ordered into the country to take command of the ranger company. Before leaving to assume his command, Lieutenant Baylor was called to Austin from his home in San Antonio and had a lengthy interview with Governor Roberts. Baylor was instructed by his excellency to use all diplomacy possible to reconcile the two factions and settle the Salt Lake War peaceably. The governor held that both sides to the controversy were more or less to blame, and what had been done could not be undone, and the restoration of order was the prime requisite rather than a punitive expedition against the mob members.

On July 28. 1879, Private Henry Maltimore and myself reached San Antonio from Austin and presented our credentials to Lieutenant Baylor, who thereupon advised us that he had selected August 2nd as the day to begin his march from San Antonio to El Paso County. In his camp on the San Antonio River in the southern part of the city the lieutenant had mustered myself as sergeant, and Privates Henry Maltimore, Dick Head, Gus Small, Gus Krimkau, and George Harold.

Early on the morning of August 2, 1879, our tiny detachment left San Antonio on our long journey. One wagon carried a heavy, old-fashioned square piano, and on top of this was loaded the lieutenant's household goods. At the rear of the wagon was a coop of game chickens, four hens and a cock, for Lieutenant Baylor was fond of game chickens as a table delicacy, though he never fought them. His family consisted of Mrs. Baylor, two daughters—Helen, aged fourteen, and Mary, a child of four or five years—and Miss Kate Sydnor, sister of

Mrs. Baylor. The children and ladies travelled in a large hack drawn by a pair of mules. Rations for men and horses were hauled in a two-mule wagon, while the rangers rode on horseback in advance of the hack and wagons.

Two men travelling to New Mexico in a two-wheeled cart asked permission to travel with us for protection. Naturally we made slow progress with this unique combination. As well as I can remember, 1879, was a rather dry year, for not a drop of rain fell upon us during this seven hundred-mile journey. When we passed Fort Clark, in Kinney County, and reached Devil's River we were on the real frontier and liable to attack by Indians at any time. It was necessary, therefore, to keep a strong guard posted at all times.

Around our camp fires at night Lieutenant Baylor entertained us with accounts of early days on the frontier. He was born August 24, 1832, at old Fort Gibson in the Cherokee nation, now the State of Oklahoma. His father, John Walker Baylor, was a surgeon in the United States Army. Lieutenant Baylor was a soldier by training and by inheritance. In 1879, he was in his forty-seventh year and stood six feet two inches tall, a perfect specimen of a hardy frontiersman. He was highly educated, wrote much for papers and magazines, was a fluent speaker and a very interesting talker and story-teller.

He was less reserved than any captain under whom I ever served. He had taken part in many Indian fights on the frontier of Texas, and his descriptions of some of his experiences were thrilling. Lieutenant Baylor was a high-toned Christian gentleman and had been a member of the Episcopal Church from childhood. In all the months I served with him I never heard him utter an oath or tell a smutty yarn. He neither drank whisky nor used tobacco. Had he written a history of his operations on the frontier and a biography of himself it would have been one of the strangest and most interesting books ever written.

I have not the power of language to describe Lieutenant Baylor's bravery, because he was as brave as it is possible for man to be. He thought everyone else should be the same. He did not see how a white man could be a coward, yet in a fierce battle fought with Apache Indians on October 5. 1879, I saw some of his rangers refuse to budge when called upon to charge up a mountainside and assault the redskins concealed above us in some rocks. George Harold, one of the attacking party, said. "Lieutenant, if we charge up that hill over open ground every one of us will be killed."

"Yes. I suppose you are right." declared Baylor, a contemptuous smile on his face. Then, pointing to some Mexicans hidden behind some boulders below us. he added. "You had better go back to them. That is where you belong."

Lieutenant Baylor was as tender hearted as a little child and would listen to any tale of woe. He frequently took men into the service, stood good for their equipment and often had to pay the bill out of his own pocket. All men looked alike to him and he would enlist anyone when there was a vacancy in the company. The result was that some of the worst San Simone Valley rustlers got into the command and gave us no end of trouble, nearly causing one or two killings in our camp.

Baylor cared nothing for discipline in the company. He allowed his men to march carelessly. A scout of ten or fifteen men would sometimes be strung out a mile or more on the march. I suppose to one who had commanded a regiment during the Civil War a detachment of Texas Rangers looked small and insignificant, so he let his men have pretty much their own way. To a man like myself, who had been schooled under such captains as Major Jones, Captain Coldwell, Captain Roberts, and Lieutenant Reynolds, commanders who were always careful of the disposition and conduct of their men, this method of Baylor's seemed suicidal. It just seemed inevitable that we would sometime be taken by surprise and shot to pieces.

Another peculiarity of this wonderful man was his indifference to time. He would strike an Indian trail, take his time and follow it to the jumping off place. He would say, "There is no use to hurry, boys. We will catch them after a while." For instance, the stage driver and passenger killed in Quitman Canyon, January, 1880, had been dead two weeks before the lieutenant returned from a scout out in the Guadalupe Mountains. He at once directed me to make a detail of all except three men in camp, issue ten days' rations, and have the men ready to move early next morning.

An orderly or first sergeant is hardly ever called upon to scout unless he so desires, but the lieutenant said, "You had better come along, Sergeant. You may get another chance to kill an Indian." It seemed unreasonable to think he could start two weeks behind a bunch of Indians, follow up and annihilate the whole band, but he did. Give Comanches or Kiowas two weeks' start and they would have been in Canada, but the Apaches were slow and a different proposition with which to deal.

Baylor was one of the very best shots with firearms I ever saw. He killed more game than almost the entire company put together. When we first went out to El Paso, he used a Winchester rifle, but after the first Indian fight he concluded it was too light and discarded it for a Springfield sporting rifle 45-70. He always used what he called rest sticks; that is, two sticks about three feet long the size of one's little finger. These were tied together about four or five inches from one end with a buckskin thong.

In shooting he would squat down, extend the sticks arm's length out in front of him with the longer ends spread out tripod-fashion on the ground. With his gun resting in the fork he had a perfect rest and could make close shots at long range. The lieutenant always carried these sticks in his hand and used them on his horse as a quirt. In those days I used to pride myself on my shooting with a Winchester, but I soon found that Lieutenant Baylor had me skinned a mile when it came to killing game at long distance. I never could use rest sticks, for I always forgot them and shot offhand.

I cannot close this description of Lieutenant Baylor without mentioning his most excellent wife, who made the long, tedious journey from San Antonio to El Paso County with us. She was Sallie Garland Sydnor, born February 11, 1842. Her father was a wholesale merchant at Galveston, and at one time mayor of that city. Mrs. Baylor was highly educated and a very refined woman and a skilful performer on the piano. Her bright, sunny disposition and kind heart won her friends among the rangers at once. How sad it is to reflect that of the twelve persons in that little party that marched out of San Antonio on August 2, 1879, only three are living: Gus Small, Miss Mary Baylor, and myself.

When we had passed Pecan Springs on Devil's River there was not another cattle, sheep or goat ranch until we reached Fort Stockton, two hundred miles to the west. It was just one vast uninhabited country. Today it is all fenced and thousands of as fine cattle, sheep and goats as can be found in any country roam those hills. The Old Spanish Trail traverses most of this section, and in travelling over it today one will meet hundreds of people in high powered automobiles where forty years ago it was dangerous for a small party of well-armed men to journey. While ascending Devil's River I learned that Lieutenant Baylor was not only a good hunter, but a first-class fisherman as well, for he kept the entire camp well supplied with fine bass and perch, some of the latter being as large as saucers.

Forty miles west of Beaver Lake we reached Howard's Well, situated in Howard's Draw, a tributary of the Pecos River. Here we saw the burned ruins of a wagon train that had been attacked by Indians a few months before. All the mules had been captured, the teamsters killed and the train of sixteen big wagons burned. Had the same Indians encountered our little party of ten men, two women and two children we would all have been massacred.

Finally, we reached old Fort Lancaster, an abandoned government post, situated on the east bank of Live Oak Creek, just above the point where this beautiful stream empties into the Pecos. We camped here and rested under the shade of those big old live oak trees for several days. From this camp we turned north up the Pecos, one of the most curious rivers in Texas. At that time and before its waters were much used for irrigation in New Mexico, the Pecos ran bank full of muddy water almost the year round. Not more than thirty or forty feet wide, it was the most crooked stream in the world, and though only from four to ten feet deep, was so swift and treacherous that it was most difficult to ford. However, it had one real virtue; it was the best stream in Texas for both blue and yellow catfish that ranged in weight from five to forty pounds. We were some days travelling up this river to the pontoon crossing and we feasted on fish.

At Pontoon Crossing on the Pecos we intercepted the overland mail route leading from San Antonio to El Paso by way of Fredericksburg, Fort Mason, Menard, Fort McKavett, Fort Concho, Fort Stockton, and Fort Davis, thence west by Eagle Springs through Quitman Canyon, where more tragedies and foul murders have been committed by Indians than at any other point on the route. Ben Fricklin was the mail contractor. The stage stands were built of *adobe* and on the same unchanging plan. On each side of the entrance was a large room. The gateway opened into a passageway, which was roofed, and extended from one room to the other. In the rear of the rooms was the corral, the walls of which were six to eight feet high and two feet thick, also of sun-dried brick. One room was used for cooking and eating and the other for sleeping quarters and storage. The stage company furnished the stage tender with supplies and he cooked for the passengers when there were such, charging them fifty cents per meal, which he was allowed to retain for his compensation.

When the stage rolled into the station the tender swung open the gates and the teams, small Spanish mules, dashed into the corral. The animals were gentle enough when once in the enclosure, but mean and as wild as deer when on the road. The stage company would buy these little mules in lots of fifty to a hundred in Mexico and distribute them along the route. The tiny animals were right off the range and real unbroken broncos. The mules were tied up or tied down as the case might be and harnessed by force.

When they had been hitched to the stage coach or buckboard the gates to the corral were opened and the team left on the run. The intelligent mules soon learned all they had to do was to run from one station to the next, and could not be stopped between posts no matter what happened. Whenever they saw a wagon or a man on horseback approaching along the road they would shy around the stranger, and the harder the driver held them the faster they ran.

On our way out our teams were pretty well fagged out, and often Lieutenant Baylor would camp within a few yards of the road. The Spanish stage mules would see our camp and go around us on the run while their drivers would curse and call us all the vile names they could lay their tongues to for camping in the road.

When we camped at a station it was amusing to me to watch the stage attendants harness those wary little animals. The stage or buckboard was always turned round in the corral and headed toward the next station and the passengers seated themselves before the mules were hitched. When all was ready and the team harnessed the driver would give the word, the station keeper threw open the gates and the stage was off on a dead run.

There should be a monument erected to the memory of those old stage drivers somewhere along this overland route, for they were certainly the bravest of the brave. It took a man with lots of nerve and strength to be a stage driver in the Indian days, and many, many of them were killed. The very last year, 1880, that the stage line was kept up several drivers were killed between Fort Davis and El Paso. Several of these men quit the stage company and joined Lieutenant Baylor's company, and every one of such ex-drivers made excellent rangers.

From Pontoon Crossing on the Pecos River we turned due west and travelled the stage route the remainder of the way to El Paso County. At Fort Stockton we secured supplies for ourselves and feed for our horses, the first place at which rations could be secured since leaving Fort Clark. Fort Stockton was a large military post and was quite lively, especially at night, when the saloons and gambling halls were crowded with soldiers and citizen contractors. At Leon Holes, ten miles west of Fort Stockton, we were delayed a week because of Mrs. Baylor becoming suddenly ill. Passing through Wild Rose Pass and up Limpia Canyon we suffered very much from the cold, though it was only the last of August. Coming from a lower to a higher altitude we felt the change at night keenly. That was the first cold weather I had experienced in the summer.

Finally, on the 12th day of September, 1879, we landed safe and sound in the old town of Ysleta, El Paso County, after forty-two days of travel from San Antonio. Here we met nine men, the remnant of Lieutenant Tays' Company "C" rangers. The first few days after our arrival were spent in securing quarters for Lieutenant Baylor's family and in reorganising the company. Sergeant Ludwick was discharged at his own request, and I was made first sergeant, Tom Swilling second sergeant, John Seaborn first corporal, and George Lloyd second corporal. The company was now recruited up to its limit of twenty men. Before winter Lieutenant Baylor bought a fine home and fifteen or twenty acres of land from a Mr. Blanchard. The rangers were quartered comfortably in some *adobe* buildings with fine corrals nearby and within easy distance of the lieutenant's residence. We were now ready for adventure on the border.

When we arrived at Ysleta the Salt Lake War had quieted down and order had been restored. Although nearly a hundred Mexicans were indicted by the El Paso grand jury, no one was ever punished for the murder of Judge Howard and his companions. In going over the papers of Sergeant Ludwick I found warrants for the arrest of fifty or more of the mob members. Though most of the murderers had fled to Old Mexico immediately after the killing of the Americans, most of them had returned to the United States and their homes along the Rio Grande. I reported these warrants to Lieutenant Baylor and informed him that, with the assistance of a strong body of rangers I could probably capture most of the offenders in a swift raid down the valley.

The lieutenant declared that he had received instructions from Governor Roberts to exercise extreme care not to precipitate more trouble over Howard's death, and, above all things, not incite a race war between the Mexican offenders and the white people of the country. He decided, therefore, that we had better not make any move at all in the now dead Salt Lake War. And of course, I never again mentioned the matter to him. Though the Salt Lake War was over, new and adventurous action was in store for us, and within less than a month after our arrival in Ysleta we had our first brush with the Apaches, a tribe of Indians I had never before met in battle.

CHAPTER 12

Our First Fight With Apaches

On October 5, 1879, at midnight, Pablo Mejia brought Lieutenant Baylor, from Captain Gregorio Garcia of San Elizario, a note stating that a band of Apaches had charged a camp of five Mexicans who were engaged in cutting hay for the stage company fourteen miles north of La Quadria stage station and killed them. As first sergeant I was ordered to make a detail of ten men and issue them five days' rations. I detailed Second Sergeant Tom Swilling, Privates Gus Small, George Lloyd, John Thomas, George Harold, Doc Shivers, Richard Head, Bill Rutherford, and Juan Garcia for the scout, and myself made the tenth man. It required an hour to arouse the men, issue the rations and ammunition and pack the two mules, so it was 1 o'clock a. m. when we finally left Ysleta.

By daylight we reached Hawkins Station, near where Fabins Station now is. Here we were told we would find the survivor of the terrible massacre. Riding up to the door of the stage house we had to thump some time before we had evidence that anyone was alive on the premises. Finally, the door opened about an inch very cautiously and a Mexican peeped out. Lieutenant Baylor asked him if he had been one of the *grameros* or hay cutters.

"*Si, senor,*" replied the sleepy Mexican.

Asked for an account of the massacre, the native said it was nearly dark when the Indians, numbering from twenty-five to fifty, charged the camp and uttered such horrid yells that everyone took to his heels and was soon in the chaparral. The speaker saw his *pobrecita papa* (poor papa) running, with the Indians about to lance him, and knew that he and the remainder of the party were killed. He himself only escaped. As he mentioned the tragic death of his beloved parent the tears rolled down his cheeks. Lieutenant Baylor comforted the weeper as best he could and asked if the Mexican would not guide the rangers to the raided camp, but the survivor declined with thanks, saying he must stay to help the station keeper take care of the stage mules, but he directed us to the ranch where some of the dead men's families lived and at which a guide could be obtained.

When we arrived at the ranch below Hawkins Station it was sunrise and we halted for breakfast after a night ride of forty miles. The people at the ranch were very uneasy when we rode up, but were rejoiced when they realised we were Texas Rangers and learned our mission. They showed us every attention. Among the first to come out to us was an old Mexican who had been in the hay camp when it was attacked. He gave a lurid account of the onset. His son had been one of the *grameros*, and when he mentioned this the tears began to flow.

"*Ah, hijo de mi cara Juan.* I shall never see him again," he lamented. "All were killed and I alone escaped!"

Lieutenant Baylor then explained to the weeping father that his son was very much alive and that we had seen him that very night bewailing the death of the father he thought killed. And it now developed that all the dead men were alive! When the camp was attacked each Mexican had scattered, and the Apaches had been too busy looting the stores to follow the fugitives. Moreover, those ranchers would fight and the Indians did not care to follow them into the brush.

A bright young Mexican went with us to the hay camp, which was about six miles toward Comales, where Don Juan Armendaris now has a cow ranch. The Apaches had made a mess of things in camp sure enough. They had broken all the cups and plates, poured salt into the sugar, this combination into the flour and beans and the conglomeration of the whole on the ground, as the sacks were all they wanted. The Indians smashed the coffee pot, the frying pan, the skillet and the water barrels with an axe. Then taking all the blankets, the raiders started eastward as though they intended to go to the Sierra Priela, but after going a mile the trail turned south.

We found the redskins had come from the north by way of Los Cormuros and were probably from Fort Stanton, New Mexico, on their way to raid Old Mexico. They were in a dry country and making for the Rio Grande, fourteen miles to the south. When they discovered the hay camp on their route, they charged it and fired on the hay cutters. The Mexicans scattered and made their escape in the darkness, each thinking himself the sole survivor and so reporting on reaching his home, though as a matter of fact not a single life was lost. Our guide went back to give the alarm to the ranches below and we followed the trail down the mesa until opposite Guadalupe.

There we crossed the overland stage route near the present Rio Grande Station and found our guide waiting for us. He had discovered the trail, and fearing the Indians might ambush the road below, he had awaited our arrival. The trail made straight for the Rio Grande, crossing about one mile west of the Mexican town of Guadalupe. From the pony and mule tracks Lieutenant Baylor judged there were fifteen to twenty Indians in the band. We had some trouble following the trail after we got to the river bottom, where loose horses and cattle ran, but a few of us dismounted and worked the trail out, crossed the river and struck camp for dinner.

Lieutenant Baylor sent Pablo Mejia into town to inform the president of Guadalupe that we had followed a fresh Apache trail to the Rio Grande going south into Mexico, and asked permission to follow the Indians into his country. The scout soon returned and reported that the president was not only pleased that we had pursued the redskins, but would willingly join us himself with all the men he could muster. Just after we crossed the river we came across a Mexican herder with a flock of goats. As soon as he heard we were trailing the Apaches he began yelling at the top of his voice and soon had the goats on the jump for town, though the Indians had passed the night before. We were quickly in saddle again, and as we rode into the *pueblo* we were kindly received by the people. We found a mare the Apaches had killed just on the edge of town and from which they had taken some of the choice steaks.

After leaving Guadalupe the trail went south, following closely the stage road from Juarez to Chihuahua. Not long after leaving town we met a courier coming to Guadalupe from Don Ramon Carandas' ranch, San Marcos de Cantarica, twenty-one miles distant, who informed us that the Apaches had killed a herder on that ranch and had taken four horses and sixteen mules of the stage company. We hurried onward and reached Cantarica at sunset, having travelled seventy-eight miles since 1 a.m. that morning. Both men and horses were rather tired.

All was confusion at the ranch. The Mexican herder had been shrouded and laid out with a cross at his head and several little lighted candles near the body. Many women were sitting around the room with black shawls pulled up over their heads. The Apaches, numbering sixteen well-armed and well mounted warriors, had slain their victim and captured the stock near the ranch just about noon. Mexican volunteers from Guadalupe and San Ignacio began to ride in until our combined force numbered twenty-five or twenty-six men. Everyone was excited at the thought of a brush with the redskins responsible for the murder.

Accompanied by our volunteer allies we left the ranch at daylight next morning and picked up the trail at once. It led off south along the base of the Armagora Mountains or Sierra Bentanos. As the Mexicans were familiar with the country, they took the lead and followed the trail rapidly. About 11 o'clock the trailers halted at the mouth of the Canyon del Moranos, an ugly black hole cut in the mountains, looking grim and defiant enough without the aid of Apache warriors. When we had joined the Mexicans—we were travelling some half a mile behind them—Lieutenant Baylor and Captain Garcia held a short conference. The lieutenant turned to me and said that Captain Garcia declared the Indians were in the canyon among the rocks, and ordered me to detail two men to guard our horses while we scaled the mountain on foot and investigated it. I could not bring myself to believe that a band of Indians that had killed a man and driven off all the stage stock the day before had gone only thirty miles and was now lying in wait for us.

"You don't know the Apaches," Lieutenant Baylor declared when I voiced my thoughts. "They are very different from the plains Indians, the kind you have been used to following. These Apaches delight to get into the rocks and lay for their enemies."

At the conference the Mexicans suggested that Lieutenant Baylor should take nine of his men and ten of their volunteers and follow the trail up the canyon, but the lieutenant declared that this would never do, as the Apaches had no doubt anticipated just such a move and hidden themselves in the cliffs where they could kill their attackers without exposing themselves in the least. He proposed scaling the mountain and following them down on top of the ridge in the Indians' rear. And this was the strategy finally adopted.

The Mexicans dismounted and started up the mountainside about one hundred yards to our left. Lieutenant Baylor and his eight rangers marched straight forward from our horses and began the ascent. As we went along the lieutenant pulled some bunch grass and stuck it all around under his hat band so his head would look like a clump of grass and conceal his head and body if he should have to flatten himself on the ground. He counselled us to follow his example. I had taken some Mexican cheese out of my saddle pockets and was eating it as we marched carelessly up the mountain.

Honestly, I did not believe there was an Indian within a hundred miles of us, but it was not long before I changed my mind. Suddenly there came a loud report of a gun and then another. I looked up to where the Mexicans had taken position behind a ledge of rocks and saw where a bullet struck the stones a foot above their heads. I did not want any more cheese. I threw down what I had in my hand and spat out what I had in my mouth.

These old Apache warriors, high in the cliffs above us, then turned their attention to our little band of eight rangers and fired twenty-five or thirty shots right into the midst of us. One of these big calibre bullets whizzed so close to my head that it made a noise like a wild duck makes when flying downstream at the rate of fifty to sixty miles an hour. Lieutenant Baylor ordered us to charge at once.

In running up the mountain I was somewhat in advance of the boys. We came to a rock ledge three or four feet high. I quickly scaled this, but before I could straighten up an Indian rose from behind a rock about fifteen to twenty yards ahead and fired point-blank at me. The bullet struck a small soap weed three feet in front of me and knocked the leaves into my mouth and face. I felt as if I had been hit but it was leaves and not blood that I wiped out of my mouth with my left hand. I turned my head and called to the boys to look out, but the warning was unnecessary—they had already taken shelter under the ledge of rock.

Just as I turned my head a second shot from the Apache carried away the entire front part of my hat brim. I saw the warrior throw another cartridge in his gun and brought my Winchester quickly to bear upon him. When he saw that I was about to shoot he shifted his position and turned sideways to me. We both fired at the same instant. My bullet hit the redskin just above his hip and, passing straight through his body, broke the small of his back and killed him almost instantly. This old brave was a big man, probably six feet tall, with his face painted in red and blue paint. He used an old octagon barrel Winchester rifle and he had with him an old shirtsleeve tied at one end in which were two hundred and fifty Winchester cartridges.

Some Indians fifty yards up the mountain now began to shell our position, so I took shelter behind the ledge of rock. Fifteen or twenty feet to our left and a little higher up the mountain, Lieutenant Baylor was sheltered behind some boulders. He raised his head slightly above his parapet for a peep at the Indians and those keen-sighted warriors saw him; a well-directed shot cut part of the grass out of his hat. Had the bullet been six inches lower it would have struck him full in the face.

"Darn that old Indian," exclaimed Baylor, ducking his head. "If I had a shot gun I would run up and jump right on top of him."

The lieutenant was mad now and ordered a charge. The boys hesitated, and George Harold, an old scout, said, "Lieutenant, if we leave this shelter and start up the mountain the Indians hidden behind those rocks seventy-five yards above will kill us all."

"Yes, I suppose you are right; they would be hard to dislodge," replied Baylor.

The Apaches evidently had plenty of ammunition, as they kept up a desultory fire all day. Seeing we were not going to fall into their trap they turned their attention to our horses. Although the animals were four or five hundred yards from the foot of the mountain, they killed Sergeant Swilling's horse, the bullet passing entirely through the body just behind the shoulders. When his horse, a large white one, staggered and tumbled over, Swilling began to mourn, for he had the horror of walking all Western men have. John Thomas, however, got the laugh on him by saying, "Sergeant, you had better wait and see if you are going back to camp." We could see the Indians' bullets knocking up dust all around the horses and the guard replying to the fire. Baylor now sent a man and had the guard move the horses out of range.

During the afternoon the Apaches moved up higher toward the crest of the mountain, and in doing so one of the Indians exposed himself. The Mexicans to our left spotted him and killed him with a well-directed shot. The warrior fell out in open ground where he was literally shot all to pieces.

We had been without water all day and when night came Lieutenant Baylor and Captain Garcia decided it was useless to continue the fight any longer, so we withdrew toward our horses. After reaching the animals we could still hear the Indians firing on our positions. We might have captured the Apaches' horses by a charge, but we would have had to go down the side of the mountain and across a deep canyon where we would have been compelled to pick our way slowly under a constant cross fire from the concealed riflemen, and neither Baylor nor Garcia thought the horses worth the sacrifice required to capture them.

As the nearest water was thirty miles away and our men and horses weary and thirsty, we rode back to our hospitable friend, Don Ramon Arrandas' ranch, where our horses were fed and we ourselves supplied with fresh milk and cheese. On our return to Guadalupe we were most kindly entertained by Mr. Maximo Arrandas, custom house officer at San Elizario, and brother to Don Ramon. We reached our headquarters at Ysleta after being out five days and travelling two hundred and twenty-two miles, sustaining no other damage than a few bruises from scaling the mountain and the loss of Sergeant Swilling's horse. This first brush with Apaches, however, was but a prelude to other expeditions after this tribe, and we were soon hot on the trail of Victorio, the Apache Napoleon.

CHAPTER 13

Scouting in Mexico

About a month after our first brush with Apaches, during November, 1879, Chief Victorio quit the Mescalero Reservation and with a party of one hundred and twenty-five warriors and a hundred women and children, travelled south into Mexico on a raid. This old chief was probably the best general ever produced by the Apache tribe. He was a far better captain than old Geronimo ever was and capable of commanding a much larger force of men. His second in command was Nana, also a very able officer.

Victorio knew every foot of the country and just where to find wood, water, grass and abundance of game, so he took his time and, coming from New Mexico down into the state of Chihuahua, stopped first at the Santa Maria. The country about this stream is very mountainous, especially to the south, and here he could find refuge in case of an attack from Mexican soldiers. Of this, however, there was not much danger at that time, for the country was thinly settled, farming and stock raising being confined to the neighbourhood of the small towns. Gradually Chief Victorio moved down into the Candelaria Mountains, approaching them from the northwest. Here he could get fresh range for his large band of horses and be near the settlement of San Jose, owned by Don Mariano Samaniego.

Here, also, he could watch the public road between Chihuahua and El Paso del Norte, the present Juarez. One of the saddest and most heartrending tragedies resulted from this move. Victorio was camped at the large tanks on the north side and almost on top of the Candelaria Mountains, where he had fine range for his stock and plenty of game and wood. From those almost inaccessible peaks he could see for twenty or thirty miles in every direction and watch every move of travellers or hostile forces. The old chief now sent a small band of

Indians, some six or seven in number, on a raid against the little settlement of San Jose. Here the Indians stole a bunch of Mexican ponies and hurried back to their camp on top of the Candelaria Mountains.

The citizens of San Jose discovered the loss of their ponies, and on examining the trail, found there was only a small band of Indians in the raiding party. A company of the principal Mexicans of San Jose, under the command of Don Jose Rodriguez, and augmented by volunteers from the little town of Carrajal, left to locate the Indians and recover the stolen horses. The little band of fifteen brave men went to the northern side of the mountains and struck the trail of Victorio's band on an old beaten route used by the Indians, which passed from the Santa Maria River to the Candelaria Mountains. This road wound between two rocky peaks and then down the side of the hills to the plain between them and the Candelaria, ending at last at the big tank.

From his position on the tall peaks Victorio had seen the little body of Mexicans long before they struck his trail and, knowing they would never come upon the Candelaria after seeing the size of his trail, sent forty or fifty of his warriors to form an ambuscade where the trail crosses the crest between the two peaks. He must have been with the braves himself, for the thing was skilfully planned and executed. On the north side of the trail there were only a few boulders, but on the south the hills were very broken, rising in rough tiers of stones. The Apaches hid in these rocks and awaited their victims. On November 7, 1879, the Mexicans entered the narrow defile and as soon as they were between the two parties of Indians concealed on each side of the pass the Apaches on the north side of the trail fired a volley upon them.

The Mexicans thereupon made for the rocks on the south, as was natural. As they sought refuge there the redskins in the cliffs above the gallant little band opened fire on them. Caught in a real death trap the entire punitive force was massacred. When I walked over the ground some time afterward, I saw where one Mexican had gotten into a crevice from which he could shoot anyone coming at him from the east or west. He was hidden also from the Indians in the cliffs above him, but his legs were exposed to the warriors on the north side and they had literally shot them off up to his knees.

I also found seven dead Mexicans in a small gulley, and on a little peak above them I discovered the lair of one old Indian who had fired twenty-seven shots at the tiny group until he had killed them all, for I found that number of 45-70 cartridge shells in one pile. Practically all the horses of the Mexicans were killed. Some of the animals had been tied to Spanish dagger plants and when shot ran the length of their rope before falling. Some of the bodies rolled down the deep canyon until they reached the bottom of what we called the Canado del Muerte (Canyon of Death), and the Indians removed none of the saddles or ropes from the dead horses.

When the company of Mexicans did not return there was great sorrow and alarm in the little town of Carrajal. As it was supposed that only a small band of Apaches bent on horse stealing was in the Candelarios, another small band of fourteen men volunteered to go and see what had become of their friends and kindred. Don Jose Mario Rodriguez was appointed commander, and the little party took the trail of their comrades with sad forebodings. Old Victorio, from his watch towers in the Candelarios, saw this rescue party and prepared for its destruction. The signs indicated that the second party had walked into the same death trap as the first, but the second band had scattered more in fighting and a good many of the Mexicans were killed on the southern slope of the hills.

Two had attempted to escape on horseback but were followed and killed. I found one of these unfortunates in an open plain some six hundred yards from the hills. He had been surrounded, and, seeing escape was impossible, had dismounted, tied his horse to a Spanish dagger plant and put up a good fight. I found thirty or forty cartridge shells near where he had fallen. His pony had been killed and the dagger plant shot to pieces. The Apaches had cut off his right hand and had carried away his gun, six-shooter, saddle and bridle.

When neither party returned then, indeed, was there sorrow in the town of Carrajal, for twenty-nine of her principal citizens had left never to return. Wives, mothers, and sweethearts mourned the loss of their dear ones. A runner was sent to El Paso del Norte and the citizens began to organise a punitive expedition at once, calling on Saragosa, Tres Jacalas, Guadalupe, and San Ignacio for their quotas. These towns responded quickly and soon a hundred Mexicans were ready to take the field. A note was sent to Lieutenant Baylor at Ysleta requesting the rangers to go with the command.

Baylor readily agreed to accompany the Mexicans, for he knew it was only a question of time before old Victorio would again be murdering and robbing on our side of the Rio Grande. A detachment of Company "C" had been in one Apache fight in Mexico and the Mexicans had a very kindly feeling for us. Lieutenant Baylor's detachment of ten rangers crossed the Rio Grande at Saragosa, a little town opposite Ysleta, and joined the Mexicans under Senor Ramos. We marched to the ranch of Don Ynocente Ochoa until the volunteers from the other towns came to Samalaejuca Springs. When they had done so the rangers moved down and our combined command amounted to one hundred and ten men.

After organising their force, the Mexicans sent Senor Ramos to inform Lieutenant Baylor that, on account of his experience as a soldier and as a compliment to the rangers, they had selected him to command the entire party. The lieutenant thanked the messenger, but declared, as the campaign was on Mexican soil to rescue or bury Mexicans, it would be more proper to appoint one of their own men commander, and that he himself would cheerfully serve under any leader so chosen. Senor Ramos returned shortly and notified Lieutenant Baylor that the Mexicans had selected Don Francisco Escapeda of Guadalupe as commander-in-chief and Lieutenant Baylor second in command.

This solution of the leadership problem pleased us, as there was an element among the Mexican party that might have caused friction. Old Chico Barelo, the *pueblo cacique* and principal commander of the mob that had killed Judge Howard, Ellis, Adkinson, and McBride at San Elizario, was with the expedition, and we had at our Ysleta headquarters warrants for the arrest of himself and many others, so we gave the old fellow to understand we were now fighting a common enemy and should act in harmony together. We did this more willingly, because we had learned that after killing Judge Howard and the others the mob wanted to murder all the rangers barricaded in an old *adobe* house, but had been dissuaded from this purpose by old Chico, who declared the rangers could only be killed after he had first been slain.

Leaving one wagon at the Ochoa ranch and taking three days' rations cooked and more in case of a siege, we went out in the night to avoid Victorio's spies. Don Francisco Escapeda with Lieutenant Baylor were at the head of the column. Sergeant James B. Gillett and eight rangers followed in Indian file, each ranger with a Mexican by his side, showing they looked on us as volunteers in the Mexican service. We rode out along the hard sand road beyond Samalaejuca and sent spies ahead to locate the Apaches if possible. Before we reached the Candelarios we halted behind some mountains to await their report, but they could learn nothing certain. It was a bitterly cold night and a few of us made fires in the deep *arroyos*. We moved on toward the mountains north of the Candelarios and reached them early next morning to find a large fresh trail about two days old going in the direction of

Lake Santa Maria, but, for fear of some stratagem, we divided our men. One party took the crest south of the trail where the massacre took place while the other went to the right.

It was soon evident that the entire Apache band had left and that nothing remained for us but the sad duty of collecting the bodies of the dead Mexicans for burial. The second, or rescue party, had found the bodies of their kinsmen killed in the first ambuscade and had collected them and put them in a big crevice in the rocks. When they began to cover the corpses with loose stones the Indians, who had been watching them all the while just as a cat plays with a mouse before killing it, opened fire on the burial party and killed the last one of the unfortunate men. The saddest scene I ever witnessed was that presented as we gathered the bodies of the murdered men. At each fresh discovery of a loved friend, brother or father and the last hope fled that any had escaped, a wail of sorrow went up, and I doubt if there was a dry eye either of Mexican or Texan in the whole command.

While the immediate relatives were hunting for those who had scattered in trying to escape, we moved south to the main tank in the Candelarios. The ascent was up a winding path on the steep mountainside to the bench where the tank, one of the largest in the west, was situated. The water coming down from a height, and big boulders falling into the tank, had cut a deep hole in the solid rock in which the water was retained. Although Victorio's band of three hundred animals and two hundred or more Indians and our command had been using the water it could scarcely be missed.

We sent scouts to the left and right to make sure no game was being put upon us, for the cunning old chief, after sending his women and children off, could have hidden his warriors in the rough cliff that towered high above and commanded the tank of water and slaughtered all those below. We remained all day and night at this place. It was the most picturesque spot I had ever seen. We rangers rambled all over this Indian camp and found many of the Mexican saddles hidden in the cliffs and several hats, each with bullet holes in it. We also discovered two Winchester rifles that had been hit in the fight and abandoned as useless. I saw a hundred or more old rawhide shoes that had been used to cover the ponies' feet and dozens of worn-out *moccasins*. This party of Apaches had killed and eaten more than seventy-five head of horses and mules in this camp.

I followed a plain, well-beaten foot path to the topmost peak of the Candelario or candle mountain, so called from the candle-like projection of rocks that shot skyward from its top. The Candelario is in an open plain fifty miles south of El Paso, Texas, and from its top affords one of the grandest views in northern Mexico. To the south one could see San Jose and Carrajal, to the north the mountains at El Paso del Norte, to the west the mountains near Santa Maria River and Lake Guzman were in plain view, while to the east the Sierra Bentanos loomed up, apparently only a few miles away. On this peak old Victorio kept spies constantly on the lookout, and it would have been impossible for a party of men to have approached without having been seen by these keen-eyed watchers.

All the bodies having been recovered they were buried in a crevice of the mountain where they had been killed. All were in good preservation owing to the pure cold air of the mountains. It is a strange fact, but one beyond question, that no wild animal or bird of prey will touch the body of a Mexican. These corpses had lain on the ground nearly two weeks and were untouched. If they had been the bodies of Indians, negroes or Americans the coyotes, buzzards and crows would have attacked them the first day and night.

Nothing of interest occurred on our return trip. The rangers, as usual, always ate up their three days' rations the first camp they made and got out of bread, but our Mexican allies divided with us. Don Ynocente Ochoa's *major-domo* or ranch boss gave us all the fresh beef we could eat and a supply of *carne seco* (dried beef) to take with us on campaign. Quite a company had come out to see us from Corrizal and we returned sadly to the widows of the brave men who fell in this, probably the most wholesale slaughter ever made by Victorio's band. The citizens of Galena were nearly as unfortunate, but it was old Hu and Geronimo who massacred them. All the Saragosa men made for their church to offer up thanks for a safe return. Men, women and children uttered their "*Gracias, senors*," as the Texas Rangers rode through their town. We arrived safely in our *adobe* quarters at Ysleta and appreciated them after sleeping out of doors.

Though Victorio had escaped us on this scout, and though he was to murder and pillage for a time, yet his days were numbered. Our company of rangers were again to cross into Mexico in pursuit of him, but, though, one year later, he and eighty-nine of his braves were killed by the Mexicans under Colonel Joaquin Terrazas, the rangers were not to take part in defeating him. However, our rangers were destined to annihilate a small band that escaped deserved destruction at that time when it resumed its depredations in Texas.

CHAPTER 14

Treacherous Braves, a Faithful Dog, and a Murder

During the latter part of January, 1880, two mining engineers named Andrews and Wiswall from Denver, Colorado, appeared at the ranger camp in Ysleta. They had a new ambulance pulled by two elegant horses and led a fine saddle pony. They were well fitted out for camping and had the finest big black shepherd dog I had ever seen. Mr. Andrews used a Springfield while Mr. Wiswall carried a Sharps sporting rifle, besides they had shotguns and six-shooters. These miners wanted to buy one hundred pack *burros* and, not finding what they wanted in the Rio Grande Valley, decided to go over in the upper Pecos Valley near Eddy or Roswell, New Mexico, for pack animals.

They consulted Lieutenant Baylor about the best route they should follow. He advised them to travel down the overland stage route to Fort Davis, thence by Toyah Creek and on up the Pecos, but the engineers thought this too much out of their way and concluded to travel by the old abandoned Batterfield stage route, which leads by Hueco Tanks, Alamo Springs, Cornudas Mountain, Crow Flat, Guadalupe Mountain and thence to the Pecos River. Lieutenant Baylor warned the men that this was a very dangerous route, without a living white man from Ysleta to the Pecos River, more than one hundred and fifty miles distant, and through an Indian country all the way.

Nevertheless, Andrews and Wiswall selected this latter route, and the third day out from our camp reached the old abandoned stage station at Crow Flat about noon. This was in an open country and from it one could see for miles in every direction. A cold north wind was blowing, so, for protection, the two men drove inside the old station walls, unhitched and hobbled their horses and pony and were soon busily baking bread, frying bacon and boiling coffee, not dreaming there was an Indian in the country, though they had been warned to look out for them. Like all men travelling in that country the two miners had the appetite of coyotes and became deeply absorbed in stowing away rations, Unnoticed, the horses had grazed off some three or four hundred yards from the station and the two men were suddenly startled by a yelling and the trampling of horses' feet. Looking up, Andrews and Wiswall saw ten or twelve Indians driving off their horses.

Seizing their guns, the two white men started after the thieves at top speed. Both being Western men and good shots, they hoped, by opening on the redskins with their long-range guns, to get close enough to prevent them from taking the hobbles off the horses. But the animals made about as good time as if they had been foot loose. This fact was well known to the Texas Rangers, who hobbled and side lined also and, even then, their horses when stampeded would run as fast as the guards could keep up with them on foot. The Apaches can't be taught anything about horse stealing—they are already past masters at the art. And while some of the Indians halted and fought Andrews and Wiswall the others ran the horses off and got away with them. The two miners returned to camp feeling very blue indeed.

A council of war was held and they were undetermined the best course to pursue. To walk back one hundred miles to El Paso and pack grub, blankets and water was no picnic. On the other hand, it was probably seventy-five miles to the Pecos, but they finally decided to take the shortest way to assistance, which proved the traditional longest way. They determined to stay within the friendly *adobe* of the old stage stand until night. To keep up appearances they rigged up two dummy sentinels and put them on guard. They had no fear of an attack at night, especially as they had a dog to keep watch.

They left the station at dark. Shep, the dog, wanted to go with them, but the men put a sack of corn and a side of bacon under the ambulance and made him understand he was to guard it. They then set out and followed the old stage route along a horrible road of deep sand. At daybreak they were near the point of the Guadalupe Peak, and after having travelled on foot about twenty-five miles they were pretty well worn out.

The old stage road here turns to the right and gradually winds around the mountain to get on the mesa land. It makes quite a circuit before getting to the next water, Pine Springs, but there was an old

Indian trail that leads up the canyon and straight through. As Andrews and Wiswall were afoot and taking all the short cuts, they took this trail. It was late in the day when, in a sudden bend of the trail, they came in full view of an entire village of Indians coming towards them. The redskins were only two or three hundred yards off and discovered the white men at once.

Under such circumstances the two pedestrians had to think quickly and act at once. They could not hope to escape by running, for most of the Indians were mounted. Fortunately, to the south of the trail there was a sharp sugar loaf peak, and for this Andrews and Wiswall made with all speed. Reaching the summit, they hastily threw up breastworks of loose rocks and as soon as the Indians came into sight they opened fire on them. The redskins returned the fire, but soon discovered they were wasting ammunition and ceased firing. The besieged, suspicious of some stratagem, kept a sharp lookout, and soon discovered the Indians were crawling upward to the barricade and pushing boulders before them to shelter their bodies. The boys decided to keep perfectly still, one on each side, and watch for a chance to kill a savage.

The watcher on the west side, where the fading light still enabled him to see, saw a mop of black hair rise cautiously over an advancing rock. He fired at once. The head disappeared and the boulder went thundering down the hill with the two white men running over the warrior, who was kicking around like a chicken with its head cut off. As good luck would have it most of the attackers were on the east side, taking it for granted the men would try to escape in that direction. Before the astonished Apaches could understand just what was occurring, the men, running like old black-tailed bucks, were out of hearing, while night spread her dark mantle over them in kindness. Being good woodsmen, the fugitives had no trouble in shaping their course to Crow Flat again.

Worn out and weary after travelling more than fifty miles on foot and with not a wink of sleep for thirty-six hours, they made the old stage stand and found their dummy sentinels still on guard with the faithful shepherd dog at his post. He was overjoyed at the return of his masters. At the old *adobe* station Andrews and Wiswall were in a measure safe, for they had water and grub and the walls of the stand, five feet or more high, would shelter them. Since the Apaches had made no attempt to kill the dog or rob the ambulance, the miners were satisfied that the Indians, after stealing their horses, had kept on their way to the Mescalero Agency, near Tularosa. This stage station was on the highway of these murderous, thieving rascals, who were constantly raiding Texas and Chihuahua, and in their raids, they had made a deep trail leading north from Crow Flat or Crow Springs, as some call it, toward the Sacramento Mountains.

After the fugitives had rested, they decided they would pull out after dark and hoof it for Ysleta. The fifty miles' walk over a rough country had pretty well worn out their shoes, so they used gunny sacks to tie up their sore and bleeding feet. Again, giving Shep his orders, with heavy hearts Andrews and Wiswall turned their faces to the Cornudos Mountains, with the next stage station twenty-five miles distant without one drop of water on the way. They were so tired and foot-sore they did not reach Cornudos until late the next day. Here they hid in the rocks, among the shady nooks of which they found cold water and sweet rest. After several days the two men dragged their weary bodies, more dead than alive, into Ysleta and to the ranger camp.

Lieutenant Baylor ordered me to take eight rangers, and with two mules, proceed to Crow Flat to bring in the ambulance Andrews and Wiswall had abandoned there. The first day we made the Hueco Tanks. Hueco is Spanish for tanks, and in the early days travellers spelled it Waco. Many wild adventures have occurred at these tanks—fights between the Mexicans and the Comanches. During the gold excitement this was the main immigrant route to California. Here, too, the overland stage route had a stand. The names of Marcy, General Lee, and thousands of others could be seen written on the rocks. The Indians themselves had drawn many rude pictures, one of which was quite artistic and depicted a huge rattlesnake on the rock under the cave near the stage stand on the eastern side of Hueco.

Many times, when scouting in the Sacramento and Guadalupe Mountains I have camped for the night in the Huecos. Sometimes the water in the tanks had been all used up by the travellers but there was always plenty of good cool rain water twenty-five feet above the main ground tanks. Often, I have watered my entire command by scaling the mountain to those hidden tanks and, filling our boots and hats with water, poured it on the flat, roof-like rocks so it would run down into the tanks below where our horses and mules would be watered in good shape. The city of El Paso, I am told, now has a fine graded road to those old historic mountains and many of its citizens enjoy an outing there.

Our next halt was at the Alamose, across the beautiful plains, at that time covered with antelope that could be seen scudding away with their swift change of colour looking like a flock of white birds. Here we found some Indian signs at the flat above the springs, but it was at Cornudos that we again saw the old signs of the Apaches. This Cornudos is a strange conglomeration of dark granite rocks shot high in the air in the midst of the plains by some eruption of the earth in ages past. This was the favourite watering place of the Tularosa Agency Indians on their raids into Texas and Mexico.

From Cornudos to Crow Flat is a long, monotonous tramp of twenty-five or thirty miles, and we arrived in the night and were promptly challenged by the faithful sentinel, old Shep. Although we were strangers, the dog seemed to recognise us as Americans and friends. He went wild with joy, barked, rolled over and over and came as near talking as any African monkey or gorilla could. We gave him a cheer. The faithful animal had been there alone for nearly fifteen days. His side of bacon was eaten and the sack of corn getting very low. The rangers were as much delighted as if it had been a human being they had rescued. The dog had worn the top of the wall of the old stage station perfectly smooth while keeping off the sneaking coyotes. Tracks of the latter were thick all around the place, but Shep held the fort with the assistance of the dummy sentinels. We found everything just as the owners, Andrews and Wiswall, had left it.

As was my custom, I walked over the ground where the Apaches and Messrs. Andrews and Wiswall had had their scrap. Near an old dagger plant, I found where an Indian had taken shelter, or rather tried to hide himself, and picked up a number of Winchester .44 cartridge shells. We secured the ambulance and our return journey was without incident. We arrived back in our camp after making the two hundred miles in a week.

Mr. Andrews presented Lieutenant Baylor with a beautiful Springfield rifle. I don't know whether Andrews or Wiswall are alive, but that Mexican shepherd dog is entitled to a monument on which should be inscribed, "FIDELITY."

In the spring of 1880, two brick masons, Morgan and Brown, stopped at our quarters in Ysleta on their way from Fort Craig, New Mexico, to San Antonio, Texas. They had heard that some freight wagons at San Elizario would soon return to San Antonio and were anxious to travel back with them. These men spent two or three days in the ranger camp and seemed very nice chaps and pleasant talkers. One of them, Mr. Morgan, owned one of the finest pistols I ever saw. It was pearl handled and silver mounted. Our boys tried to trade for it, but Morgan would not part with the weapon.

After the two men had been gone from our camp three or four days, word was brought to Lieutenant Baylor that two men had been found dead near San Elizario. The lieutenant sent me with a detail of three rangers to investigate. At San Elizario we learned that the dead men were at Collins' sheep ranch, four miles from town. On arriving there we found, to our surprise and horror, that the dead men were Morgan and Brown, who had left our camp hale and hearty just a few days before. It was surmised that the men had camped for the night at the sheep ranch and had been beaten to death with heavy *mesquite* sticks. They had been dead two or three days and were stripped of their clothing, their bodies being partly eaten by coyotes.

On repairing to his sheep ranch Mr. Collins found the dead bodies of Morgan and Brown, his shepherds gone and his flocks scattered over the country. Mr. Collins gave the herders' names as Santiago Skevill and Manuel Moleno. After beating out the brains of their unfortunate victims the Mexicans robbed the bodies and lit out for parts unknown.

As the murderers were on foot and had been gone three or four days, I found it very difficult to get their trail, as loose stock grazed along the *bosques* and partially obliterated it. As there was a number of settlements and several little *pueblos* along the river, I knew if I did not follow the Mexicans' tracks closely, I could never tell where they had gone, so I spent the remainder of the day trying to get the trail from camp. We were compelled to follow it on foot, leading our horses. We would sometimes be an hour trailing a mile.

On the following day I was able to make only ten miles on the trail, but I had discovered the general direction. I slept on the banks of the Rio Grande that night, and next morning crossed into Mexico, and found that the murderers were going down the river in the direction of Guadalupe. I now quit the trail and hurried on to this little Mexican town. Traveling around a short bend in the road I came suddenly into the main street of Guadalupe, and almost the first man I saw standing on the street was a Mexican with Morgan's white-handled pistol strapped on him.

I left two of my men to watch the suspect and myself hurried to the office of the president of Guadalupe, made known my mission and told him I had seen one of the supposed murderers of Morgan and Brown on the streets of his city, and asked that the suspect be arrested.

The official treated me very cordially and soon had some police officers go with me. They found the two suspected Mexicans, arrested them and placed them in the *housgow*. The prisoners admitted they were Collins' sheep herders and said their names were Moleno and Skevill but, of course, denied knowing anything about the death of Morgan and Brown.

All my rangers recognised the pistol taken from the Mexican as the weapon owned by Mr. Morgan. The Mexican officers reported to the *alcalde* or town president that the suspects had been arrested. The latter official then asked me if I had any papers for these men. I told him I did not, for at the time I left my camp at Ysleta we did not know the nature of the murder or the names of the parties incriminated. I declared I was sure the men arrested had committed the murder and that I would hurry back to Ysleta and have the proper papers issued for the prisoners' extradition. The *alcalde* promised to hold the suspects until the proper formalities could be complied with.

From Guadalupe to Ysleta is about fifty or sixty miles. I felt the importance of the case, and while I and my men were foot-sore and weary, we rode all night long over a sandy road and reached camp at Ysleta at 9 o'clock the following morning. Lieutenant Baylor at once appeared before the justice of the peace at Ysleta and filed a complaint of murder against Manuel Moleno and Santiago Skevill, had warrants issued for their arrest and himself hurried to El Paso, crossed the river to El Paso del Norte and, presenting his warrants to the authorities, asked that the murderers be held until application for their extradition could be made.

Within a week we learned, much to our disgust, that the two murderers had been liberated and told to *vamoose*. I doubt whether the warrants were ever sent to the *alcalde* at Guadalupe. A more cruel murder than that of Morgan and Brown was never committed on the Rio Grande, yet the murderers went scot-free. This miscarriage of justice rankled in my memory and subsequently it was to lead me to take the law into my own hands when dealing with another Mexican murderer.

CHAPTER 15

Victorio Becomes a Good Indian

As soon as the summer rains had begun in 1880, and green grass and water were plentiful, old Victorio again began his raids. He appeared at Lake Guzman, Old Mexico, then travelled east to Boracho Pass, just south of the Rio Grande. This old chief was then reported making for the Eagle Mountains in Texas. The Mexican Government communicated this information to General Grierson at Fort Davis, Texas, and Lieutenant Baylor was asked to cooperate in the campaign to exterminate the wily old Apache.

General Grierson, on receipt of this information, at once put his cavalry in motion for Eagle Springs, and on August 2, 1880, Baylor left his camp at Ysleta with myself and thirteen rangers equipped for a two weeks' campaign. On August 4th our little band reached old Fort Quitman, eighty miles down the Rio Grande from El Paso, and Lieutenant Baylor reported to General Grierson by telegraph. His message was interrupted, for the Apaches had cut the wires between Bass's Canyon and Van Horn's Well, but the general ordered him by telegram to scout toward Eagle Springs until his command should meet the United States cavalry.

We were to keep a sharp lookout for Indian trails, but we saw none until we reached Eighteen Mile water hole, where General Grierson's troops had had an engagement with Victorio. From here the Indians went south and around Eagle Mountains, so we continued down the road beyond Bass's Canyon and found the Apaches had crossed the road, torn down the telegraph wire, carried off a long piece of it, and destroyed the insulators. The Indians also dragged some of the telegraph poles two or three miles and left them on their trail. The signs indicated they had from one hundred and eighty to two hundred animals. After destroying the telegraph, the raiders finally moved north toward Carrizo Mountains.

At Van Horn, Lieutenant Baylor could learn nothing of General Grierson or his movements. We thereupon took the general's trail leading north and overtook him in camp at Rattlesnake Springs, about sixty-five miles distant. Here we joined Company "K," Eighth Cavalry, and Captain Nolan's company, the Tenth. The cavalry camped at Carrizo Springs and our scouts found Victorio's trail the next day leading southwest toward the Apache Tanks. We left camp at dusk and rode all night and struck the redskins' trail next morning at the stage road where General Grierson had fought. The Indians crossed the road, but afterwards returned to it and continued toward old Fort Quitman.

The overland stage company kept a station at this abandoned frontier post, situated on the north bank of the Rio Grande, eighty or ninety miles east of El Paso, Texas. On August 9, 1880, Ed Walde, the stage driver, started out on his drive with General Byrnes occupying the rear seat of the stage coach. The stage, drawn by two fast running little Spanish mules, passed down the valley and entered the canyon, a very box-like pass with high mountains on either side—an ideal place for an Indian ambuscade. Walde had driven partly through this pass when, around a short bend in the road, he came suddenly upon old Victorio and his band of one hundred warriors.

The Indian advance guard fired on the coach immediately, and at the first volley General Byrnes was fatally wounded, a large calibre bullet striking him in the breast and a second passing through his thigh. Walde turned his team as quickly as he could and made a lightning run back to the stage stand with the general's body hanging partly out of the stage. The Apaches followed the stage for four or five miles trying to get ahead of it, but the little mules made time and beat them into the shelter of the station's *adobe* walls.

It was a miracle that Walde, sitting on the front seat, escaped without a scratch and both of the mules unharmed. At old Fort Quitman I examined the little canvas-topped stage and found it literally shot to pieces. I noticed where a bullet had glanced along the white canvas, leaving a blue mark a foot long before it passed through the top. Three of the spokes of the wheels were shot in two and, as well as I remember, there were fifteen or twenty bullet marks on and through the stage. Lieutenant Baylor and his rangers buried General Byrnes near old Fort Quitman and fired a volley over his grave. Subsequently Walde joined Lieutenant Baylor's command and made an excellent ranger. It was from him that I obtained the particulars of the fight that resulted in the general's death.

En route the Apaches raided Jesus Cota's ranch, killed his herder and drove off one hundred and forty head of cattle. In crossing the river forty of the animals mired in the quicksands. The heartless Indians thereupon pounced upon the unfortunate cattle and cut chunks of flesh out of their living bodies. Many of the mutilated animals were still alive when we found them. The redskins, with a freakish sense of humour, perpetrated a grim joke on the murdered herder. He was rendering out some tallow when surprised and killed, so the murderers rammed his head into the melted tallow to make him a greaser!

After the fight at Quitman, Victorio and his band crossed into Mexico and there found temporary safety, as the United States troops were not permitted to enter that country in pursuit of Indians, though negotiations to permit such pursuit of Indians were even then pending between the two governments. Alone, we were no match for Victorio's hundred braves, so we returned to our camp.

Victorio, however, did not remain idle in Mexico. He made a raid on Dr. Saminiego's San Jose ranch and stole one hundred and seventeen horses and mules, besides killing two Mexican herders. Don Ramon Arranda, captain of the Mexican Volunteers, invited the rangers to Mexico to cooperate with him in exterminating the Apaches, so, on September 17, 1880, Lieutenant Baylor with thirteen rangers, myself included, entered Mexico and marched to Tancas Cantaresio, Don Arranda's ranch. Here we were joined by Mexican volunteers from the towns of Guadalupe, San Ignacio, Tres Jacalas, Paso del Norte, and from the Texan towns of Ysleta, Socorro, and San Elizario, until our combined force numbered over a hundred men.

On the night of the 19th we crossed an Indian trail south of the Rancheria Mountains, but could not tell the number of redskins in the party, as it was then dark and the trail damaged by rain. The same night we saw Indian signal fires to the east of the Arranda ranch. Next morning, with a detail of five rangers and ten Mexican volunteers, I scouted out in the direction of the fires but did not have time to reach the sign, as I was ordered to take and hold the Rancheria Mountains before old Victorio and his band reached them.

At Lucero, the first stage stand, the Apaches were reported within a league of Carrizal. We made a night march with our rangers and seventy-three volunteers, but found the Indians had left, and, as a heavy rain had put out the trail, we struck east toward El Copra Mountains. Here we again picked up the trail and, following it until night, we found a few loose horses of Saminiego's. The marauders now went west toward some tanks and we returned to Candelario, where Victorio's entire band had crossed the Chihuahua stage road. Thence we marched back to San Jose and went into camp to await the arrival of General Joaquin Terrasas.

The Mexican general made his appearance on the 3rd day of October with two hundred cavalry and one hundred infantry. This general, a member of a well-known family of Chihuahua, was more than six feet in height, very dark and an inveterate smoker of cigarettes. He used four milk white horses, riding one while his *aides* led three. His cavalry, well-armed with Remington pistols and carbines, was nicely uniformed and mounted on dark coloured animals of even size. The infantry were Indians from the interior of Mexico. These foot soldiers wore rawhide sandals on their feet and were armed with Remington muskets. Each soldier carried two cartridge belts, containing one hundred rounds of ammunition. I was impressed with the little baggage and rations these infantrymen carried.

On the march each man had a little canvas bag that held about one quart of ground parched corn, sweetened with a little sugar—and a tablespoonful of this mixture stirred in a pint cup of water made a good meal. Of course, when in a cattle country plenty of beef was furnished them, but when on the march they had only this little bag of corn. This lack of baggage and rations enabled them to move quickly and promptly. This light infantry had no trouble at all in keeping up with the cavalry on the march and in a rough country they could move faster than the horsemen.

With General Terrasas' three hundred soldiers and our hundred volunteers we could bring to bear against Victorio about four hundred men. From San Jose the combined command marched to Rebosadero Springs, twenty miles south of El Caparo, on the new Chihuahua stage road. There we rested two days and then marched forty miles to Boracho Pass, where the Apaches had camped after killing General Byrnes and stealing Jesus Cota's stock. We crossed the Indians' trail twenty miles west of the pass and formed our line of battle, as we expected the enemy was camped at some tanks there. He did not appear, so we camped at the pass to await supplies.

When the supply wagons arrived, General Terrasas sent an orderly to Lieutenant Baylor and invited him to send his men to draw ten days' rations. While I was standing in my shirtsleeves near the wagon one of the Mexican soldiers stole from my belt a fine hunting knife that I had carried ten thousand miles over the frontier. I discovered the loss almost immediately and reported it to Lieutenant Baylor, who, in turn, mentioned it to General Terrasas. The Mexican general at once had his captains form their respective companies and had every soldier in camp searched, but the knife was not found. The thief had probably hidden it in the grass.

The Mexican volunteers remained with General Terrasas until after the defeat of Victorio, and one of them told me afterward he had seen a Mexican soldier scalping Apaches with it. Just one year later an orderly of General Terrasas rode into the ranger camp at Ysleta and presented Lieutenant Baylor, then a captain, with the missing weapon and a note stating that Terrasas was glad to return it and to report that the thief had been punished.

While at Boracho we were joined by Lieutenant Shaffer, the Twenty-third United States Cavalry (negroes), Lieutenant Manney, Captain Parker and sixty-five Apache scouts. These latter were Geronimo's Chiricauhaus, who later quit their reservation and wrought such death and destruction in Arizona, New Mexico, and Old Mexico. From the first General Terrasas viewed these Indian allies with distrust, and as soon as we had scouted southeast from Boracho to Los Pinos Mountains, about seventy-five miles distant, and learned that Victorio's trail turned southwest toward Chihuahua, General Terrasas called Captain Parker, Lieutenants Baylor, Shaffer and Manney to his camp and informed them that, as the trail had taken a turn back into the state of Chihuahua and was leading them away from their homes, he thought it best for the Americans to return to the United States. I was present at this conference and I at once saw my chance for a scrap with old Victorio go glimmering. But there was nothing to do but obey orders, pack up and vamoose.

While on scouts after Victorio's band I met many United States officers, and often around the camp fire discussed this old chief. The soldiers all agreed that for an ignorant Indian Victorio displayed great military genius, and Major McGonnigal declared, with the single exception of Chief Crazy-horse of the Sioux, he considered Victorio the greatest Indian general that ever appeared on the American continent. In following this wily old Apache Napoleon, I examined twenty-five or more of his camps. Victorio was very particular about locating them strategically, and his parapets were most skilfully arranged and built. If he remained only an hour in camp, he had these defences thrown up. He had fought in over two hundred engagements, but his last fight was now very close at hand.

The very next morning after the United States troops, the Apache scouts and the Texas rangers turned homeward General Terrasas' scouts reported to him that Victorio with his entire band of followers was camped at Tres Castilos, a small group of hills about twenty-five miles southwest of the Los Pinos Mountains. General Terrasas at once set his column in motion for that place. Captives afterward declared that Victorio's spies reported the presence of the Mexican cavalry early in the day and thereafter kept him informed hour by hour as to the movements of the approaching enemy.

Victorio had just sent his war chief, Nana, and fifty of his best young warriors away on a raid, so he had left in his camp just an even hundred braves, some of them very old men. He also had ninety-seven women and children and about five hundred head of horses and mules, yet the remarkable old Indian made no move to escape. By nightfall General Terrasas drew up near the Apache camp, surrounded the three hills as best he could and waited until morning before assaulting the enemy. During the night twelve of Victorio's warriors, with four women and four children, deserted the old chief and made their way back to the Eagle Mountains in Texas. Here they committed many depredations until exterminated three months later in the Diablo Mountains by Lieutenants Baylor and Nevill.

Early the following morning Victorio mounted a white horse and, in making some disposition of his braves to meet the expected onset of the enemy forces, exposed himself unnecessarily. The Mexicans fired on him at long range and two bullets pierced his body. He fell from his horse dead—a good Indian at last.

The loss of Victorio and the absence of Nana demoralised the Apaches, and a vigorous assault by Terrasas and his army resulted in a complete victory for the Mexicans. Eighty-seven Indian warriors were killed, while eighty-nine squaws and their children were captured with a loss of only two men killed and a few wounded. This victory covered General Terrasas with glory. The Mexican Government never ceased to shower honors upon him and gave him many thousands of acres of land in the state of Chihuahua. The general was so elated over the outcome of the battle that he sent a courier on a fast horse to overtake Lieutenant Baylor and report the good news. The messenger caught us in camp near old Fort Quitman. Every ranger in the scout felt thoroughly disgusted and disappointed at missing the great fight by only two days after being with General Terrasas nearly a month.

The captured women and children were sent south of Mexico City into a climate perfectly unnatural to them. Here they all died in a few years. When Nana heard of the death of Victorio and the capture of the squaws and children he fled with his fifty warriors to the Sierra Madre Mountains in the State of Sonora, Mexico. There he joined forces with old Geronimo and massacred more people than any small band of Indians in the world. To avenge himself on Terrasas for killing his friends and carrying away their wives and children, Nana and his band killed more than two hundred Mexicans before joining Geronimo. Nana, with his new chief, surrendered to General Lawton in 1886, and, I believe, was carried away by our government to Florida, where he at last died.

On our return to camp at Ysleta a commission as captain was waiting Lieutenant Baylor, since Captain Neal Coldwell had been named quartermaster of the battalion, his company disbanded and its letter, "A," given to our company.

Though we missed the fight with Victorio it was not long before we were called upon to scout after the band of twelve warriors that had deserted the old chief on the night before the battle of Tres Castilos. However, we had first to clean up our company, for many undesirable recruits had seeped into it. This accomplished, we were ready to resume our Indian warfare.

CHAPTER 16

Some Undesirable Recruits

In the early fall of 1880, two well mounted and well-armed men appeared at the ranger camp at Ysleta and applied to Captain Baylor for enlistment in his company. After questioning the applicants at some length, the captain accepted them and swore them into the service. One gave his name as John (Red) Holcomb and the other as James Stallings. Unknown to us, both these men were outlaws and joined the rangers solely to learn of their strength and their methods of operations. Holcomb was a San Simone Valley, Arizona, rustler and was living under an assumed name. Stallings, though he went by his true name, had shot a man in Hamilton County, Texas, and was under indictment for assault to kill.

These two recruits came into the service just before we started on our fall campaign into Mexico after old Victorio and were with us on that long scout. Although one was from Texas and the other from Arizona, the two chummed together and were evidently in each other's confidence. Stallings had not been long in the company before he showed himself a trouble maker.

As orderly sergeant it was my duty to keep a roster of the company. Beginning at the top of the list and reading off the names in rotation, I called out each morning the guard for the day. We had in the company a Mexican, Juan Garcia, who had always lived in the Rio Grande country, and Captain Baylor had enlisted him as a ranger that he might use him as a guide, for Garcia was familiar with much of the country over which we were called upon to scout. It so happened that Jim Stallings and Garcia were detailed on the same guard one day. This greatly offended Stallings, and he declared to some of the boys that I had detailed him on guard with a Mexican just to humiliate him and he was going to give me a d—n good whipping. The boys advised him he had better not attempt it. I could see that Stallings was sullen, but it was not until months afterward that I learned the cause.

After our return from our month's scout in Mexico, Captain Baylor received a new fugitive list from the adjutant-general, and in looking over its pages my eyes fell on the list of fugitives from Hamilton County, Texas. Almost the first name thereon was that of James Stallings with his age and description. I notified Captain Baylor that Stallings was a fugitive from justice. Baylor asked me what Stallings had been indicted for and I replied for assault to kill.

"Well, maybe the darned fellow needed killing," replied the captain. "Stallings looks like a good ranger and I need him."

Not many days after this I heard loud cursing in our quarters and went to investigate. I found Stallings with a cocked pistol in his hand standing over the bed of a ranger named Tom Landers, cursing him out. I could see Stallings had been drinking and finally persuaded him to put up his pistol and go to bed. The next morning, I informed Captain Baylor of the incident, and suggested that if we did not do something with Stallings, he would probably kill someone. The captain did not seem inclined to take that view. In fact, I rather believed Captain Baylor liked a man that was somewhat "on the prod," as the cowboys are wont to say of a fellow or a cow that wants to fight.

John Holcomb soon found out as much about the rangers as he desired and, fearing he might be discovered, asked Captain Baylor for a discharge. After obtaining it he took up his abode in El Paso.

Not long afterwards one morning at breakfast, while the twenty rangers were seated at one long dining table, Jim Stallings had a dispute with John Thomas, who was seated on the opposite side of the table and, quick as a flash, struck Thomas in the face with a tin cup of boiling coffee. Both men rose to their feet and pulled their pistols, but before they could stage a shooting match in the place the boys on either side grabbed them.

I at once went to Captain Baylor and told him that something had to be done. He seemed to be thoroughly aroused now and said, "Sergeant, you arrest Stallings, disarm and shackle him. I'll send him back where he belongs."

I carried out the order promptly and Captain Baylor at once wrote to the sheriff of Hamilton County to come for the prisoner. Hamilton County is seven hundred miles by stage from El Paso and it took a week to get a letter through. There was no jail at Ysleta at that time, so we were compelled to hold this dangerous man in our camp.

Stallings was shrewd and a keen judge of human nature. We would sometimes remove the shackles from him that he might get a little exercise. Finally, it came the turn of a ranger named Potter to guard the prisoner. Potter had drifted into the country from somewhere up north, and Captain Baylor had enlisted him. He knew very little about riding and much less about handling firearms. Stallings asked Potter to go with him out into the corral. This enclosure was built of *adobe* and about five feet high. It was nearly dark and the prisoner walked leisurely up to the fence with Potter following close behind with Winchester in hand. All of a sudden Stallings turned a handspring over the fence and hit the ground on the other side in a run.

Potter began firing at the fugitive, which brought out all the boys in camp. Stallings had only about one hundred yards to run to reach the Rio Grande, and before anything could be done, he was safe in Mexico. He yelled a goodbye to the boys as he struck the bank on the opposite side of the river. Captain Baylor was furious over the prisoner's escape and promptly fired Potter from the service and reprimanded me for not keeping Stallings shackled all the time.

Though we had lost the man we had his horse, saddle, bridle and arms. Stallings at once went to Juarez and John Holcomb met him there. The fugitive gave his pal an order on Captain Baylor for his horse, saddle, and pistol, and Holcomb had the gall to come to Ysleta and present this order. He reached our camp at noon while the horses were all in the corral. At the moment of his arrival I happened to be at Captain Baylor's home. Private George Lloyd stepped over to the captain's and said to me, "Sergeant, John Holcomb is over in camp with an order from Jim Stallings for his horse and outfit."

"Gillett, you go and arrest Holcomb and put him in irons and I'll see if I can find where he is wanted," ordered Captain Baylor, who heard what Lloyd said.

Holcomb, seeing Lloyd go into Captain Baylor's, got suspicious, jumped on his horse and left for El Paso in a gallop. I detailed three men to accompany me to capture Holcomb, but by the time we saddled our horses and armed ourselves the fugitive was out of sight. We hit the road running and after travelling two or three miles and inquiring of people we met in the road I became convinced that Holcomb had quit the road soon after leaving our camp and was striking for Mexico. I turned back in the direction of camp and followed the bank of the river.

We had probably travelled a mile on our way home when we discovered Holcomb coming up the river toward us. He was about four hundred yards away and discovered us about the same time. Turning his horse quickly he made a dash for the river. Where he struck it, the bank was ten feet high, but he never hesitated, and both man and horse went head first into the Rio Grande. The three men I had with me outran me and when they reached the point where the fugitive had entered the water, they saw him swimming rapidly to the Mexican side and began firing at him. I ran up and ordered them to cease, telling them not to kill Holcomb, as he was in swimming water and helpless. Just at this moment the swimmer struck shallow water and I ordered him to come back or I would shoot him.

"I'll come if you won't let the boys kill me," he called back.

I told him to hit swimming water quickly, which he did, and swam back to the American side. He was in his shirtsleeves and with his hat gone. His horse, meantime, had swam back to our side of the river.

We all mounted and started back to camp, two of the rangers riding in front with Holcomb. I had not searched the prisoner because he was in his shirtsleeves. As we rode along Holcomb reached into his shirt bosom and pulled out an old .45 pistol and handed it to one of the boys, saying, "Don't tell the sergeant I had this." The rangers at camp gave the prisoner some dry clothes and dinner, then put him in chains and under guard.

Captain Baylor went on to El Paso, crossed the river to Juarez and had Stallings arrested. In two days, we had him back in camp and chained to Holcomb. The captain then wrote to Bell County, Texas, as he had heard John Holcomb was wanted there for murder. Holcomb had a good horse and he gave it to a lawyer in El Paso to get him out of his trouble. Of course, we had no warrant for Holcomb's arrest and Judge Blacker ordered our prisoner brought before him. The county attorney made every effort to have Holcomb held, while his lawyer tried his best to have the suspect released.

The judge finally said he would hold Holcomb for one week and unless the officers found some evidence against him during that time, he would order the prisoner freed. It was nearly dark before we left El Paso on our return to Ysleta, twelve miles distant. Holcomb had, in some manner, gotten two or three drinks of whisky and was feeling the liquor. I had one ranger with me leading the prisoner's horse. The road back to camp followed the river rather closely and the country was very brushy all the way.

As soon as we had gotten out of El Paso Holcomb sat sidewise on his horse, holding the pommel of his saddle with one hand and the cantle with the other, all the while facing toward Mexico. I ordered him to sit straight in his saddle, but he refused. We were riding in a gallop and I believe he intended to jump from his horse and try to escape in the brush. I drew my pistol and hid it behind my leg. Although Holcomb had the cape of his overcoat thrown over his head he discovered I had a pistol in my hand and began a tirade of abuse, declaring I had a cocked gun in my hand and was aching for a chance to kill him. I told him I believed from his actions he was watching for a chance to quit his horse and escape, and that I was prepared to prevent such a move. We reached camp safely and chained Holcomb to Stallings.

These boys, although prisoners, were full of life, and laughed and talked all the time. Holcomb played the violin quite well. We held the two suspects several days and finally one night one of the rangers came to my room and said, "Sergeant, I believe there is something wrong with those prisoners. They are holloaing, singing and playing the fiddle."

I was busy on my monthly reports and told him to keep a sharp lookout and before I retired, I would come and examine the prisoners. On examination I found that while Holcomb played the violin Stallings had sawn their shackles loose. They laughed when I discovered this and said that when the boys had all gone to bed, they intended to throw the pack saddle, which they used for a seat, on the guard's head and escape. We could get no evidence against John Holcomb and the judge ordered his release.

While a prisoner Holcomb swore vengeance against myself and Prosecutor Neal. Mr. Neal heard of this threat, met Holcomb on the streets of El Paso afterward and, jerking a small Derringer pistol from his pocket, shot Holcomb in the belly. Holcomb fell and begged for his life. He was not badly hurt, and as soon as he was well, he quit El Paso, went to Deming, New Mexico, where he stole a bunch of cattle. He drove the stolen herd to the mining camp of Lake Valley and there sold them. While he was in a saloon drinking and playing his fiddle the owner of the cattle appeared with a shotgun and filled the thief full of buckshot. As he fell Holcomb was heard to exclaim, "Oh, boys, they have got me at last."

Jim Stallings was sent to Fort Davis and placed in the jail there, from which he and half a dozen other criminals made their escape.

A man named John Scott came to Captain Baylor, told a hard luck story, and asked to be taken into the service. Captain Baylor enlisted the applicant and fitted him out with horse, saddle, bridle and armed him with gun and pistol, himself standing good for the entire equipment. Scott had not been in the service two months before he deserted. I was ordered to take two men, follow him and bring him back. I overtook Scott up in the Canutillo, near the line of New Mexico, and before I even ordered him to halt, he jumped down, sought refuge behind his horse and opened fire on us with his Winchester. We returned the fire and killed his horse. He then threw down his gun and surrendered. We found the deserter had stopped in El Paso and gotten a bottle of whisky. He was rather drunk when overtaken, otherwise he probably would not have made fight against three rangers. Captain Baylor took Scott's saddle, gun and six-shooter away from him and kicked him out of camp, but was compelled to pay $75 for the horse that was killed.

Another man, Chipman, deserted our company and stole a bunch of horses from some Mexicans down at Socorro. The Mexicans followed the trail out in the direction of Hueco Tanks, where it turned west and crossed the high range of mountains west of El Paso. The pursuers overtook Chipman with the stolen horses just on the line of New Mexico. The thief put up a fierce fight and killed two Mexicans, but was himself killed. Captain Baylor had a scout following the deserter but the Mexicans got to him first and had the fight before our men arrived. However, the ranger boys buried the body of Chipman where it fell. This chap had made a very good ranger and we all felt shocked when we learned he had stolen seven ponies and tried to get away with them single-handed.

Yet another San Simone Valley rustler, Jack Bond, enlisted in the company. A band of rustlers and cow thieves were operating up in the Canutillo, eighteen miles above El Paso, about the time he joined the command. I did my best to break up this band and made scout after scout up the river, but without success. Finally, Captain Baylor learned that Bond and another ranger, Len Peterson, were keeping the thieves posted as to the rangers' movements. The captain fired these two men out of the company and within ten days I had captured Frank Stevenson, the leader of the Canutillo gang, and broken up the nest of thieves. Stevenson was later sent to the penitentiary for fifteen years. Bond and Peterson went to El Paso, stole Mayor M. C. Goffin's fine pair of carriage horses and fled to New Mexico. Subsequently Bond was killed at Deming by Deputy Sheriff Dan Tucker in an attempted arrest.

Captain Roberts, Coldwell or Lieutenant Reynolds would never have let such a bunch of crooks get into their companies, for they had to know something about a man before they would enlist him. However, there was some excuse for Baylor at the time he was on the Rio Grande. It was a long way from the centre of population and good men were hard to find. Then, too, it looked as if all the criminals in Texas had fled to New Mexico and Arizona, from which states they would ease back into the edge of Texas and join the rangers. Captain Baylor was liberal in his views of men: they all looked good to him until proven otherwise. If there was a vacancy in the company any man could get in. And if they lacked equipment the captain would buy the newcomer a horse, saddle, and arms and then deduct the cost thereof from the man's first three months' pay. However, Baylor had generally to pay the bill himself. The captain also liked to keep his company recruited to the limit and this made enlistment in his command easy.

In all the years I was with Captain Baylor I never knew him to send a non-commissioned officer on a scout after Indians. He always commanded in person and always took with him every man in camp save one, who was left to guard it, for he liked to be as strong as possible on the battlefield.

Captain Baylor never took much interest personally in following cattle thieves, horse thieves, murderers and fugitives from justice. He left that almost entirely to me. Sometimes we would have as many as six or eight criminals chained up in camp at one time, but the captain would never come about them, for he could not bear to see anyone in trouble. His open, friendly personality endeared Baylor to the Mexicans from El Paso down the valley as far as Quitman. They were all his *compadres* and would frequently bring him venison, goat meat and mutton. Always they showed him every courtesy in their power.

Now, having freed the company of its undesirable recruits, we were once more a homogeneous force ready and anxious to perform our duty in protecting the frontier and bringing criminals to justice. Almost as soon as the last undesirable had been fired from Company "A" we started on the scout that was to culminate in our last fight with the Apaches.

CHAPTER 17
Last Fight Between Rangers and Apaches

Despite General Terrasas' great victory at Tres Castillos as recorded in a preceding chapter, he did not entirely destroy all the Apaches that had been with old Victorio. Nana and fifty warriors escaped and finally joined Geronimo in his campaign of murder and destruction. On the night preceding the battle in which Victorio was killed and his band of warriors exterminated twelve braves with four squaws and four children deserted the old chief and made their way to those rough mountains that fringe the Rio Grande in the vicinity of Eagle Springs. At once this band of twenty Indians began a series of pillages and murders that has no parallel considering the small size of the party.

The little band of Apaches soon appeared at Paso Viego and began their depredations by an attack on Lieutenant Mills and his cavalry. Paso Viego is a gap in the mountains that parallel the Rio Grande from Eagle Mountains on the west to Brites' ranch on the east, and is situated ten or twelve miles west of and in plain view of the present little town of Valentine, Texas, on the G., H. & S. A. Railroad. The tribe of Pueblo Indians has lived at the old town of Ysleta, El Paso County, Texas, for more than three hundred years. They have always been friends to the Americans and inveterate enemies to the Apaches.

It was customary, therefore, for the United States troops at Fort Davis to employ the Pueblos as guides during the Indian disturbances along the border. In 1881, Bernado and Simon Olgin, two brothers, were the principal chiefs of this tribe. Bernado was the elder and looked it. Both chiefs dressed in the usual Indian fashion, wore moccasins, buckskin leggins and had their long black hair braided and hanging down the back. Simon was a very handsome Indian, and he, with four of his tribe—all nephews of his, I think—were employed by General Grierson during the troublesome times of 1880-1881.

Simon and his four scouts had been detailed to make scouts down on the Rio Grande with Lieutenant Mills, commander of the Tenth United States Cavalry (coloured). On their way out the troops reached Paso Viego early in the evening, and after they had eaten supper Simon Olgin advised the lieutenant to move out on the open plains three or four miles north of the pass where they would be safe from attack. Olgin declared Paso Viego was a favourite camping place for the Indians going to and returning from Mexico because of the fine water and good grass. He stated that should a band of redskins appear at the pass during the night and find it occupied by soldiers they would attack at daylight and probably kill some of the troopers.

Lieutenant Mills, fresh from West Point, replied that he was not afraid of Indians and did not propose to move. During the night the little band of twenty Apaches reached the pass, just as Olgin had prophesied, and hid themselves in the rocks. The next morning the soldiers had breakfast, packed their mules, and as they were standing by their horses ready for the order to mount a sudden fusillade of bullets was fired into their midst at short range. Other volleys came in quick succession. At the very first fire that grand old Indian, Simon Olgin, was shot down and killed, as were five or six of the negro cavalry. The remainder of the company thereupon fled, but the four Pueblo scouts, Olgin's nephews, took to the rocks and fought until they had routed the Apaches and saved the bodies of their old beloved uncle and the soldiers from falling into the hands of the attackers to be mutilated.

Repulsed at Paso Viego the twenty Apaches next appeared at Bass's Canyon, a gap in the mountains on the overland stage road about twelve or fourteen miles west of Van Horn. Here the redskins waylaid an immigrant train on its way to New Mexico. At the very first fire of the Indians Mrs. Graham, who was walking, jumped upon the tongue of the wagon and reached for a Winchester, but was shot and killed. A man named Grant was killed at the same time, while Mr. Graham had his thigh broken. From Bass's Canyon the Indians turned south, crossed around the east end of the Eagle Mountains and again entered Old Mexico, where they were for a time lost to view.

We next hear of this band at Ojo Calienta, some hot springs on the Rio Grande southwest from Eagle Mountains. A captain of cavalry with some coloured troops near old Fort Quitman detailed seven men and instructed the sergeant in charge to scout down the river as far east as Bosque Bonita, keep a sharp lookout for Indian signs and report back to camp in one week. These troopers followed orders, and on their return journey, camped for the night at Ojo Calienta. Next morning at break of day the soldiers were preparing to cook breakfast when the Apaches fell upon them and killed all save one at their first assault. This single survivor made his escape on foot, and after two days in the mountains without food finally reached the soldier camp and reported to his captain. The Indians evidently located the soldier scout the evening before but, as they never make a night attack, waited until daylight to massacre their victims. The redskins captured all the soldiers' equipment and baggage, including seven horses and two pack mules. They pillaged the camp and took everything movable away with them.

Before resuming their journey, the Apaches took six stake-pins made of iron and about twenty inches long that were used by the soldiers to drive into the ground as stakes to which to fasten their horses and drove one through each soldier's corpse, pinning it firmly to the earth. The captured stock was killed and eaten, for the soldiers' animals were fat while most of the ponies and little mules of the Apaches were worn out by constant use in the mountains, and consequently very poor. This band was not heard of again for nearly two months—until the warriors set upon the stage at Quitman Canyon and killed the driver, Morgan, and the gambler, Crenshaw, a passenger.

The reports about this stage robbery and murder were so conflicting and the impression so strong that the driver and the passenger had themselves robbed the stage and made Indian signs to avert suspicion that Captain Baylor deemed it best to go down to the canyon and investigate for himself. Accordingly, the captain made a detail of fourteen privates and one corporal, and with ten days' rations on two pack mules left Ysleta on January 16th to ascertain if possible whether the stage had been robbed and the driver and passenger killed by Indians or by white men, and to punish the robbers if they could be caught. To keep down disorder and violence threatened at El Paso, the captain left me and a detail of three men in our camp at Ysleta.

At Quitman, Captain Baylor learned that the trail of the stage robbers bore southwest to Ojo Calienta, and as the foothills of Quitman Mountains are very rough, he went down the north bank of the Rio Grande, as he felt quite certain he would cut signs in that direction. About twenty-five miles below Quitman he struck the trail of a freshly shod mule, two barefooted ponies and two unshod mules, and within fifty yards of the trail he found the kid glove thought to have been Crenshaw's. The trail now bore down the river and crossed into Mexico, where the Indian band made its first camp. Captain Baylor followed, and the next day found the Apaches' second camp near the foothills of the Los Pinos Mountains, where we had left General Terrasas the fall before.

Here all doubts about the Indians were dispelled, as the rangers found a horse killed with the meat taken as food and a pair of old *moccasins*. Besides, the camp was selected on a high bare hill after the custom of the Indians. The same day Captain Baylor found another camp and a dead mule, and on the trail discovered a boot-top recognised as that of Morgan, the driver. Here also was the trail of some fifteen or twenty mules and ponies, quite fresh, coming from the direction of the Candelario Mountains with one small trail of three mules going toward the Rio Grande. The rangers passed through some very rough, deep canyons and camped on the south side of the Rio Grande, this being their second night in Mexico.

Next morning the trail crossed back into Texas. Going toward Major Carpenter's old camp above the Bosque Bonito the scouting party found a camp where the Indians had evidently made a *cache*, but Captain Baylor only tarried here a short time and followed on down the river a few miles when he found the Apaches had struck out on a bee line for the Eagle Mountains. The captain felt some hesitation about crossing the plains between the Eagle Mountains and the Rio Grande in the daytime for fear of being seen by the Indians, but as the trail was several days old, he took the risk of being discovered. He camped within three or four miles of the mountains and at daybreak took the trail up a canyon leading into the peaks.

The party came suddenly upon an Apache camp which had been hastily deserted that morning, for the Indians left blankets, quilts, buckskins and many other things useful to them. They had just killed and had piled up in camp two horses and a mule, the blood of which had been caught in tin vessels. One mule's tongue was stewing over a fire and everything indicated the redskins were on the eve of a jolly war dance, for the rangers found a five-gallon can of *mescal* wine and a horse skin sunk in the ground that contained fifteen or twenty gallons more. Here Captain Baylor found the mate to Morgan's boot-top and a bag made from the legs of the passenger's pantaloons, besides express receipts, postal cards and other articles taken from the stage. The night before had been bitterly cold and the ground had frozen hard as flint rock, so the rangers could not get the trail, though they searched the mountains in every direction, and the three Pueblo Indians, Bernado Olgin, Domingo Olgin, and Aneseta Duran, looked over every foot of the ground. The scouting party now turned back toward Mexico to scout back on the west side of the Eagle Mountains around to Eagle Springs in search of the trail.

At Eagle Springs, as good luck would have it, Captain Baylor learned that Lieutenant Nevill and nine men had just gone toward Quitman to look for him. As soon as Lieutenant Nevill returned to the Springs he informed Baylor that he had seen the trail six miles east of Eagle Springs and that it led toward the Carrizo Springs or Diablo Mountains.

Captain Baylor's rations were out and Lieutenant Nevill had only supplies enough to do the combined force five days, but the two commanders trusted either to catch the Indians or get in striking distance of the Pecos settlements within that time. The Apaches made pretty good time across the plain in front of Eagle Springs, and did not seem to recover from their scare until they reached the Diablo Mountains. Here they killed and cooked meat from one horse and obtained water by melting snow with hot rocks.

The trail led northward by Chili Peak, a noted landmark to be seen from Eagle Station. Here the rangers quit the trail and went into the Diablo Mountains to camp at Apache Tanks, where General Grierson cut off Victorio from the Guadalupe Mountains the summer before. Next morning Captain Baylor followed the trail north and camped on the brow of cliffs overlooking Rattlesnake Springs. The sign now led to the edge of the Sierra Diablo, where the Indians camped and slept for the first time since leaving Eagle Mountains. They were still watchful, as they were near a most horrible looking canyon down which they could have disappeared had the scouting party come upon them.

Their next camp was about ten miles farther on, and Captain Baylor saw they were getting more careless about camping. On the 28th he came across another horse and fire where the Apaches had eaten some meat. The leg of the horse was not yet stiff and blood dropped from one when picked up. The chase was getting to be exciting, and Captain Baylor and his men felt their chance to avenge the many outrages committed by this band was now near at hand.

The trail led off north as though the redskins were going toward the Cornudos in New Mexico, but turned east and entered Sierra

Diablo Mountains. In a narrow gorge the rangers found where the Indians had eaten dinner, using snow to quench their thirst, but their horses had no water. From this camp the Apaches made for the cliffs on the northeast side of Devil Mountains. The scouting party now felt the Indians were nearby, as they were nearly all afoot. The danger of being discovered if they passed over the hills during the daylight was so apparent that the rangers decided to make a dry camp and pass the mountain's brow before day the next morning. All the signs were good for a surprise; the trail was not over two hours old, and a flock of doves passing overhead going in the direction of the trail showed that water was nearby.

The morning of the 29th of January the party was awakened by the guard, and passed over the mountain's brow before daylight. There was some difficulty in picking up the trail, though Captain Baylor, Lieutenant Nevill and the Pueblo trailers had been up the evening before spying out the land. By stooping down with their faces close to the ground the Pueblos got the trail leading north along the crest of the mountains. Soon the Indian guides said in low voices: "*Hoy esta los Indias.*" And Captain Baylor perceived the Apaches' camp fires not over half a mile distant.

Leaving a guard of five men with the horses the rangers advanced stealthily on foot. By taking advantage of the crest of the mountain they crept within two hundred yards of the camp, supposing the Indians were camped on the western slope of the hill. The Apaches, however, were cautious enough to put one *tepee* on the eastern slope overlooking the valley and the approaches from that direction. Captain Baylor thereupon ordered Sergeant Carruthers of Lieutenant Nevill's company to take seven men and make a detour to the left and attack that wigwam while Lieutenant Nevill and himself with seventeen men advanced on the eastern camp. Sheltering themselves behind some large Spanish dagger plants and advancing in Indian file the attackers got within one hundred yards of the enemy, who was apparently just out of bed, for it was then sunrise. Halting the men deployed to the right and left and then, kneeling, the rangers gave the astonished Indians a deliberate volley. At the second fusillade the Apaches broke and fled, the rangers charging the flying foe with a Texas yell.

Sergeant Carruthers executed his orders in gallant style. The Apaches on his side, alarmed and surprised by the fire of Captain Baylor's force, huddled together and three were killed within twenty yards of their camp fire. The redskins ran like deer and made no resistance, for it was each man for himself. Nevertheless, as they fled, they were thickly peppered, as there were but two or three out of the party of sixteen or eighteen but left blood along their trail as they ran off.

One Indian the rangers named Big Foot (from his enormous track) ran up the mountain in full view for four hundred yards, and not less than two hundred shots were fired at him, but he passed over the hill. Sergeant Carruthers and several men pursued the fugitive for a mile and a half and found plenty of blood all the way. Another warrior was knocked down and lay as though dead for some time, but finally regained his feet and made two-forty time over the hills with a running accompaniment of Springfield and Winchester balls. One brave stood his ground manfully, principally because he got the gable end of his head shot off early in the action.

Of course, the women were the principal sufferers. As it was a bitterly cold, windy morning and all ran off with blankets about them few of the rangers could tell braves from squaws, and in the confusion of battle two women were killed and one mortally wounded. Two children were killed and a third shot through the foot. One squaw with three bullets in her hand and two children were captured. Seven mules and nine horses, two Winchester rifles, one Remington carbine, one United States cavalry pistol and one .40 double action Colt's, six United States cavalry saddles taken from the troops killed at Ojo Caliente and some women's and children's clothing, American made,—evidently those of Mrs. Graham,—a Mexican saddle with a bullet hole in it and fresh blood thereon and over a hundred and fifty yards of new calico fell as spoil to the victors. All the Indians' camp equipage was burned.

The victorious rangers breakfasted on the battleground, as they had eaten nothing since dinner the day before. Some of the men found horse meat good, while others feasted on venison and roasted *mescal*. The band of scouts could not remain long at this camp for water was very scarce. They had forty head of stock to care for, and the Indians, in their flight, ran through the largest pool of water and liberally dyed it with their blood, and as none of the men were bloodthirsty enough to use this for making coffee or bread, they were short of water.

However, the rangers found enough pure good water for their use but the horses had to wait until the force reached Apache Tanks, thirty miles distant. This scarcity of water made it impossible to remain at this Apache camp, otherwise Captain Baylor could have added three or four scalps to his trophies. The return march was begun, and at

Eagle Station Lieutenant Nevill and Captain Baylor separated. The captured squaw and the two children were sent to Fort Davis to be turned over to the post commander for medical attention, for the rangers had neither a surgeon nor a hospital.

On their return from the Battle of the Diablos, Captain Baylor's Pueblo Indian scouts, Chief Bernado Olgin, Domingo Olgin, and Aneseta Duran, suddenly halted about one mile from Ysleta, unsaddled and unbridled their tired little ponies and went into camp. This was their custom after a successful campaign against their Apache enemies so that their comrades might come out and do honour to the returning heroes. For three days and nights a feast and a scalp dance was held by the whole of the Pueblo tribe of Ysleta. They feasted, wined and dined their returning warriors and invited the rangers to the festivities. The boys all went and reported they had a fine time generally. This celebration was the last scalp dance the Pueblo Indians ever had, for the destruction of the Apaches in the Diablos exterminated the wild Indians and there were no more of them to scalp.

CHAPTER 18

An International Episode

The American citizens of Socorro, New Mexico, during Christmas week of 1881, held a church festival, and Mr. A. M. Conklin, editor of the *Socorro Sun*, was conducting the exercises. Abran and Enofrio Baca appeared at the church under the influence of liquor. Their talk and actions so disturbed the entertainment that Mr. Conklin went to them and requested them to be more quiet, at the same time telling the offenders they were perfectly welcome in the church but that they must behave. The brothers, highly indignant, invited Mr. Conklin to fight, but Mr. Conklin declined and again assured the two that they were welcome but must act as gentlemen. Abran and Enofrio at once retired from the church.

After the social had ended and as Mr. Conklin with his wife at his side passed out of the church door, Abran Baca caught Mrs. Conklin by one arm and jerked her away from her husband. At the same instant Enofrio shot and killed the editor on the church steps.

This foul murder created no end of indignation in the little town of Socorro. Scouting parties were sent in all directions to try and effect the capture of the murderers. However, the two Bacas managed to elude their pursuers and made their way into the Republic of Mexico. The governor of New Mexico at once issued a proclamation offering $500 for their capture and the citizens of Socorro offered a like amount for the murderers, dead or alive. The proclamation, with a minute description of the Baca boys, was sent broadcast over the country. And, of course, the rangers at Ysleta received several of the circulars.

In the spring of 1881, the county judge of El Paso County was Jose Baca, an uncle of the two murderers. He was also a merchant at Ysleta, then the county seat of El Paso County. Captain Baylor's company of rangers was quartered in the west end of Ysleta, about one-half mile from the public square. On receiving the New Mexico proclamation, I set a watch over the home and store of Judge Baca and kept it up for nearly a month but without success. We finally concluded that the Baca boys had not come our way and almost forgot the incident.

However, one morning in the latter part of March, 1881, Jim Fitch, one of our most trustworthy rangers, hurried back to camp from Ysleta and informed me that he had seen two well-dressed Mexican boys, strangers to him, sitting on the porch of Judge Baca's home. I at once made a detail of four men. We saddled our horses, rode to town, rounded up the Baca home and captured two strange Mexicans. I believed them to be the Baca brothers, and left at once for New Mexico with my prisoners.

Before we had reached El Paso on our journey, we were overtaken by Judge Baca, who had with him an interpreter. He asked me to please halt as he wished to talk with the prisoners. After a short conversation with the boys the judge asked me what was the reward for the capture of Abran Baca. I replied, "Five hundred dollars."

"If you will just let him step out in the *bosque* and get away I will give you $700," Judge Baca finally said with some hesitation.

Subsequently the judge raised the bribe to one thousand dollars, but I informed him there was not enough money in El Paso County to buy me off, so he returned to Ysleta and I continued my journey to New Mexico, feeling assured I had at least captured one of the Conklin murderers. On arriving at Socorro, I was at once informed that I had Abran all right but my second prisoner was Massias Baca, a cousin of the murderers, but not incriminated in the crime.

I was treated royally by the citizens and officers of Socorro. They were delighted that one of the murderers had been captured and promptly counted out to me $250 as their part of the reward offered for the apprehension of one of the criminals. Colonel Eaton, head deputy sheriff of the county, issued me a receipt for the body of Abran Baca delivered inside the jail of Socorro County, New Mexico. This receipt, forwarded to the governor of the territory, promptly brought me a draft for $250 and a letter of thanks from His Excellency.

Early in April, about one month after the capture of Abran Baca, I learned from Santiago Cooper, a friend that lived in Ysleta, that he had seen a man at Saragosa, Mexico, who, from the description, he believed to be Enofrio Baca. I told Cooper I would give him $25 if he would go back to Saragosa and find out to a certainty if the person he had seen was Enofrio Baca. A week later Cooper came to me and said the man at Saragosa was Baca and that the murderer was clerking in the one big store of the town. This store was a long *adobe* building situated against a hill with the front facing so that one riding up to the front of it would bring his saddle skirts almost on a level with the building because of the terraces in front of it made necessary by the slope of the hill. Enofrio was of florid complexion with dark red hair, which made it easy to identify him.

I kept this information about the murderer to myself for nearly a week while I pondered over it. I was anxious to capture Baca, yet I well knew from previous experience that if I caused him to be arrested in Mexico the authorities there would turn him loose, especially when the influence of wealthy relatives was brought to bear. Knowing he would follow the law to the letter I dare not take Captain Baylor into my confidence. Saragosa, a little town of about five hundred inhabitants, is situated about four miles southwest of Ysleta.

While it is only about a mile from the Rio Grande as the crow flies, yet, because of the many farms and big irrigation ditches, it was impossible to enter or leave the town only by following the public road between Ysleta and Saragosa. It has always been the delight of border Mexicans to get behind an *adobe* wall or on top an *adobe* house and shoot to ribbons any hated *gringo* that might be unfortunately caught on the Mexican side of the river. I knew only too well from my own experience that I could not go into Saragosa, attempt to arrest a Mexican, stay there five minutes and live, yet I determined to take the law in my own hands and make the attempt.

I took into my confidence just one man, George Lloyd. If ever there was an ace in the ranger service, he was one. I unfolded my plans to him. I did not have to point out the danger to him for he had lived on the Rio Grande ten times as long as I.

"Sergeant, that is an awful dangerous and risky piece of business and I will have to have a little time in which to think it over," he said when I talked with him.

The next day Lloyd came to me and said, "Sergeant, I will go anywhere in the world with you."

Though willing to accompany me I could tell he doubted our ability to execute the capture.

I planned to attempt the capture of Baca the next morning and sent Cooper back to Saragosa to look over the situation there once more. He informed me on his return that Baca was still clerking in the store. I now told Lloyd to keep our horses up when the animals were turned out to graze next morning. This move caused no especial thought or comment, for the men frequently would keep their horses to ride down town. As soon as we had crossed the Rio Grande into Mexico, I planned to quit the public road, travel through the *bosques*, pass around on the west side of Saragosa and ride quickly up to the store in which our man was working. Lloyd was to hold the horses while I was to dismount, enter the store and make the arrest. Then, if possible, I was to mount Baca behind Lloyd and make a quick get-away.

Our plans were carried out almost to the letter. We reached Saragosa safely, and while Lloyd held my horse in front of the store I entered and discovered Baca measuring some goods for an old Mexican woman. I stepped up to him, caught him in the collar, and with a drawn pistol ordered him to come with me. The customer promptly fainted and fell on the floor. Two other people ran from the building, screaming at the top of their voices. Baca hesitated about going with me, and in broken English asked me where he was to be taken.

I informed him to Paso del Norte. I shoved my pistol right up against his head and ordered him to step lively. When we reached our horses, I made Baca mount behind Lloyd. I then jumped into my saddle and, waving my pistol over my head, we left Saragosa on a dead run. Our sudden appearance in the town and our more sudden leaving bewildered the people for a few minutes. They took in the situation quickly, however, and began ringing the old church bell rapidly, and this aroused the whole population.

As I left Saragosa I saw men getting their horses together and knew that in a few minutes a posse would be following us. When we had gone two miles almost at top speed, I saw that Lloyd's horse was failing, and we lost a little time changing Baca to my mount. We had yet two miles to go and through deep sand most of the way. I could see a cloud of dust and shortly a body of mounted men hove in view. It was a tense moment. Lloyd thought it was all off with us, but we still had a long lead and our horses were running easily. As our pursuers made a bend in the road, we discovered nine men in pursuit. As soon as they had drawn up within six hundred yards they began firing on us. This was at long range and did no damage.

In fact, I believe they were trying to frighten rather than to wound us as they were just as likely to hit Baca as either of us. We were at last at the Rio Grande, and while it was almost one hundred yards wide it was flat and shallow at the ford. I hit the water running and as I mounted the bank on good old Texan soil, I felt like one who has made a home run in a world series baseball game. Our pursuers halted at the river so I pulled off my hat, waved to them and disappeared up the road.

We lost no time in reaching camp, and our appearance there with a prisoner and two run-down horses caused all the boys in quarters to turn out.

Captain Baylor noticed the gathering and hurried over to camp.

"Sergeant, who is this prisoner you have?" he asked, walking straight up to me.

I replied it was Enofrio Baca, the man that had murdered Mr. Conklin. The captain looked at the run-down horses, wet with sweat, and asked me where I had captured him.

"Down the river," I replied, trying to evade him.

"From the looks of your horse I would think you had just run out of a fight. Where down the river did you capture this man?"

I saw the captain was going to corner me and I thought I might as well "fess up." I told him I had arrested Baca at Saragosa and kidnaped him out of Mexico. Captain Baylor's eyes at once bulged to twice their natural size.

"Sergeant, that is the most imprudent act you ever committed in your life! Don't you know that it is a flagrant violation of the law and is sure to cause a breach of international comity that might cause the Governor of Texas to disband the whole of Company "A"? Not only this, but it was a most hazardous undertaking and it is a wonder to me that the Mexicans did not shoot you and Lloyd into doll rags."

Captain Baylor was plainly out of patience with me.

"Gillett, you have less sense than I thought you had," he declared, heatedly. "If you have any explanation to make, I would like to have it."

I reminded the captain of the tragic fate of Morgan and Brown and how the authorities at Guadalupe had turned their murderers, Skevill and Molina, loose. I declared that had I had Baca arrested in Mexico he would have gone scot-free with his rich and influential friends to help him. Baylor declared that two wrongs did not make one right, and said I should have consulted him. I finally told the captain frankly that I had been in the ranger service six years, had risen from the ranks to be orderly sergeant at a salary of only $50 a month. I pointed out that this was the highest position I could hope to get without a commission, and while one had been promised me at the first vacancy yet I could see no early hope of obtaining it, as every captain in the battalion was freezing to his job. This remark seemed to amuse Captain Baylor and somewhat eased his anger.

I went on to say that I not only wanted the $500 reward offered for Baca, but I wanted the notoriety I would get if I could kidnap the murderer out of Mexico without being killed in the attempt, for I believed the notoriety would lead to something better than a ranger sergeancy. And this is what really happened, for I subsequently became First Assistant Marshal of El Paso under Dallas Stoudemire at a salary of $150 per month, and in less than a year after my arrest of Enofrio Baca I was made Chief of Police of that city at a salary that enabled me to get a nice start in the cattle business.

"Sergeant, you can go with your man," Captain Baylor finally said, "but it is against my best judgment. I ought to escort him across the Rio Grande and set him free."

I lost no time in sending a ranger to the stage office at Ysleta with instructions to buy two tickets to Masilla, New Mexico, and one to El Paso. The stage was due to pass our quarters about 12 o'clock, so I did not have long to wait. I took Lloyd as a guard as far as El Paso and there turned him back, making the remainder of the journey to Socorro, New Mexico, alone with the prisoner. I reached the old town of Masilla, New Mexico, at dark after a rather exciting day. I was afraid to put Baca in jail at that place, as I had no warrant nor extradition papers upon which to hold him and feared the prison authorities might not redeliver Baca to me next morning. The stage coach from Masilla to Rincon did not run at night so I secured a room at the hotel and chaining the prisoner to me we slept together.

On the following day we reached Rincon, the terminus of the Santa Fe Railroad at that time. I wired the officers of Socorro, New Mexico, from El Paso that I had captured Baca and was on my way to New Mexico with him. Baca's friends had also been informed of his arrest and lost no time in asking the Governor of New Mexico to have me bring the prisoner to Santa Fe as they feared mob violence at Socorro. When I reached San Marcial, I was handed a telegram from the governor ordering me to bring Baca to Santa Fe and on no account to stop with him in Socorro.

Because of delay on the railroad I did not reach Socorro until late at night. The minute the train stopped at that town it was boarded by twenty-five or thirty armed men headed by Deputy Sheriff Eaton. I showed Eaton the governor's telegram, but he declared Baca was wanted at Socorro and that was where he was going. I remonstrated with him and declared I was going on to Santa Fe with the prisoner. By this time a dozen armed men had gathered around me and declared, "Not much will you take him to Santa Fe." I was furious, but I was practically under arrest and powerless to help myself, Baca and I were transferred from the train to a big bus that was in waiting. The jailer entered first, then Baca was seated next to him and I sat next the door with my Winchester in my hand. The driver was ordered to drive to the jail.

It was a bright moonlight night and we had not travelled far up the street before I looked out and saw at least a hundred armed men. They came from every direction. Boys, did you ever encounter a mob? I assure you it is far from a pleasant feeling when you face one. The men swarmed around the bus, three or four of them grabbed the horses by the bridle reins and held them, while others tried to force the bus doors. I asked the jailer if I could depend on him to help me stand the mob off, but he replied it would do no good. I was now madder than ever, and for the first time in my life I ripped out an oath, saying, "G— d—n them, I am going to stand them off!"

As the doors were forced, I poked my Winchester out and ordered the mob to stand back or I would shoot. The men paid no more attention to my gun than if it had been a brown stick. A man standing beside the bus door seized the muzzle of my rifle and, with a quick jerk to one side, caused it to fly out of my hand and out upon the ground.

By this time another of the mob grabbed me in the collar and proceeded to pull me out of the bus.

I spread my legs and tried to brace myself, but another hard and quick jerk landed me out on the ground, where one of the men kicked me. I was tame now and made no effort to draw my pistol. One of the crowd said to me, "What in h— do you mean? We do not wish to hurt you but we are going to hang that d—n Mexican right now!"

I then informed the mob of the nature of Baca's arrest and told them that the hanging of the prisoner would place me in an awkward position. Then, too, the reward offered by the territory of New Mexico was for the delivery of the murderer inside the jail doors of Socorro County. The leaders of the crowd consulted for a few minutes and then concluded I was right. They ordered me back into the bus, gave me my Winchester and we all started for the jail. As soon as Baca had been placed in prison Deputy Sheriff Eaton sat down and wrote me a receipt for the delivery of Baca inside the jail doors.

By this time day was just beginning to break and I tried to stay the hanging by making another talk. The mob interpreted my motive and invited me to step down a block to their community room where they would talk with me. I started with them and we had gone only a hundred yards before the whole mob broke back to the jail. I started to go with them but two men held me, saying, "It's no use; they are going to hang him."

The men took Baca to a nearby corral and hanged him to a big beam of the gate. The next morning Baca's relatives came to me at the hotel with hats in their hands and asked me for the keys with which to remove the shackles from the dead man's legs. As I handed them the keys, I felt both mortified and ashamed. A committee of citizens at Socorro waited on me just before I took the train for home, counted out to me $250 as their part of the reward and thanked me for capturing the two murderers. The committee assured me that it stood ready to help me financially or otherwise should I get involved with the Federal Government over the capture and kidnapping of Enofrio Baca.

I presume the relatives of young Baca reported his kidnapping to our government, for a few weeks after his capture Mr. Blaine, Secretary of State, wrote a long letter to Governor Roberts regarding a breach of international comity. Governor Roberts wrote Captain Baylor for a full explanation of the matter. Captain Baylor, while never countenancing a wrongdoing in his company, would stand by his men to the last ditch when they were once in trouble. He was a fluent writer and no man in Texas understood better than he the many foul and outrageous murders that had been committed along the Rio Grande, the perpetrators of which had evaded punishment and arrest by crossing over into Mexico. Baylor wrote so well and so to the point that nothing further was said about the matter. Only an order came to Captain Baylor admonishing him never again to allow his men to follow fugitives into Mexico.

Soon afterward the Safety Committee of Socorro, New Mexico, wrote to Captain Baylor saying, "We are informed by a reliable party that Jose Baca of Ysleta, Texas, has hired a Mexican to kill Sergeant Gillett. Steps have been taken to prevent this. However, he would do well to be on the lookout." Baylor at once went to Judge Baca with this letter, but the jurist denied in the most emphatic terms any knowledge of the reported plot. Also, there was a report current in both Ysleta and El Paso that a reward of $1,500 had been offered for the delivery of Sergeant Gillett's body to the Mexican authorities at El Paso del Norte.

Upon investigation I found that no such offer had ever been made, but for safety's sake I kept out of Mexico for several years.

The kidnapping of Baca aroused much comment and gave me a deal of notoriety and, as I had anticipated, it was not long in bearing the fruit I desired—promotion into larger and more remunerative fields of work.

CHAPTER 19

Last Scoutings

During the summer of 1881, Captain Baylor's company made several scouts out to the Sacramento and Guadalupe Mountains. These were reported to the Adjutant-General as scouts after Indians, but there were no more redskins in Texas, for the rangers had done their work effectively. These expeditions were, therefore, more in the nature of outings for the boys. And it was quite a pleasure to get away from camp in the hot Rio Grande Valley and scout in those high mountains covered with tall pine timber that teemed with game such as deer, bear and wild turkey. The plains between the Guadalupe Mountains and Ysleta contained hundreds of antelope, thus affording the rangers the best of sport.

Turning over the pages of my old scrap book I find this little announcement taken from the *El Paso Times*:

> Colonel Baylor and twenty of his rangers have just returned from a scout in the Guadalupe Mountains, in which they killed twenty-five turkeys, fifteen deer and two antelope.

On one of these hunting expeditions we had with us George Lloyd, who had been a ranger under Lieutenant Tays when his company was first mustered into service in El Paso County. We camped at Los Cornuvas, and here Lloyd had had an engagement with Indians. He went over the ground and gave us an interesting account of his fight. He said there were but twelve men in the scout, including Lieutenant Tays. In marching from Crow Springs to Los Cornuvas, a distance of thirty miles, six of the rangers were riding nearly a mile ahead of the others and on approaching Los Cornuvas made for some *tinajas* (water holes) up in those mountains. They rode around a point of rocks and met face to face some ten or twelve Indians coming out from the water. Indians and rangers were within forty feet before they discovered each other's presence and paleface and redskin literally fell off their horses—the Indians seeking cover in the rocks above the trail while five of the rangers turned a somersault into a friendly *arroyo*.

A ranger said to be a Russian nobleman and nihilist was killed early in the fight and buried on the spot where he fell. A headboard was placed to mark the grave, but the Indians soon defaced it by hacking at it with their knives whenever they passed the spot. Though he could have had splendid cover, the Russian stood upright according to the etiquette prevailing among British officers in the Transvaal and was shot through the brain.

In dismounting, Lloyd held on to the end of a thirty-foot stake rope that was tied around his horse's neck. Four of the dismounted scout wriggled their way down the creek and got away. In reloading his Winchester after shooting it empty Lloyd unfortunately slipped a .45 Colt's pistol cartridge into the magazine of his .44 Winchester and in attempting to throw a cartridge into his gun it jammed—catching him in a serious predicament. However, taking his knife from his pocket this fearless ranger coolly removed the screw that held the side plates of his Winchester together, took off the plates, removed the offending cartridge, replaced the plates, tightened up the screw, reloaded his gun and began firing. It takes a man with iron nerve to do a thing like that, and you meet such a one but once in a lifetime. Is it any wonder, then, that when I cast around for a man to go into Mexico with me to kidnap Baca, I selected Lloyd out of the twenty men in camp?

Seeing that the Russian was dead and his companions gone, Lloyd crawled back down the *arroyo*, pulling his horse along the bank above until he was out of danger. The five rangers' horses, knowing where the water was, went right up into the rocks, where they were captured, saddles, bridles and all, by the Indians.

The redskins, as soon as Lloyd was gone, came out of hiding, took the Russian's Winchester and pistol and left. Lloyd was the only man of the six to save his horse, for the Indians, with their needle guns high up in the rocks, held Lieutenant Tays and the remainder of his force at bay.

In the latter part of the summer of 1881, Captain Baylor moved his company of rangers from Ysleta to a site three miles below El Paso. While camped there the captain was warned by the sheriff of Tombstone, Arizona, to be on the lookout for four San Simone Valley rustlers, supposed to be a part of Curley Bill's gang. The robbers' names were given as Charley and Frank Baker, Billie Morgan and a fourth person supposed to be Curley Bill himself. These outlaws had stolen sixteen big work mules and four horses at a wood camp some twelve miles from Tombstone. They had also robbed a store and, assaulting the proprietor with pistols, left him for dead. A $500 reward was offered for the capture of the *desperadoes* and the stolen stock. The robbers' trail led down into New Mexico and it was believed Curley Bill and his gang were headed for western Texas, where they would try to dispose of their stolen stock at some of the railroad grading camps near El Paso.

Captain Baylor at once ordered me to take seven men and five days' rations and scout up the Rio Grande to the line of New Mexico for the bandits' trail, and, if I found it, to follow it up. I worked up the river but found no trail. Neither could I learn anything about any strange men driving stock through the country. My time was nearly up and I concluded to return to camp through a gap in the Franklin Mountains, some thirty or forty miles north of El Paso. We left the Rio Grande late in the evening, passed out through the gap and made a dry camp on the plains east of the mountains.

Early the following morning we rode to a watering place known as Monday's Springs and stopped for breakfast. Here the boys discovered some horse and mule tracks. At first, we thought nothing of this, supposing the trail had been made by some loose stock grazing near the water. From Monday's Springs a dim road led along the east side of the mountains to El Paso and we took this route home. Before we had travelled very far, we noticed that some of the stock was travelling the same road, though even then I never suspected that these tracks might be the trail of the bandits for whom we were scouting. Finally, we came to footprints made by some men as they adjusted their saddles or tightened their packs. It here dawned upon me that the tracks might have been made by the parties we wanted.

I thereupon followed the trail carefully and it led me through what is today the most beautiful residential portion of the city of El Paso. The tracks led to a big camp yard where now stands the $500,000 Federal building and post office. In the description of the stolen stock we were told one of the mules carried a small Swiss stock bell. As I neared the wagon yard, I heard the tinkle of this bell and felt sure we had tracked our quarry. We dismounted, and with our Winchesters cocked and ready for action, our little party of rangers slipped quickly inside the large corral gate and within ten feet of it we came upon three heavily armed men bending over a fire cooking their breakfast. Their guns were leaning against the *adobe* fence near at hand, so the surprise was complete.

The outlaws rose to their feet and attempted to get their guns, but my men held their cocked Winchesters at their breasts. I told our captives that we were rangers ordered to arrest them and demanded their surrender. The robbers were undecided what to do; they were afraid to pull their pistols or seize their guns, yet they refused to hold up their hands. Finally, one of the Baker brothers turned slightly toward me and said they would rather be shot down and killed than give up—surrender meant death anyway. I thereupon answered that we had no desire to hurt them, but declared that the least attempt to pull a gun would mean instant death to them all, and again ordered them to raise their hands. They slowly obeyed. I stepped up to them, unbuckled their belts and took their weapons.

In looking over their camp I found four saddles and Winchesters but I had captured only three men. I mentioned this fact to the prisoners and they laughingly said one of their number had stepped down town to get a package of coffee, had probably noticed our presence and lit out. The two Baker boys and Billie Morgan were the men captured, and I asked if the missing man was Curley Bill himself. They replied it was not, but refused to tell who the fourth member of their party was. As we had no description of him and he was on foot in a town full of armed men we had no means of identifying him and he was never captured.

From the captured robbers we learned that they had run out of provisions, and for this reason they had not camped at Monday Springs. They had risen early and come into El Paso for breakfast.

They declared it was a good thing for us that they had built their camp fire so near the gate, for had they been thirty feet from it they would have put up a fight we should have remembered for a long time. I replied that the eight of us could have held our own no matter where they had camped.

These robbers were held in our camp some ten days or more until the proper extradition papers could be had from the State Capitol at Austin, as they refused to be taken back to Arizona without the proper authority. They owned horses, which they gave to some lawyers in El Paso to prevent their being taken back to the scene of their crimes. We secured all the stolen stock—sixteen mules and four horses. The owners came and claimed them and paid the rangers $200 and the Arizona sheriff paid a like amount for the capture of the rustlers.

Our rangers became well acquainted with these thieves while we held them in our camp. The robbers admitted they were going under assumed names and said they were Texans but refused to say from what part of the state they came. The three of them were taken back to Arizona, tried for assault to kill and the theft of the horses at Tombstone and sent to the prison at Yuma for twenty-five years. They frequently wrote to our boys from there and seemed to hold no grudge against us for capturing them. The scout to capture these men was the last one of importance I took part in, for my work with the rangers was now growing toward its close.

In the fall of 1881, Captain Baylor received word from Israel King of Cambray, New Mexico, that a band of thieves had stolen a bunch of cattle from him and at last reports were headed toward El Paso with them. With a detail of four men I was ordered to make a scout up the river and into the Canutillos to intercept the rustlers. After travelling some ten miles up the Rio Grande we crossed the river into New Mexico to get on more even ground. Some eighteen miles above El Paso we found the trail of the stolen stock and followed it back across the Rio Grande into Texas.

While working our way along the trail through almost impassable brush we entered a small glade and came upon the stolen stock quietly grazing. On the opposite side of them a Mexican with a Winchester stood guard while his horse grazed nearby. The guard fired on us as he ran to his horse and we were compelled to run around the cattle to get to the thief. We fired our guns as we ran and this sudden noise frightened the loose pony so the fugitive was unable to mount. He was then forced to dive into the brush on foot. Knowing we could make no headway through the heavy *tornilla bosque* we dismounted and charged it on foot. The fleeing Mexican undertook to run through a muddy slough formed by back water from the Rio Grande. Here he bogged but, extracting himself, he backed out the way he had entered and found safety in the friendly brush. In running to where he was last seen we found his gun abandoned in the mud. Some twenty or thirty shots were fired at him and while none found the mark, we captured his Winchester, his pony and thirty-six head of stolen cattle and gave him a scare that he will remember so long as he lives. The cattle were returned to Mr. King, who kindly presented us with $200 for their recovery.

We learned later that Frank Stevenson, a notorious rustler, whose rendezvous was in this Canutillo brush, had stolen these cattle and had left the Mexican in charge of them while he had gone into El Paso to effect their sale. As described in a previous chapter, I finally captured Stevenson and he was sent to the penitentiary for fifteen years for horse stealing. His capture and imprisonment broke up the Canutillo gang, and today, forty years after his arrest, the upper Rio Grande Valley is almost an Eden on earth with its fine apple and peach orchards, its *alfalfa* fields, big dairy herds and elegant homes. It is one of the beauty spots adjacent to the now fine city of El Paso. The Santa Fe Railroad traverses this valley, and I sometimes travel over it. As I sit in an easy seat in the Pullman and look out over the country I always reflect on the past and wonder how many of its present inhabitants know what a wilderness and what a rendezvous it once was for all kinds of cutthroats, cattle thieves and murderers.

While the rangers were camped near El Paso during the fall of 1881, I met Captain Thatcher, then division superintendent of the Santa Fe Railroad. He told me, because of the stage and train robberies in New Mexico and Arizona, the railroad and the Wells-Fargo Express companies feared that their trains would be held up near El Paso. To protect themselves they had, therefore, decided to place armed guards of three men on the main line of the Santa Fe to run between Deming and Las Vegas, New Mexico, and a similar guard on the branch from El Paso, Texas, to Rincon, New Mexico. Captain Thatcher had known me as a ranger and my kidnapping of Enofrio Baca out of Mexico had won me no little notoriety, so he now offered me a position with the railroad company as captain of the guard at a salary of $150 per month. I would be allowed to select my own men for guards and would be responsible for their acts.

I requested time to consider the proposition. While the position as captain of the railroad guard might not be permanent—might not hold out more than six months—yet the salary attached was exactly three times what I received from the State of Texas as sergeant of rangers. I discussed Thatcher's offer with Captain Baylor and finally prevailed upon him to give me my discharge. And on the 26th of December, 1881, after serving the State of Texas as a ranger for six years and seven months I laid down my Winchester with the satisfied consciousness that I had done my duty ever. My term of service embraced one of the happiest portions of my life, and recollections of my ranger days are among my most cherished memories. Among my dearest possessions, though preserved in an old scrapbook, is my discharge. It reads simply:

Discharge

This is to certify that James B. Gillett, 1st Sergeant of Captain Geo. W. Baylor's Company "A" of the Frontier Battalion of the State of Texas, is hereby honourably discharged from the service of the state by reason of his own request. I take great pleasure in testifying to his uniform good conduct and gallant service in my company.

Given at El Paso, Texas, this, the 26th day of December, 1881.

George W. Baylor
Commanding Company.

The personnel of Captain Baylor's company changed rapidly, so that at the time of my discharge there was scarcely a man in the company that had served longer than six months. There was, therefore, no wrenching or straining of strong friendship ties when I left the command, save only for my leaving of Captain Baylor. To part from him did, indeed, make me feel sad. My farewell and departure was simple and unimpressive. I sat down with my comrades for a last ranger dinner of beans, bacon, bread and black coffee. After the meal I arose from the table, shook hands with Captain Baylor and the boys, mounted my horse and rode away from the ranger camp forever. Yet, though my term of actual service was over and though I had garnered a host of memories and experiences, I had not quite finished with the rangers—I had not gathered all the fruits of my rangership,—an appointment to the police force of El Paso in the vicinity of which city I had so often scouted.

CHAPTER 20

Fruits of Ranger Service

Early in the spring of 1881, the old town of El Paso awoke out of her Rip Van Winkle sleep to find that four grand trunk railroad lines,—the Santa Fe, Southern Pacific, G., H. & S. A., and the Texas & Pacific—were rapidly building toward her and were certain to enter the town by the end of the year. Situated as it was, many hundreds of miles from any other town, it was a foregone conclusion that El Paso had the making of a great city and was a fine field for investment. Bankers, merchants, capitalists, real estate dealers, cattlemen, miners, railroad men, gamblers, saloon-keepers and sporting people of both sexes flocked to the town. They came in buggies, hacks, wagons, horseback and even afoot. There was not half enough hotel accommodations to go around, so people just slept and ate at any old place. El Paso Street, the only business thoroughfare at that time, was flooded with crowds.

At night there was not enough room for people to walk on the sidewalks and they filled the streets. To me it looked just a miniature midway at a world's fair. A saloon was opened on almost every corner of the town with many in between. Each drinking place had a gambling house attached where the crowds played *faro* bank, *monte*, roulette, chuck-a-luck, stud poker and every gambling game on the calendar. If one wished a seat at the gaming tables he had to come early or he could not get within thirty feet of them. Two variety theatres, the Coliseum, operated by the Manning Brothers—the largest in the southwest—and Jack Doyle's, were quickly opened.

An election was called in El Paso and the city was duly incorporated and a mayor and board of aldermen installed. George Campbell was elected city marshal and given one assistant, Bill Johnson. The new marshal had come to El Paso from Young County, Texas, where

DALLAS STOUDENMIRE

he had been a deputy sheriff. Campbell had done some good detective work and was a fairly good and efficient officer, but his assistant was much below ordinary.

The city marshal soon found that with but one man to aid him he had the biggest kind of a job on his hands with something doing every hour in the twenty-four, Campbell decided he was not getting enough pay for the work he had to do and asked the City Council for a raise in his salary, but the council refused it. The marshal at once resigned and left Bill Johnson to hold the town. Campbell was very friendly with the sporting element in El Paso, especially with the Manning Brothers, who were running two saloons and a big variety theatre. Campbell and his friends decided to use strategy to force the council to increase his salary and planned to shoot up the town, thinking this would cause the city fathers to reinstate Campbell in his old position with a substantial increase in pay. At 2 o'clock one morning the town was shot up, some three or four hundred shots being fired promiscuously and with no attempt to make arrests.

The following morning Mayor McGoffin sent a hurry call to Captain Baylor at Ysleta and asked that a detachment of Texas Rangers be sent to El Paso to help police the town. At that time, I had not severed my connection with the rangers, so I was ordered to make a detail of five rangers, issue them fifteen days' rations and have them report at once to the mayor of El Paso.

The peace-loving citizens of the town welcomed the rangers, secured nice quarters for them and furnished the detachment with a stove on which to cook its meals. The rangers had been in El Paso on police duty about a week when there appeared in the town from New Mexico the famous Dallas Stoudenmire. The newcomer was six feet two inches in height, a blonde and weighed one hundred and eighty-five pounds. Stoudenmire had a compelling personality and had been a Confederate soldier, having served with General Joe Johnston at Greensboro, North Carolina. Mr. Stoudenmire applied to the mayor and City Council for the position of city marshal. He presented good references and was duly appointed town marshal.

George Campbell now saw his chances for reinstatement as an officer in El Paso go glimmering. Marshal Stoudenmire called on Bill Johnson for the keys of the city jail, but the latter refused to surrender them. Thereupon Stoudenmire seized the recalcitrant assistant, shook him up and took the keys from his pocket, thereby making his first enemy in El Paso.

About ten days after the new marshal had been installed it was reported in El Paso that two Mexican boys had been found murdered some ten or twelve miles from town on the Rio Grande. The rangers stationed in the city went out to the ranch to investigate. The bodies were brought to El Paso and a coroner's inquest was held in a room fronting on El Paso Street. Johnnie Hale, manager of Manning's little ranch, was summoned to appear before the coroner, and it was believed by the rangers that Hale and an ex-ranger named Len Peterson had committed the double murder.

The inquest, being held in such a public place, attracted a crowd of onlookers. Besides the rangers, Marshal Stoudenmire, ex-Marshal Campbell, and Bill Johnson were present. A man named Gus Krempkau acted as interpreter. The trial dragged along until the noon hour and the proceedings were adjourned for dinner. The rangers went at once to their quarters to prepare their meal, though there was still a crowd standing about the scene of the inquest. Krempkau came out of the room and was accosted by John Hale, who had become offended at the way the interpreter had interpreted the evidence. After a few hot words Hale quickly pulled his pistol and shot Krempkau through the head, killing him instantly. Marshal Stoudenmire ran up, shot at Hale but missing him killed a Mexican bystander. At the second shot from the marshal's pistol John Hale fell dead. George Campbell had pulled his pistol and was backing off across the street when Stoudenmire suddenly turned and shot him down. Four men were thus killed almost within the twinkling of an eye.

Stoudenmire was held blameless by the better class of citizens for the part he had played, but a certain sporting element—mostly friends of Campbell—was highly indignant at Marshal Stoudenmire for killing Campbell, and declared the latter had been murdered. The Manning Brothers were especially bitter against the marshal, as he had killed their ranch foreman, Hale, and their friend, Campbell. This feeling against Marshal Stoudenmire never subsided, and just a little more than one year after, Dallas Stoudenmire was shot and killed in a street fight by Jim and Dr. Manning within fifty feet of the spot where Stoudenmire himself had killed the three men the year before.

The friends of George Campbell now sought to take the life of Marshal Stoudenmire, and they used as their instrument Bill Johnson, a man almost simple mentally. The plotters furnished Johnson with plenty of free whisky and when they had made him drunk, they told him Stoudenmire had no right to catch him in the collar and shake him as if he were a cur dog. Johnson finally agreed to kill the marshal. Armed with a double-barrelled shotgun the tool of the plotters took up a position one night behind a pile of bricks in San Antonio Street where it enters El Paso and lay in wait for his intended victim.

Marshal Stoudenmire was then down at Neal Nuland's Acme saloon, and it was well known he would soon make his round up the street. Shortly afterward he was seen coming, and when he had approached within twenty-five feet of the brick pile Bill Johnson rose to his feet and fired both barrels of his shotgun. Unsteady with drink, Johnson's fire went over the marshal's head and left him unharmed. The marshal pulled his pistol and with lightning rapidity filled Johnson's body full of holes. At the same moment Campbell's friends, posted on the opposite side of the street, opened fire on Stoudenmire and slightly wounded him in one foot, but the marshal charged his attackers and single-handed put them to flight.

From this day Marshal Stoudenmire had the roughs of El Paso eating out of his hand. There was no longer any necessity for the rangers to help him police the town and they were withdrawn. Stoudenmire's presence on the streets was a guarantee of order and good government. He was a good man for the class of people he had to deal with, yet he knew there were those in El Paso that were his bitter enemies and always on the alert for a chance to take his fife. This caused him to drink, and when under the influence of liquor, he became mean and overbearing to some of his most ardent supporters, so much so that by the spring of 1882, he was asked to resign. In a dramatic and fiery speech Stoudenmire presented his resignation and declared he had not been treated fairly by the City Council and that he could straddle them all.

Immediately on leaving the rangers, as narrated at the close of the preceding chapter, I accepted a position of captain of guards on the Santa Fe Railroad under my friend, Captain Thatcher. I did not long remain in the railroad's employ, and after a few months I resigned my position there to become assistant city marshal under Mr. Stoudenmire.

Upon the resignation of Mr. Stoudenmire I was appointed city marshal of El Paso. Upon my appointment the ex-marshal walked over, took me by the hand and said, "Young man, I congratulate you on being elected city marshal and at the same time I wish to warn you that you have more than a man's size job on your hands."

Stoudenmire at once secured the appointment as United States deputy marshal of the Western District of Texas with headquarters at El Paso. Stoudenmire always treated me with the greatest consideration and courtesy and gave me trouble on only one occasion. I reproduce here a clipping from an El Paso paper of the time:

> Last Thursday night a shooting scrape in which ex-Marshal Stoudenmire and ex-Deputy Page played the leading parts occurred at the Acme saloon. It seems that early in the evening Page had a misunderstanding with Billy Bell. Stoudenmire acted as peacemaker in the matter. In doing so he carried Page to Doyle's concert hall, where the two remained an hour or so and got more or less intoxicated. About midnight they returned to the Acme and soon got into a quarrel. Stoudenmire drew his pistol and fired at Page; the latter, however, knocked the weapon upward and the ball went into the ceiling. Page then wrenched the pistol from Stoudenmire and the latter drew a second pistol and the two combatants were about to perforate each other when Marshal Gillett appeared on the premises with a double-barrel shotgun and corralled both of them. They were taken before court the following morning and fined $25 each and Stoudenmire was placed under bond in the sum of $250 to keep the peace.

My election to the marshalship of El Paso I attribute solely to my training as a ranger and to the notoriety my kidnapping of Baca out of Mexico had given me, so that the marshalship of the town was one of the direct fruits of my ranger service.

I was an officer of El Paso for several years. Not very long after my acceptance of the marshalship Captain C. L. Nevill, with whom I had served in Lieutenant Reynolds' company, resigned his ranger command and became sheriff and tax collector of Presidio County, Texas. The Marfa country was now seen to be a very promising cattle section, so Captain Nevill and myself formed a partnership and embarked in the cattle business. This did not in the least interfere with our duties as sheriff and marshal, respectively, and we soon built up a nice little herd of cattle.

In the spring of 1885, General Gano and sons of Dallas, Texas, formed a company known as the Estado Land and Cattle Company. The new concern arranged to open a big ranch in Brewster County and General Gano wrote to Captain Nevill, asking him please to secure a good cattleman as ranch manager for the new company. Nevill at once wrote me and advised me to accept this position. In his letter he jokingly remarked:

> Jim, you have had a quart cup of bullets shot at you while a ranger and marshal, and now that you have a chance to quit and get something less hazardous, I advise you to do it. Besides you will be near our own little ranch and can see your own cattle from time to time.

I considered the proposition seriously, and on the 1st day of April, 1885, I resigned from the police force of El Paso and became a cowboy again. In accepting the marshalship I reaped the fruits of my ranger service and now, in resigning from that position I completely severed all my connection with the ranger force and all that it had brought me. Henceforth my ranger days and ranger service were to be but a memory, albeit the most happy and cherished one of my life.

I was manager of the Estado Land and Cattle Company's ranch for nearly six years and during that period the herd increased from six to thirty thousand head. When I resigned the ranch managership it was that I might attend to my own ranch interests, which had also grown in that period. Though today, (1921), I own a large and prosperous ranch in the Marfa country and though my business interests are many and varied, I still cherish the memory of my ranger days and am never too busy to see an old ranger comrade and re-live with him those six adventurous, happy and thrilling years I was a member of the Frontier Battalion of the Texas Rangers.

Life and Adventures of Sam Bass the Notorious Union Pacific and Texas Train Robber

Sam Bass

Contents

Early Life of Bass	199
Fatal Mistake	202
Life in the Black Hills	205
Launching into Crime	210
Fated	212
James Berry	218
Escape of Bass and Davis	223
Texas Train Robberies	226
Hutchins and Eagle Ford	229
Robbers' Fastness	233
Texas Band	241
Spy in Camp	245
Mesquite	248
Gathering Them in	253
The Great Campaign against Bass	258
The Great Campaign against Bass Continued	266
Pipes and Herndon	275
The Betrayal	278
The Betrayer with the Band	282

The Last Fight	287
Capture and Death	292
Notes and Comments	297

Chapter 1

Early Life of Bass

Sam Bass was born July 21st, 1851, in Lawrence County, Indiana, on a farm two miles north of Mitchell. He was the son of Daniel Bass, who in 1840, had married Elizabeth J. Sheeks and settled upon a farm, where by industry and economy he acquired a competency. They had ten children, the two oldest of whom died in infancy. The third son, Geo. W. Bass, enlisted in the 16th regiment Indiana volunteers and was killed in the Battle of Richmond, Ky., August 30th, 1862. The rest of the children, with the exception of the wayward subject of this sketch, are still living, (1878), in Lawrence and Martin Counties, Indiana. Their names are John, Denton and Sallie Bass, Euphema Beasley, Mary Hersey and Clarissa Hersey, "all doing well," so the chronicles state, "and highly respectable."

In 1861, Bass lost his mother, but a few months after his father made haste to supply the loss by marrying "a pious young widow and devoted member of the M. E. Church." This union seems to have been attended by excellent results, as we are informed that soon after the marriage "Daniel Bass joined the M. E. Church and was a praying Methodist up to the time of his death which occurred February 20th, 1864." One child was born from this last marriage, Charles Bass, who now lives at Kansas City, Missouri.

After the death of the elder Bass, Daniel L. Sheeks, an uncle of the heirs, took charge of the estate and the children. Mr. Sheeks, being one of the largest, and most respectable farmers in the country, trained the children up to the habits of industry and gave them all the advantages of education and improvement conferred upon his own children. But as Bass could not read and could barely sign his name, these advantages could not have been great.

There seems to be no question that the Bass and Sheeks families were highly respectable and had the esteem of all the people with whom they lived.

Up to the time of the death of his father and for two or three year afterward, young Bass maintained an excellent character, but after that he began to associate with bad companions and soon acquired evil habits.

In 1869, tired of the restraints of his guardian or longing to see more of the world, he left his Hoosier home and went to St. Louis, a very bad place to go to at any time, as everybody in Chicago would testify, even upon oath. But the great city had but few attractions for the country boy, and hence he took passage on a steamboat and floated down the Mississippi, landing at Rosedale, Mississippi. Here the young adventurer remained a year, working at Charles' Mill and forming bad habits with reckless rapidity. It is said that he became an expert at card playing and revolver shooting and was noted for his dissipation.

In 1870, he bundled together his little effects again and left for the Lone Star State, arriving at Denton in the latter part of the year. His advent in the Empire State seems to have had a subduing effect upon his mind, for he at once sought employment and began a sober, industrious life. His first engagement was with Mrs. Lacy, proprietress of the Lacy House in Denton. He continued in her employ about a year and a half, giving entire satisfaction and greatly endearing himself to the good lady of the house by his kind and obliging disposition and his excellent conduct.

He was next employed by a man named Wilkes, and shortly after this by Sheriff W. F. Eagan, with whom he remained until the beginning of his downward career. Sheriff Eagan speaks of him as a very sober and industrious young man. He frequently entrusted him with considerable sums of money to go to Dallas and other neighbouring places to purchase lumber and supplies. His habits of economy were so great that his employer found fault with him for starving himself and team. He never would wear a suit of clothes that cost more than five dollars. In all his service he was very much devoted to his employer's interests. He was also retired and quiet in his disposition, never was absent from home in the evening or away on the Sabbath unless sent upon an errand. His only companion was a little boy, who taught him to write and assisted him in his efforts to make a man of himself.

But unfortunately for himself, on an evil day in 1874, he became the owner of a "little sorrel mare." This was the beginning of a downward career, which has made Bass one of the most noted criminals of this or any age; for the mare proved to be fast and Bass soon became faster than the mare. After he had run a few races around Denton his employer saw that driving a team and running races would not go together. Hence, he told Bass that he must take his choice between the race mare and the team. Bass at once concluded to keep the mare and abandoned the employment in which he had been industriously and respectively engaged for four years. This was in 1875, and from that time on he gave himself up to a life of dissipation. Soon afterwards he made the acquaintance of Henry Underwood, who became his boon companion, and later was one of the most noted of his gang.

His evenings were spent at saloons, all business was neglected and he was constantly with wild, reckless fellows. His neighbours say that he became wholly unlike himself. This remark explains much of his career; for he evidently had one of those headstrong earnest natures which do nothing by halves. Whatever he did was done with all his might. As a boy at cards he became the most skilful of all his companions; as an employee he was faithful to his employer; as a bandit he outstripped all the daring characters who have wrought deeds of violence upon Texas soil.

It is said that when he was but nine years of age, he witnessed a noted criminal trial at his home in Indiana. It apparently made a great impression on his mind and may have excited an evil passion for notoriety, even if it was infamous; at all events he is said to have remarked one day in Denton, when seeing some horse thieves sent to the penitentiary, that when "he committed a crime, it would amount to something. He would never be sent to the penitentiary for so small a thing as stealing a horse."

CHAPTER 2

Fatal Mistake

It was in March, 1875, that Bass left the employ of Sheriff Eagan. After horse racing, gambling and dissipating for some time in and around Denton, he went to Fort Sill, accompanied by five or six companions. He was absent on this trip two or three months, but what transpired during the time, is not known, though it is not believed that he carried his dissipation beyond horse racing and other forms of gambling.

When next heard of he was in the Indian Territory, that beautiful paradise of nature, the government's home for civilized Indians and the hiding place of uncivilized white men.

It is not to be supposed that these races, like the great Ten Broeck-McCarty fiasco, drew all the governors, senators, members of Congress, and other people in the whole region round about, nor is there any record of a heavy gate fee for the privilege of a grand sell. But in spite, of his rudeness the red-skinned racer is up to the tricks of the profession and has no trouble with a superabundance of honest scruples.

Bass found it easy enough to beat their scrubby little couriers with his sorrel mare. But how to get possession of the ponies he had won was a much more difficult matter. It was in vain that he reasoned, cursed and threatened. They were not playing a losing game, they had the ponies and meant to keep them. But Bass was equally determined to have what the mare won. Therefore, when night came, he took all the ponies he had won and as many more as he could get his hands on and started for Texas. This is the first act of robbery recorded in his career. The ponies were driven across the State toward San Antonio, where. Bass arrived in the latter part of '75, or early in '78.

Here horse racing and gambling were resumed, the sorrel mare still doing the honours of the course. But shortly afterwards this fatal piece of horse flesh, which had so rapidly carried her owner down the course of ruin, was sold. Bass remained in and about San Antonio during the summer, but nothing of note occurred until about August 1st, when he joined Joel Collins, afterwards leader of the gang which robbed the Union Pacific train, in gathering up a drove of cattle for the Northern market. The nucleus, at least, of the drove was purchased, but how many mavericks, old or young, with or without brands, voluntarily or otherwise, slipped into the drove as it moved across the country, no one can tell. But very loose notions on such points prevail in the stock ranges, and it is not to be supposed that Collins and Bass played a puritanical part as they followed their herd across the wide prairies.

The cowboy is a *sui generis* of the Southwest. Usually he is tall and slim, with sunburnt face, keen glittering eye and handsome moustache. His dress is of the simplest kind. A half-acre of hat, more or less, covers his head. His feet are enclosed in a heavy pair of cow-hide boots, at the heels of which are a pair of clanking, clattering spurs, and in the tops, he stows away the surplus ends of his pantaloons. His shirt is a flannel or calico and abhors mansard collars, and other "neck fixins." He rides a tough little animal called a Texas or Mexican pony, which he purchases for fifteen or twenty-five dollars. It can stand more riding and less feeding than almost any kind of horse living. At his saddle is strapped a Sharp's or Winchester rifle, and at either hip is a six shooter, while around his waist is a belt filled with cartridges. Intervening space is filled up with daggers, bottles or whiskey and plugs of tobacco.

When on the drive he stops wherever night overtakes him, sleeping as sweetly with his body stretched upon the greensward, his head upon his saddle and the glittering stars above, as if tucked away in the softest bed. He always stops at "the store," takes a drink, buys some more tobacco and replenishes his bottle.

When he arrives in a town or city, if he is flush, he always finds his way to a gambling saloon, where he plays more recklessly than successfully, or to a house of prostitution, where he falls an easy victim to the blandishments of some fair enchantress, and usually retires heavy in head and light in pocket.

But with all his weakness, he has some of the best qualities of manhood. He is generous, brave, and faithful to his friends, selfishness and small meanness find but little place in his everyday life.

There is no doubt that, as a cowboy, Bass snugly filled out the proportions of the type.

But not to make a further digression, we find that the drovers arrived in Kansas sometime during the fall. Here they sent their cattle on to Sidney, Nebraska, while they took the cars for the same place. It is said, by detectives that his was done because the ownership of some of the cattle was a disputed question, and that they were afraid at that time and place to be seen with them. But it is quite probable that they were tired of the drive and took this method of obtaining a rest.

At Sidney they met the herd and drove it from there to the Black Hills, where it was disposed of.

This ended the cattle business and introduces us to another phase of the bandit's career.

CHAPTER 3

Life in the Black Hills

After disposing of the herd of cattle, Bass and Collins purchased two four-horse teams, and began freighting between Dodge City, Yankton and the Black Hills. In this business they continued until January, 1877, when they sold out and opened a gambling saloon and house of prostitution in Deadwood.

There is nothing puritanical or bigoted about Deadwood society. The widest latitude of opinion and practice is allowed on all—moral questions. The conscience is not harassed with scruples and no prudential considerations harness the passions. Nobody seems to have the slightest recollection of a father's solemn admonitions or a mother's prayers. Religious teaching is a withered tradition, tossed among the other rubbish of abandoned sobriety. Sunday is no better than any other day, and every other day is as bad as it can be, but night is still worse.

Every man who goes to Deadwood is shadowed by the presentiment that he will either be shot or that the mad fever in his blood will break out in the slaughter of somebody else. When he arrives in the city he needs no introduction, but to hang out his revolvers, call for a drink and lay down a greasy pack of cards. He is asked his name, for convenience sake, but nobody thinks of inquiring where he came from, why he left or what his name was before he left.

Most of the houses are saloons. The rest are theatres, faro banks and dance houses. Prostitution is not confined to special quarters but has full sweep of the range. Only respectability and virtue are crowded into corners.

The queens of society are the most brilliant of the demimonde. The further they have fled from the modesty of their sex, the more dashing and daring they are, the more recklessly they can handle a revolver and the straighter they can throw a dagger; the more men rave over them and the more ready they are to kill or be killed for their sake.

To show that this picture of Deadwood society is not overdrawn, and to present a fair type of the leaders of the sex, we give below a description of one of the queens who reigned in the height of her glory at the time Bass and Collins kept the dance house. This was Kitty LeRoy, a woman who has been much written about and whose tragical fate shortly after this sent her name throughout the press of the country. A Black Hills letter speaks of her thus:

> Kitty LeRoy, who was killed by her husband only a short time ago, who then killed himself, was a small figure, and had previously been noted us a jig-dancer. She had a large Roman nose, cold, grey eyes, a low, cunning forehead, and was inordinately fond of money. I saw her often in her "Mint," which was opposite my office, where men congregated to squander their money; and as Kitty was a good player, like the old gravedigger, "she gathered them in!" that is, their money. Men are, in a general sense, fools. A small tress of golden hair, or a bright eye or soft cheek will precipitate them into an ocean of folly, and women of the world (and some out of the world) know this fact and play upon the weak string of men's hearts until all is gone—money, character and even life. Kitty had seen much of human nature, entering upon her wild career at the age of ten. She was married three times and died at the age of twenty-eight.
>
> A polite and intelligent German met her. He was going well with his gold claim; she knew it. Like the spider, she spun her delicate web about him until he poured into her lap $8,000 in gold, and then when his claim would yield no more, she beat him over the head with a bottle and drove him from her door. One and another she married, and then when their money was gone, discarded them in rapid succession. Yet there was something peculiarly magnetic about Kitty. Men did love her and there are men living today, (1878), who love her memory. Well, she's gone. I saw her only a short time since, lying dead by the body of her inanimate husband, with whom she would not live, but with whom she was obliged to pass quietly to the grave.

Another correspondent writes of Deadwood society and very

gushingly of Kitty as follows:

> There are dance houses and theatres, where the gay society congregates, and it is at such houses, as well as at the gambling houses, that the fair sex may be seen. The women, though not so bad as the men, are all strong minded, which, from a henpecked point of view, is the worst thing you can say of a female. Some keep bars, taverns, boarding houses, and variety shows, while a few keep gambling dens, like 'The Mint,' which was kept by poor Kitty LeRoy, lately killed by one of her husbands, which was the tragic end of a brilliant career; for, barring the wild, Gipsy-like attire, which fashion would fail to appreciate as intensely picturesque, Kitty LeRoy was what a real man would call a starry beauty. Her brow was low and her brown hair thick and curling; she had five husbands, seven revolvers, a dozen bowie-knives and always went armed to the teeth, which latter were like pearls set in coral. She was a terrific gambler, and wore in her ears immense diamonds, which shone most like her own glorious eyes. The magnetism about her marvellous beauty was such as to drive her lovers crazy; more men had been killed about her than all the other women in the Hills combined, and it was only a question whether her lover or herself had killed the most,
>
> She could throw a bowie-knife straighter than any pistol bullet except her own, and married her first husband because he was the only man of all her lovers who had the nerve to let her shoot an apple off his head as she rode by him at full speed. On one occasion she disguised herself in male attire to fight a man who had declined to combat with a woman. He fell, and she then cried over him, and married him in time to be his widow. Kitty was sometimes rich and sometimes poor, but always lavish as a prince when she had money. She dealt '*vautoom*' and '*faro*,' and played all games and cards with a dexterity that amounted to genius.

Kitty is supposed to have been the wife of Capt. E. H. Lewis, of Bay City, Michigan. But in 1872, she left her husband, and after that time figured as a public dancer in various part of the Union. In the winter of 1875-6, she was engaged at Thompson's variety den in Dallas. While there she created quite a sensation among the lewd habitues of that resort, by her artistic dancing and gay rollicking and dashing manners. After a few months stay she ran away with a well-known saloon man, and together the two visited California, where they remained a few months and then proceeded to Deadwood. Subsequently she quarrelled with her *paramour* and married Samuel R. Curley, a noted *faro* dealer.

But the couple proved to be badly mated, and soon after their marriage Curley went to Denver, and almost immediately thereafter the broken friendship between Kitty and her paramour was restored, a fact that was communicated to Curley, who undoubtedly went to Deadwood for the express purpose of killing his wife, her paramour and himself, for he travelled under an assumed name; alighted from the coach in South Deadwood, telling the driver if asked if any passengers other than those delivered at the office had come up, to say no. He walked direct to the hotel at which the unfortunate woman was a guest, remained there all day, and in the evening sent for his rival, who refused to visit him. He then told a coloured man employed in the house that he intended to kill his wife and himself, and true to his word went upstairs and did so.

When the bodies of the murderer and his victim were found the woman rested upon her back, in a position and with a quiet facial expression that indicated naught of the bloody deed that had been enacted but a moment before. Close examination revealed a small bullet hole in the waist of her dress, which, upon being opened, disclosed the fatal wound in the centre of her chest. In the opposite corner of the room lay the murderer upon his face, in a sickening pool, of blood, his brain oozing out and pieces of skull protruding from a ghastly wound. His, right arm was doubled up behind him, the hand grasping a Smith & Wesson, by which the fatal deed was committed.

It is not strange that in such society as this Bass soon became fit for crimes of the first magnitude. But before entering on his career of daring deeds he seems to have made one more effort to follow a respectable occupation. For about this time he wrote to Henry Underwood, then in Denton, that he and Collins had purchased a quartz mine, for which they had been offered $4,000, but it was a big thing and he would not sell, but when he got it worked up, he would let him know all about it. He assumed his friend in the phraseology of the cattle ranch, that he had the world by the tail, with a downhill pull. He also informed him that he would return to Texas in the Fall and would then pay off his creditors. But whether the "tail holt", of which he boasted, slipped or whether the mine had been salted for his special benefit by men shrewder than cowboys, is not known. But this was the last respectable piece of business in which he engaged. After this he is known to the world only as a bold highwayman, undertaking deeds of daring which but few bandits have the audacity to attempt or the nerve to execute.

What led immediately to his final plunge into a career of bold outlawry is known only from the statement which he made on his death bed. When asked the question why he began to rob he replied that he had won some money gambling and had been robbed of it and wanted to get even with them. Whether this occurred at Deadwood or elsewhere is open to conjecture, but there is some reason to believe that he referred to some occasion on which he had been beaten out of his money by sharpers. The fact that both he and Collins got rid of their cattle money so fast, indicates that if there were none more reckless and daring, yet there were much shrewder gamblers and sharpers in the Hills than Bass and Collins.

CHAPTER 4

Launching into Crime

While in the Black Hills Bass made the acquaintance of Nixon and Jack Davis, and probably of all the men who assisted in the Union Pacific train robbery. But according to his own statement only Jack Davis and Nixon were engaged with him in stage robbing.

There were seven of these robberies in all, and some money was realised from them, but how much is not known.

It is apparent that but a short time elapsed between the stage robberies and the capture of the railroad train at Big Spring, Nebraska.

This was one of the most daring and successful train robberies ever committed.

Collins formed the plan of the robbery, though it is believed Jack Davis first suggested it. He had come from San Francisco, and was familiar with the fact that large sums of gold were constantly passing over the route. The names of the gang, six in number, have all been ascertained since, Bass himself testifying to the correctness of the list in his dying moments. They were Joel Collins, formerly from Dallas County, Texas; Sam Bass, from Denton County, Texas; Jack Davis, from San Francisco; Bill Heffridge, who went from San Antonio with Collins and Bass; James Berry, from Mexico, Mo., and Nixon, of whose previous history but little is known.

A more daring and desperate band of outlaws was never gotten together in this country. Collins acted as leader of the band and it has been charged that he spent three or four weeks previous to the robbery at Ogalalla, Neb., gambling and associating with desperate men, from whom he organised the gang. It has also been said that he had a cattle ranch near Big Spring Station, and thus became acquainted with the habits of the station men, the operations of trains and the surroundings of the office. But this has been denied.

The time selected for the robbery was Tuesday night, the 19th of

September last. As Big Spring was only a water station, the plan evidently was, to capture the few men employed about the station and keep them under guard until after the train was robbed.

At the appointed hour the bandits boldly rode down towards the station, hitched their horses conveniently near, and at once proceeded to business. With a small flourish of revolvers and the well-known command, "throw up your arms," the station agent and assistant were soon made secure.

As train time, 10 o'clock, drew near, the bright rays of the headlight were seen falling upon the distant track. Then came the long sound of the whistle, the rushing train checked its speed and, in a moment, more stood still upon the track. It was but the work of an instant for one of the gang to mount the engine, command the engineer and fireman to throw up their hands and there hold them helpless under the muzzle of a cocked revolver. But even before this had been accomplished, two of his confederates had boarded the express car and were ransacking its contents. They soon found a large quantity of gold in one of the safes, but the other could not be opened. It was in vain that they ordered the messenger to open it. He assured then that he had no key, that it was a time lock and could only be locked or opened at each end of the route. Jack Davis cursed and raved, beat him over the head, thrust his revolver into his mouth knocking out one of his teeth and lacerating the flesh, and threatened to blow the top of his head right off if he didn't open it. But Bass said he reckoned the messenger was telling the truth, and that they had better give it up.

After going through the coaches and robbing the terrified passengers the bandits slowly backed away, keeping their arms presented until they were lost to view in the darkness.

A number of shots were fired during the transaction and a few wounds were inflicted, but no one was killed.

The gold taken from the express car amounted to the sum of $60,000, no small weight for the robbers to handle under the circumstances. It consisted entirely of twenty dollar gold pieces, of the coinage of 1877, a fact which was afterwards of material assistance in ferreting out the perpetrators of the crime.

Shortly after the robbery, the gang divided the money and separated, going two together by different routes. Bass, Davis, and Nixon, for a time vanished from view. Of the others we shall speak in the succeeding chapters.

Chapter 5

Fated

The Big Spring robbery created intense excitement among railroad officials and caused a general sensation throughout the country.

The large amount of money secured was looked upon as a temptation which would soon lead to another like attempt. This in connection with the heavy shipments of gold over the line would be likely to excite the cupidity of every bandit in the West, at the same time the long stretch of road through waste and desert regions, with here and there a lonely station, made it very difficult to afford adequate protection. It was determined, therefore, to capture the robbers at any cost and hazards. Large rewards were at once offered by the State authorities of Nebraska and by the railroad companies. This brought forward detectives from almost every quarter. Telegrams were sent to all officers along railroad lines, to sheriffs and officers in command of U. S. troops.

At first it was not wholly known who the robbers were or whence they came. But it so chanced that among the passengers on the plundered train was a young man named Andy Riley, a resident of Omaha. During the attack upon the train, Riley stood upon the platform and received a wound in the hand from one of the flying bullets, he was also robbed along with the rest of the passengers. He had travelled with Joel Collins on the way to Deadwood and knew him well. He had also seen him and conversed with him only a few days before, while on a visit to Ogalalla. Great was his surprise, therefore, when the robbers came through the train, to find Joel Collins among them. Immediately upon his return to Omaha he notified the officials of the fact and Collins' name and description of his person were accordingly telegraphed in all directions.

It was shortly learned also that after leaving the railroad, the robbers crossed the Platte River, in Nebraska and were next heard of at

Young's ranch on the Republican River in Kansas.

✶✶✶✶✶✶

Detective Leech, of Ogalalla, afterwards claimed that he was in the camp of the gang on the night they divided the money, and that he knew by sight all the robbers. He said that he escaped capture at their hands only by hasty flight on his horse

✶✶✶✶✶✶

This was on the 23rd, the next Saturday after the robbery. Intelligence of this fact having reached Sheriff Bardsley, of Ellis County, Kansas, he at once started from Hays City, on the Kansas Pacific road, with a squad of ten cavalrymen and a detective from Denver and made his headquarters at Buffalo Station, on the Kansas Pacific. This is sixty miles west of Hays City, in the centre of a wild and dreary waste. Nearby is a large ravine, in which the sheriff and his posse camped. While there, about nine o'clock in the morning of the 26th, Joel Collins, the chief of the train robbers, and a single adherent, rode up to the lonely station.

The following account of their capture and tragical death we take from a Western daily of the 28th:

When first seen they were riding from the north, coming boldly over a high ridge of open prairie. They led between them a pony heavily laden with something which, while it was not bulky, seemed to tax the strength of the pony to carry it. The men were dusty and travel stained. They appeared to be and might have been taken for two Texas "cow boys" out on a hunt for cattle or on their way to join a herd. Had they rode straight across the track and continued their journey without stopping, no suspicion would have been aroused; but they were led instinctively to their death. They rode their jaded horses to the shady side of the principal building of the station, and one of the two dismounted, leaving his partner in charge of the horses and the pack pony.

The man left in charge of the horses said they were Texas cattle men on their way home, and enquiring the way to Fort Larned. The dismounted man walked up to the station agent and enquired the way to Thompson's store. The building was pointed out to him, but as he stood conversing, he took out his handkerchief, which revealed a letter in his pocket upon which was plainly visible he superscription "Joel Collins." This was the name of the leader of the Union Pacific train robbers, and the brands upon their horses assured the station agent that these were the men wanted by the sheriff and his soldiers encamped a few hundred yards away. Sheriff Bardsley was notified at once, and he came up to the station and examined the horses and made other satisfactory observances. He conversed with the robber chief for some time, and asked many questions, which were freely answered.

They walked together to the station and took a drink, and conversed upon various inconsequential subjects. Collins made no effort to conceal his real name. He had no suspicion whatever that the telegraph had given his name and description at that little station in the middle of the buffalo plains. Bardsley then left his prey and started back to the camp of the soldiers, who were under the command of Lieut. Allen, and ordered them to saddle up and follow him, and he would bring back the Texans.

In the meantime, the two horsemen with their heavily burdened pony had started out on the open plains southward. Sheriff Bardsley and his posse started out in pursuit.

When Collins and his companions saw the sheriff and his blue coated posse of cavalry appear on their trail, they manifested no excitement. They did not even attempt to run. On the contrary, they rode on leisurely on the Texas trail until Sheriff Bardsley rode up and halted them. Even then they gave no sign of trepidation or excitement. Collins looked at Bardsley with the coolest effrontery and demanded his business. Sheriff Bardsley said:

"I have a description of some train robbers which answers well to your appearance. I want you and your partner to return with me to the station. You need fear nothing if you are innocent, and if you are the man I want, then I am $10,000 better off. Please come back to the station, gentlemen."

"You are mistaken in your men, gentlemen," said Collins, laughingly, "but, of course there is no use to object. We will go back and have the mistake explained. We are Texas boys going home—that's all."

Then they turned their tired horses back towards the station. As they returned, they exchanged a few brief words which were undistinguishable even by the nearest trooper. They rode a few hundred yards over the level plain towards the solitary station, when suddenly the leader, Joel Collins, broke the silence. Turning to his companion he said:

"Pard, if we are to die, we might as well die game."

Then he drew his revolver. His partner followed his example, but before either could fire, the troops had fired a volley into them and they fell from their horses riddled with bullets. The robbers died instantly and were taken to the station for burial, but were afterwards taken to Ellis station, where an inquest was held upon the bodies.

The body of Collins was identified by a dozen of his old Texas acquaintances but for a long time the body of his accomplice could not be identified. It was at first believed to be that of Sam Bass himself, and was so telegraphed over the country and published in the papers.

Finally, Anna Langs appeared in the depot, where the bodies were lying, and stated, under oath, that she recognised the body as being that of William Cotts, formerly of Pottsville, Pa., but more recently of San Antonio, Texas, and that his father resided in Pottsville. He was a light complexioned man, about thirty years of age, light hair and sandy beard, about five feet seven inches high and weighed 135 pounds.

Whether Anna had any real knowledge of the man, or whether she thought so "because she thought so," or whether the true name of Heffridge was Cotts, is difficult to say. But there is no doubt now that the man who fell with Joel Collins under a shower of bullets, was the member of the gang known as Bill Heffridge.

At the time of his death Collins was described as being dark complexioned, with black hair and beard, about five feet eleven inches high, weighed one hundred and fifty pounds, and was supposed to be twenty-eight years old. He was also said to have been affable, of pleasing address, intelligent, and very handsome. Upon his body a small piece of paper was found upon which was written a poetical effusion by a lady and dedicated to Joel Collins.

But the richest discovery was made upon the pony. When the tired little animal was stripped of the blanket which covered the pack saddle, an old pair of pantaloons was found underneath. The ends of the legs had been tied together, then they were filled with gold and thrown across the saddle. When the glittering metal was turned out upon the ground and counted, it was found that the amount was no less than twenty-five thousand dollars. It was all of the mintage of 1877, and in twenty dollar pieces.

This fact, taken in connection with the other circumstances, furnished the strongest evidence that the lucky Bardsley had struck the right man. Railroad officials were in high glee and congratulations were exchanged all along the line.

But in a few days serious doubts began to creep into many minds and it was gravely feared that the deadly rifle had struck down an innocent man. A leading law firm at Topeka, Kansas, was retained to investigate the circumstance attending the bloody tragedy. It was alleged in Collins' defence that he obtained a large sum of money from the drove of cattle which had been disposed of the previous year, that he had written to his father that he had obtained twenty-five cents per pound for them and would soon start home with the money. It was also stated that he had amassed a considerable fortune in the cattle business with his brother near San Antonio and that this precluded all temptation to commit robbery.

In addition to this it was said there was unquestionable evidence as to the time Collins started for home, and of his movements, which tended to show that he could not have been in the vicinity of Big Spring at the time of the robbery. Collins' conduct at the moment of his death was accounted for on the supposition that he believed himself in the hands of a gang of outlaws who intended to rob and murder him, and that he was determined to sell his life as dearly as possible.

About this time, also, an old Texan came out with a short newspaper article defending Collins from many of the charges which had been made against him and stating it to be the belief of those who had long known young Collins and his parents, that he was not the guilty man.

But a few days later the dying statement of one of his captured confederates forever set at rest all doubt in regard to the matter. Since then, the deathbed statement of Bass himself has been added to the proof.

As Joel Collins, so far as known, participated in but one noted crime, few events in his life have been preserved on record.

He was born in Dallas County, Texas where his parents still reside, his father being a farmer of some means and a man who has long enjoyed the respect and sympathy of his neighbours.

In 1868, Young Collins left home and went to the southwest part of the State where he had a brother in the cattle business. From 1868 to 1870, he was in the employ of Allen and Poole, the great cattle men of the coast, and stood well as a young man.

In 1871, he took a herd of one thousand cattle to Kansas for Bennet and Schoate, of North Texas.

In 1872, he took up a large herd for P. T. Adams, Joel receiving one half the profits. In 1873, he did the same thing and on the same favourable terms for James Reed.

In 1874, he bought a drove from Bennet and Akard, partly on time and was induced (if not forced) to ship them to Chicago at a heavy loss. This he did against his will in order to meet the deferred payment, when the cattle were poor and the market down.

This is the statement made by his friends, while others give a different version of the matter.

In 1875, he kept a saloon in San Antonio for a few months. The house is said to have been a disreputable one.

In 1876, as we have already seen, he took his last drove North in company with Bass. In the Spring of 1877, he is said to have opened a provision store at Polato Gulch, thirty-five miles from Deadwood. His friends claim that he remained there until he "started for Texas." But there is much reason to doubt whether it was known to them what he was doing during his last stay in the North. His letters were not always intended to give the exact situation of affairs. It has been charged that he killed several men during his life, but this is probably an exaggeration as there is no authentic account of more than one such act. In 1869, he killed a Mexican in Victoria County, but surrendered himself, was tried and acquitted. As is well known it is very difficult for an American to murder a Mexican. It is a principle with jurists that such acts are always for self-defence.

Before closing this chapter, we pause for a moment to note the fatal chain of apparently trivial circumstances which so quickly tightened around the unfortunate Collins. Never was the perpetrator of a great crime stricken down by a more unerring blow of retribution at the very moment when escape seemed well night assured. It must be admitted that he showed a singular lack of shrewdness, first in not thoroughly disguising himself when he boarded the train, and secondly in not giving a wide berth to all telegraph stations.

But still, had he rode through Buffalo Station without stopping he would have passed unnoticed; or had he left the dust and sweat upon his face and allowed his handkerchief to remain in his pocket, or had the tell-tale envelope not clung to it, he might soon have been beyond the reach of detectives and soldiers. But the unseen hand of fate had marked him for her own and at that very hour.

His bold attempts to defend himself against a whole troop of soldiers may be called bravery, but it was the extreme of folly. In a country like this, where jails are weak and the law weaker than the jails, where the whole criminal jurisprudence seems to be run for the protection of criminals rather than the public, it would have been better to submit quietly and await a better opportunity. There is reason, however, to believe that this reckless leader of bandits feared Judge Lynch and preferred to "die game."

Chapter 6

James Berry

The capture and death of Collins and Heffridge occurred September 26th, but no further clue to the remaining robbers was obtained until about the 8th or 9th of October, when suspicion was aroused in Mexico, Mo., by a large sale of gold which was made there. While at Boonville October 11th, Col. A. B. Garner, General Superintendent of the M. K. & T. railway, received the following telegram:

> To Col. A. B. Garner, Boonville, Mo.:
> Mexico, Mo., Oct. 11.—James Berry, an old resident of Callaway County, is one of the Union Pacific train robbers. He was at Williamburg Monday night. He is six feet high, weighs about 190 pounds, is forty years old, has a red face, yellowish red hair, moustache and goatee, just recently shaved, round, full face, blue eyes and freckly hands. We will pay $500 for his arrest and ten *per cent* of the money recovered. He had about $9,000. Think he is making for Texas. Have all crossings closely watched. He has a pacing bay horse and new saddle.

On the same day the *Moberly Monitor* published the following:

> A man by the name of Jim Berry, of Callaway County, has just returned from the Black Hills to Mexico, Mo. Suspicion has been directed to him of complicity in the Union Pacific robbery, by a financial transaction in which he was engaged immediately on his return. The morning after his arrival in Mexico he visited the banks at the hour of opening and sold gold to the amount of $9,000. Berry remained in Mexico all day Friday and until Sunday evening. He was princely extravagant with his money. Meeting an old mining acquaintance, he gave him $250; he delighted a clothier by purchasing a fine suit

of clothing without higgling at the price, and bought a $300 bill of groceries, which were sent to his family in Callaway. Saturday evening, he took his departure, and Monday morning the bankers received news that the gold he had exchanged, and which they had shipped to St. Louis, had been identified as part of the treasure captured by the Union Pacific robbers. The next day (Tuesday) a corps of detectives from St. Louis and Chicago arrived at Mexico, and with the Audrain County sheriff at their head, started in pursuit of Berry.

After a long rough ride, the vicinity of his house was reached and the party so disposed as to completely surround it. They now felt sure of their game and the rich reward that awaited his capture. But they were doomed to disappointment. Narrowing the circle and gradually closing in, a rush was finally made for the house. They encountered no opposition where they had calculated upon a fierce resistance, and, upon entering, they found that the bird had flown. A thorough search of the premises revealed no trace of the daring robber, and, though the whole country had been scoured by different parties, his trail had not been struck up to yesterday There is not a particle of doubt that Berry was one of the robbers and his capture is only a question of time.

This prophecy was shortly fulfilled, as the following account of his capture, published in the *Mexico Ledger,* October 15th, will show:

We have just interviewed H. Glascock and J. Berry, concerning the arrest of Berry, Sunday morning, and we give you the facts as near as possible below:

It appears that last Saturday night as our sheriff was eating supper, about half-past six o'clock, he received a message that a man was in town after the suit of clothes Berry had left at Blum's The man's name was Bose Cazy; he lived near Berry's. He told Blum that Berry had told him that he could have the clothes if he would pay the balance of $30 due on them. This was the way he had his "job" fixed up. Glascock ran right down to Kabrich's hall and hid behind the corner and saw Cazy come out; this was half past seven. Glascock followed him to Wallace and McKamy's livery stable. Just as Glascock got near the stable he met J. Carter, and told him to come along. Carter, Glascock and Cazy all got to the stable at the same time. Cazy paid for his horse feed and started to get on his horse.

Sheriff Glascock took Cazy by the collar, presented a pistol to his head and told him he would shoot him if he moved. Cazy did not move. Glascock ordered two more horses saddled. They then tied Cazy on his horse. The sheriff and Carter then got on their horses and the cavalcade moved off, Glascock leading Cazy's horse. They went down to the branch near Tom Smith's in South Mexico, and as they thought no one would get wind of them there, they stopped. Glascock then went and got John Coons, Bob Steele and a young man named Moore. All got horses and double-barrel shot guns which were loaded with buck shot. They then told Cazy they would have to know where Berry was. He said he had not seen him since he (Berry) had told him he could have the clothes, which was about a week before.

The men started out towards Cazy's house, and passed Jeff Jones about 12 o'clock Saturday night. About three o'clock they got to James Armstrong's. Sheriff Glascock told him what they had done, and he wanted Armstrong to go with them and show them where Cazy lived, as he was afraid that Cazy would fool them. Armstrong said he did not know where Cazy lived, and so would not go. We don't know whether Armstrong knew or not. It was then three o'clock Sunday morning. The posse then all got around Cazy, put their guns to his heart and told him if he led them into any trap, or did not take them at once to his house they would shoot him down in a minute. He said he would take them to his house if it would do them any good.

When they got within about a half a mile of Cazy's house they took Cazy off, tied him and left Bob Steele to guard him; then Glascock placed two men north of the house and stable, Moore and himself going to the south and west side, and as the open timber was there they thought he might be over in that. They did not alarm Cazy's house at all, it was not quite daylight yet. They all secreted themselves in thickets, as mentioned above, to await results. Glascock told his men: "Boys if you see him halt him; if he shows fight shoot him down; if he runs shoot him in the legs; catch him at all hazards." In about half an hour Glascock heard a horse "nicker" about a half a mile off, as he thought. Moore and Glascock then crept toward the noise, went 300 yards down the branch, came to a fence, saw fresh horse tracks. Glascock got over the fence and got into a thicket; heard the horse snort about fifty yards off in the brush.

Glascock took off his hat and crept up twenty yards closer; then he raised up and saw Berry unhitching the horse from a tree. Berry then led his horse aslant toward Glascock, as Berry now says, to lead him to water. Glascock cocked both barrels of his gun, ran out about twenty yards, within about twenty feet of Berry, and demanded him to halt. Berry started to run; Glascock shot, but aimed too high, which caused the charge to go over Berry's head. He shot again and seven buckshot lodged in Berry's left leg below the knee. Berry fell to the ground. When Glascock got to him he was trying to get his pistol out but he could not get it out before Glascock was on him and snatched it away from him. He then asked Glascock to shoot him, that he did not want to live.

Glascock told him no; that he did not want to kill him, he wanted him to have justice. Just then Moore came up.

After Moore came up, Glascock called for the rest of the posse when they all gathered around Berry. Glascock then searched him and found in his belt five $500 packages, and in his pocketbook was found $340. He had a gold watch and chain, one dressing coat, three overcoats and comfort. He had doubtless slept there within ten feet of the horse. They took him to Cazy's house, when Mrs. Cazy got breakfast for the men, while a messenger was sent to Williamsburg for medical assistance.

Immediately after breakfast Sheriff Glascock and John Carter started for Berry's house to look for the balance of the money. Upon arriving there Glascock inquired of Mrs. Berry the whereabouts of Berry; she replied that she did not know, as she had not seen him for four or five days, and thought he had left the country. Glascock then showed her the watch and chain, when one of the children said: Oh, I thought that was papa's. Glascock then told her he had got Berry, when she asked if he had been taken alive, and receiving an affirmative reply, said: I never thought he would be taken alive. He has said a good many times he would never be taken alive. At this they all began to cry—the wife, one little boy and five little girls. It was a very distressing scene.

Glascock searched the house, but found no money. The house was well provisioned for the winter—hams without number, sacks of flour and coffee, kegs of molasses, etc.

After Glascock left Cazy's about forty of Berry's friends came around and made threats about taking him away, but they did not make any attempt at all; it all ended in talk.

At first it was not thought that Berry's wounds were serious, but gangrene set in and on the night of the 18th his sufferings became very great. It was apparent that he had not long to live, but he maintained a determined and bravado spirit to the last. As the deep silence of night settled down upon all without, he lay in his gloomy cell, alternately writhing in paroxysms of pain or coolly talking to the officers who remained with him to the last, anxious to secure a dying confession.

This wish was partly gratified, as he stated in his dying moments, that he was one of the parties who committed the Big Springs robbery; that Collins had planned the robbery and that the names of the rest of the gang were correct, as given by the Express Company. He said that they all travelled together two hundred miles and then separated in squads of two, that his partner came to Mexico with him and then went on to Chicago. This partner must have been Nixon, as it is well known that it was not Davis. After much suffering Berry died at one o'clock in the morning. He left a wife and six children. He is said to have been very respectably connected in Gallaway County.

Thus, it is seen that in less than a month three of the Big Spring robbers had been consigned to bloody graves. They had lost their booty and paid the penalty of their crimes with their lives.

There is little reason to doubt Berry's statement that Nixon went to Chicago. From that city he probably went to Canada, as Henry Underwood stated to the officers at Omaha, December 30th, that Nixon was a Canadian and that he was then in Canada. Bass also made the statement at Round Rock.

Chapter 7

Escape of Bass and Davis

According to the dying statement of Davis, the whole gang travelled together two hundred miles and then separated. Where this separation occurred is not known, though it was probably somewhere near the Republican River in Kansas, where the gang was seen four days after the robbery.

In the separation Bass and Davis chose to go together. Like the ill-fated Collins, they also started for Texas, but by a different route. It is said that they visited Sidney, Neb., after the robbery, and left the city suddenly. But this is doubtful, as it would have been attended by very great danger. Be this as it may, it is certain that they purchased a one-horse hack, loaded their gold in it and turned their course southward just as soon as circumstances would permit. Months after this when Bass was safe in Denton, while lounging the day away in camp, he told the boys, that soon after they set out in the buggy they fell in with a company of soldiers and detectives. They at once assured them that they too were detectives hot in pursuit of the bold bandits, who had robbed the Union Pacific train, and that they hoped to come up with them, for there would be a big thing in the capture.

This threw the officers off their guard, and the two were allowed to join the squad. They continued with them four days, while twenty thousand dollars of ill-gotten gold clanked under their seat as the old hack rattled over the road. The officers with whom they laughed and joked all day long, would have given thousands of dollars to have known this secret, but it remained concealed, and finally the wily robbers bade them goodbye and drove gayly away.

The next heard of them was in Cooke County, where Bass passed under the name of Samuel Bushon. Here they separated, Bass going to his old home in Denton and Davis departing for the gay metropolis of the South. Here he seems to have lived a fast life, spending his money freely, and enjoying himself as passion led or vice dictated.

But it was not long before he suspected that detectives were shadowing his track. This led to his return to Texas, where he met Bass and the two proceeded to Fort Worth. Here Jim Murphy exchanged $4,000 of the stolen gold for greenbacks. Bass divided the money with his old partner, and that night Davis took the train, and now a score or more of detectives would give much to know where he is.

Early in December Sam Bass, Henry Underwood and Frank Jackson went to San Antonio. Thither they were followed by Sheriff Everheart of Sherman, Tom Gerren, a rather noted character of Denton, and Tooney Waits, a detective who had come from the north to identify the parties connected with the Big Springs robbery. Waits believed that Underwood was connected with that affair, and declared his readiness to swear that he was Tom Nixon. Sheriff Everhart also acted on the same belief, and went to San Antonio for the purpose of arresting Underwood for Nixon. The name of Bass does not figure conspicuously in the controversy which afterwards sprung up in regard to this matter.

Tom Gerren says that he had a warrant in his pocket for the arrest of Underwood on another charge, and that was his object in pursuing him. He says that he knew that Underwood could not be the man who was known in the robbery as Nixon, because Underwood slept at Jim Hall's ranch in Denton County on the 16th or 17th of September and could not, therefore, have been in Nebraska on the 15th.

There can be no doubt that harmonious action and shrewd management would have resulted in the arrest of all the party. But the officers did not act in unison. One or two prostitutes were let into the secret, which helped to mix matters much. In the meantime, Capt. Lee Hall was telegraphed to hurry up with his rangers. But Bass was not the man to be captured by any such hesitating methods, and suddenly he and his associates vanished.

The newspaper controversy between Everhart and Gerren in regard to their failure to make the capture has been extensively published and to that public opinion is referred for a settlement of the question as to who played a bad part.

Bass and party soon returned again to Denton where they remained sometime as will be seen further on.

A freebooter, with ten thousand dollars in ready cash at his command, is apt to prove a great demoralizer to any community not steeled in moral integrity. As he passes here and there among his friends and neighbours, with a pocket full of gold pieces which he deals out with a free hand, buying without pricing and loaning without hesitation, he soon becomes such a convenience and desideratum that men of easy morals and scant conscience do not care to see him driven out of the country or lugged off to jail.

This proved true of Bass'ss stay in Denton County. His gold made him many friends. "He was always so kind and obliging" that they were "ready to do almost anything for him." No greater curse ever befell that county than this stolen gold. It brought reproach to the whole people, ruin to individuals, and sorrow to many homes. It was an evil which the thousands of good people who live there still deeply deplore, an evil, too, which it will require years to eradicate from the young and susceptible mind.

Chapter 8
Texas Train Robberies

We come now to one of the most daring series of train robberies which ever disgraced this country. The deeds of the old highwaymen, who used to stop unwary travellers at some lonely place in the road and rifle their pockets pale into utter insignificance before the highhanded acts of these modern bandits who dare step upon the iron track of commerce, stop the rushing engine, plunder express and mail cars, while the officers stand pale and trembling before the muzzle of a cocked revolver, and a whole train of terrified passengers sit shivering in their seats until the bold transaction is over. For outrageous audacity and cool and deliberate proceedings the Texas robberies have never been surpassed not even in the notorious carer of the James and Younger brothers, nor in the bold assaults made upon Union Pacific trains. Blow after blow was struck, even when it was known that the officers on all trains were on the alert, and that all the express and mail cars were guarded by heavily armed men.

The first of these robberies was committed at Allen Station, a very small place on the Houston & Texas Central Railroad, six miles south of McKinney and twenty-four miles north of Dallas. This robbery occurred between 9 and 10 o'clock on the night of February 22nd. When the South bound train arrived at the station it was immediately boarded by four masked men, one of whom leaped upon the engine and in a twinkling had the engineer and fireman under the influence of a cocked revolver. The other members of the band made a rush for the express car and attempted to enter it, but were repulsed by Mr. J. L. A. Thomas, the messenger. Mr. Thomas says that he had some express matter for the agent at that place, and was standing in the door of the car when the train stopped. The masked men ordered him to throw up his hands, crying out, "Your money or your brains." He jumped back in the car and drew his pistol.

The robbers then began firing, he returned the fire, discharging his revolver three or four times. The robbers fired several shots and then sprang into the car, previously threatening to burn it if Thomas did not surrender. The bell rope was then cut, the express car uncoupled from the rest of the train and the engineer was ordered to draw it over the switch, when the safe was rifled of its contents. The amount secured was sad at the time to be $2,500. It is known now that it was nearly $3,000.

There was a large number of passengers on board, but they considered prudence the better part of valour and made haste to stow away whatever valuables they had upon their persons, all momentarily expecting to see the robbers coming through the train. But as soon as they had finished the express car they made their escape, moving off in a westerly direction.

This bold deed produced much excitement all along the line of the road. Texas had seen much stage robbing and many deeds of violence, but this was a kind of lawlessness to which the people had not become habituated and did not care to see successfully inaugurated. But still not much effort was made to capture the robbers, except by the officers of the Texas Express Company. They at once instituted a vigorous pursuit, and on February 27th captured Tom Spotswood at what he called his cattle ranch on Little Elm Creek, in Denton County. This arrest was effected under the leadership of Mr. W. K. Cornish, agent at Dallas, and Mr. Thomas, the messenger.

Spotswood was taken to McKinney where he had a preliminary examination, and in default of $2,500 bail, he was remanded to jail to await his trial at the next term of the District Court.

The trial began in the latter part of June and ended July 2nd. Mr. Thomas, the express messenger, was the principal witness against Spotswood. He testified that one of the men who entered the car on the night of the robbery was not masked, and this man he recognized as Tom Spotswood, the prisoner. He said that he had ample opportunity to see him, as Spotswood held a revolver in his face, while the other men robbed the safe. He noted his peculiar appearance, especially his glass eye. It is something of a question how straight a man can see with a cocked revolver in his face, but the evidence had great weight with the jury.

Mr. Newman, a saloon keeper at Allen station, testified that Spotswood visited his saloon the day before the robbery and asked him whether there was any gaming done in town, and said that he was a sporting man. He also asked at what hour the train came from the North.

An attempt was made to prove an alibi. Bill Spotswood, brother of the prisoner, and another man testified that Tom slept at the house of the former on the night of the robbery. But two other witnesses testified that they met Bill Spotswood and his companion in the woods the next morning, where they were chopping wood, and they said they had not slept at home the night before because they couldn't get across the creek. The jury returned a verdict of guilty, and the prisoner was sentenced to ten years in the penitentiary.

But since then, he has obtained a new trial. If he lives long enough to wear out all the continuances which the laws of the State permit, the delays which the lawyers ask, and gets safely over the frequent "reversing and remanding" of higher courts, he may go back to his cattle ranch, or he may join some of the boys at Huntsville. But these are things which "no fellow can find out" until he lives long enough.

CHAPTER 9

Hutchins and Eagle Ford

Nearly a month passed quietly away after the Allen robbery and the public began to feel that the capture of Spotswood, who was regarded as the chief of the band, had put an end to the desperate business. But on the night of March 18th the whole country was startled by the intelligence which flashed over the wires, that still another train had been successfully captured and robbed. This act was also committed on the Houston & Texas Central, at a small station named Hutchins, ten miles south of Dallas. The train selected for the attack was again the southbound through express and mail train from Chicago and St. Louis, which passed the station about 10 o'clock at night.

The following account of the robbery appeared in one of the daily papers the next day:

> The robbers understood their business well, had evidently planned the assault deliberately, and the manner of its execution was prompt and effective. They first took into their possession the railroad agent at Hutchins and a negro, then the engineer and fireman of the train. They also captured two tramp printers from Dallas, who were stealing a ride on the front of the locomotive, and added them to the crowd.
>
> This squad they marched in front of them to the express car door, so that, should the messenger on board the car fire, the discharge would take effect not on the robbers but on the innocent agent, negro, fireman and engineer, or puncture the valuable epidermis of the newspaper fraternity. The messenger barred the car doors and extinguished the lights, but the robbers soon burst asunder the door. The messenger then fired into the mob, with what effect is not known, but the fire was returned and the messenger wounded in the face. One of the

printers also received a wound in one of his limbs, which for the present will operate as a serious check to his perambulatory tendencies.

Messenger Thomas, being wounded and seeing the futility of attempting any further resistance, surrendered to the mob. The safe was rifled of its contents and the mail car ransacked for whatever plunder the robber's saw fit to appropriate. In regard to the amount of money obtained in the express car there are several rumours. One is that they only obtained a small amount, the express messenger having secreted the bulk of money and valuables in the stove while the lights were out. Another rumour is to the effect that they obtained several thousand dollars. Messenger Thomas continued on his route as far as Corsicana, where he stopped off on account of his wound.

Mr. Thomas is a brother of the agent who was in charge of the car that was robbed some time ago at Allen station. (He was afterwards rewarded by the company for his bravery.)

Word of the robbery was dispatched in all directions, but up to noon today no trace of the daring scoundrels had been obtained Marshal Morton, of this city, with several members of the police force, kept a lookout all last night, but their watching resulted in nothing satisfactory. The marshal rode about thirty-five miles last night, taking in Hutchins and the adjacent country.

The passengers on board the train were not molested. The robbers, it is said, after transacting their business, took off toward Trinity Bottom, but efforts to track them in that direction for any great distance failed.

Later reports confirm the statement that the train robbers secured but a small amount of money, probably not over $300.

The great drought prevailing at that time made it impossible to follow the trail of the robbers, and active search for them was soon given up. It was wholly unknown at the time who they were, whence they had come or whither they went.

Matters were now beginning to wear a serious aspect. The repetition of such acts was bringing disgrace upon the State, the traveling public was becoming alarmed, while the express and railroad companies were put to heavy expense to protect their property. As no clue to the robbers had been obtained, and as no great effort was made by the State authorities to ferret them out and effect their capture, it was feared that they might at any time strike another blow.

These fears were soon realised. This time the blow fell upon the Texas & Pacific Railroad, at Eagle Ford, a small station six miles west of Dallas. This robbery was one of the best planned and most coolly perpetrated crimes ever committed. It is almost impossible to believe that the masked men who moved about the train as deliberately as employees of the road engaged in the ordinary operations of the track, were actually robbers coolly plundering cars in the presence of the train men, the express company's guards and a score or so of passengers.

The attack was made on the night of April 4th, and was reported as follows the next day:

> The western bound train was robbed last night at 11:30, at Eagle Ford, by four masked men. The train from the east, on the Texas & Pacific Railroad, passed through Dallas last night a few minutes after 11 o'clock. It arrived at Eagle Ford, six miles west of Dallas, about thirty minutes past eleven. As the depot agent for the Express Company, came out of his office he saw a man come round the corner of the depot upon the platform with a pistol in his hand closely followed by two other men.
>
> The first one presented his pistol at the agent and kept him quiet until the other two arrested the engineer and fireman, whom they brought round to where the agent and first man were standing. The fourth man was placed near the passenger coach with a view, it is supposed, to prevent the approach of the passengers. The agent, engineer and fireman were then placed in front of the express door, two of the robbers' (one standing at either end of the men under guard), covering them with their pistols, while the leader ordered the local agent to ask the messenger to open the door.
>
> The messenger refused to open the door when the leader took a stick of wood and broke the door in. On the express car—so we are informed by Col. C. T. Campbell, the Superintendent of the Express Company—were the messenger and a man lately hired as guard. The guard had a shot-gun and the messenger his pistol. Neither made any attempt to fight so far as we can learn. They were both ordered out and into line with the other prisoners. Then the leader, with the express messenger following, entered the car and the safe was opened. The amount taken

from the express will not exceed fifty dollars. The mail car was also robbed of several registered packages, but the amount received from this source we are unable to ascertain.

We are indebted to Col. Campbell for the information above. We also met Mr. Ely, who checks baggage on the train, who informed us that, observing the delay, he went out with the conductor, when they were arrested and held under guard by one of the robbers. He says when the robbers left, they retreated with their guns cocked and presented and facing the parties, in readiness for an attack. They went in a north-westerly direction."

Had the guard and messenger made good use of their weapons on this occasion, two of the robbers, at least, would never have rode away in the darkness again.

Chapter 10

Robbers' Fastness

The Eagle Ford robbery greatly increased public excitement and aroused an intense determination to capture the hidden bandits at all hazards.

As yet the State authorities had taken no action except to offer a reward of five hundred dollars each for the capture of the guilty parties. Stimulated by the hope of securing this reward and the desire to rid the country of such dangerous outlaws, a few private individuals, whose names will appear hereafter, made an earnest effort to follow the robbers to their hiding place.

Great effort was also made by the officers of the Texas Express Company to ferret out the bandits. This effort was attended with such success that a few days after the Eagle Ford robbery, they believed themselves in possession of a full knowledge, not only of the whereabouts of the robbers, but also of their names. But they were also convinced that their capture by any means at their hand, or by civil process, would be well-nigh impossible and that the aid of the State administration must be called into requisition.

They determined, therefore, to appeal at once to the governor for assistance and to afford a proper justification to public opinion for the movement, they called upon the managing editor of the *Dallas Commercial* and requested a full publication of all the facts which they had discovered and the conclusions to which they had come after a long and expensive investigation. The request was complied with and the article at once appeared, on Tuesday following the Eagle Ford robbery. As this article threw much light on a question then wrapped in doubt and mystery and turned public attention to the hiding place of the robbers, and as its statements have been proven almost absolutely true by subsequent developments, we give it below:

Robbers' Fastness.

After a most thorough investigation of all the circumstances attending the late railroad robberies and a careful following up of every clue, the detectives are fully convinced that the band of robbers who perpetrated these daring deeds are located in Denton County. The direction taken by the band in the three successive robberies establish the correctness of this conclusion, beyond a doubt. The band which robbed the train at Allen moved off in the direction of Denton County, and shortly afterwards Spotswood, who is now believed by all the detectives to have been the leader of the gang, was arrested there.

When the train was waylaid at Hutchins, the roads were so dry and hard that it was impossible to track the gang, but the indications were that they also went in the same direction. But the next morning after the affair at Eagle Ford a hot track was found and the maskers were followed directly to their present hiding place.

The fastness in which these highwaymen have each time successfully taken refuge is an extensive tract of woodland, full of undergrowth and very difficult of ingress. It is described as a place where a man could live for a year and nobody ever see him. This forest contains many log cabins standing among the trees and in such isolated places that nothing but a long search can discover them. It is believed that there are many good people among the inhabitants, but fear of their desperate neighbours compels them to keep their lips closed.

But many of the people are thought to be more or less in sympathy with the gang. Their houses are always open to them, and when compelled to stay in the woods, they carry them meals and act as spies for them. A detective fully acquainted with the character of the people says there are women among them who would ride fifty miles in a night to warn one of the gang of approaching danger. It is said, too, that they have couriers scattered through all the neighbouring country, who keep them constantly informed of every movement of the authorities. Some of these couriers are supposed to be here in Dallas, and constantly act as spies to gather and report the sentiments of the people.

They are also believed to have regular lines and stations extending as far west as Palo Pinto and northwest to the Indian

Territory.

As is well known, Bass, Underwood and Jackson, who were implicated in the Union Pacific robbery, live in Denton County Underwood alias Nixon, was arrested some time since and taken to the scene of the robbery for trial. But two weeks ago, he made his escape and is now at home again. Not long since this gang went into the town of Denton, and hearing that the authorities were trying to capture them, they retired to a mill near the town and sent word to the officers and the whole town of Denton to come out and take them.

To show the difficulty of capturing the *desperadoes* in their present hiding place by a posse of civil officers, it is related that a few days since two or three citizens were passing through the woods and upon firing a pistol they heard an answering shot, and repairing to the spot they suddenly found themselves confronted by several men who stood behind trees with Winchester rifles levelled at them and ready to pull the trigger.

The authorities of Denton County confess their inability to capture the gang.

There is now no doubt that all the robberies were perpetrated by the same gang. At Allen there were five robbers, at Hutchins and Eagle Ford there were but four—Spotswood having been arrested in the meantime. It is also fully believed that the same parties perpetrated the stage robberies and other deeds of daring in western counties.

In each case they were traced in the direction of the Denton County rendezvous. It is to be feared, too, that they will next make raids upon neighbouring cities, probably going through a bank or two, and startling the whole country with their bold burglaries.

The Texas Express and Railroad Companies have spent large sums of money in ferreting out the robbers, and the duty now devolves upon the State to arrest or break up the gang.

Detectives can do no more, for they have traced the robbers to their hiding place, and can almost name the guilty parties. The local authorities are powerless to capture the robbers, therefore the matter should at once be taken in hand by our State authorities and a sufficient force should be sent into Denton to arrest the guilty parties or drive them out of the country.

The companies are now compelled to keep a heavily armed

guard on all leading trains. This, of course, involves them in a very heavy expense. The additional expense of the Express Company alone is said to be a hundred dollars per day. As these companies are engaged in legitimate business, they should be protected by the State, no matter what the expense. The state of Texas must protect all its commercial business or it might as well quit. If *desperadoes* defy local authorities, then the State police might be called upon to assist in the enforcement of law. The name of the State is suffering greatly from these repeated and daring robberies.

The news of each successful attempt flashes at once to every town and city in the country, and another black mark is scored against Texas.

Every good citizen deplores this, and we believe that the Governor would be upheld by public sentiment in a determined effort by means of the State police to break up this desperate gang.

This article was extensively quoted by State exchange and republished by different papers throughout the West, and it did much to direct attention to the guilty parties.

The parties mentioned above as meeting the *desperadoes* in the woods were private detectives from Dallas. The history of the adventures of this squad in Denton County is as follows: The next morning after Eagle Ford robbery Samuel Finley, June Peake, James Curry and one other from Dallas, struck a hot trail leading northward from the railroad, and followed it to the Cross Timbers in Denton country. They continued through the timbers towards Denton, when within about three miles of that place, near the farm of Capt. B. H. Hopkins, they suddenly came upon two men asleep in the woods. They had ridden past them, when someone discovered the men and their horses which were picketed nearby.

The men immediately sprang to their feet and fired at the approaching party. The fire was returned by James Curry, but no one was hurt on either side. A parley then ensued. The detectives did not feel sure of their men, and were afraid to shoot them down for fear of killing innocent parties. While they were manoeuvring with a view to ascertaining who the men were, the two saddled their horses, sprang upon them, raised a whoop and dashed through the woods. The Dallas party supposing that the remainders of the gang were near did not pursue them, but sent for more force.

Continuing on to Denton, they stopped at the Lacy House on Saturday afternoon, (once the home of Bass) while there the notorious Sam Bass and a number of his associates appeared on the outskirts of the town and, according to one statement, rode into the city. They had heard that the Dallas party were looking for outlaws, and were anxious to know if they were the men whom they sought; if so, they would like to have them come out and try and take them. Messengers galloped back and forth between the excited and defiant crowd and their friends in the city. Finally, later in the evening Bass and company sent a messenger to the Dallas men to inform them that:

> They would remain in sight of them for two hours and a half, and challenged them to come out and fight. They stood near the residence of John S. Lovejoy, Jr., (we quote from the *Denton Monitor* of a few days late) in the eastern suburbs of the city, plain to view from the public square. More than a hundred men saw them.

But as the Bass party outnumbered the Dallas squad, they did not think it best to attempt their arrest without more assistance. Whether this assistance was tendered them by the officials of Denton is a question which we do not care to discuss. It is evident, however, that Mr. Geo. Smith, City Marshall, made an attempt to raise a posse and go to the mill, where Bass had lodged his men and was breathing out defiance to every man from Dallas, but failing in this, he started to the mill alone, and was afterwards followed by a few others. He soon returned with the report that Bass and party had skedaddled. Sheriff Eagan also offered to go out with a posse if the detectives would loan him their weapons, which they declined to do for the reason that they thought they had particular need of them themselves.

It was also stated afterwards by the city paper that assistance would have been freely given to make the arrests, if the detectives had furnished the proper papers. But this was impossible, as they had obtained such description of the robbers at Eagle Ford as could be given by the agent and train men, and then followed the trail, hoping to capture the men who answered the description, the names of the robbers being at this time unknown to them. As Sheriff Eagan afterwards spent many weary days and nights endeavouring to capture these same men, there can be no doubt that if he had felt convinced that they were the right parties, he would freely have offered his assistance to make the arrest.

He has the reputation of a brave and efficient officer and does not hesitate to do his duty when he sees it clearly.

But it is certain that the citizens of Denton were greatly in the dark at this time in regard to the guilt of the men, who were thus audaciously defying pursuit in their very midst. That Bass was one of the Union Pacific robbers was generally suspected, and to very many well-known. For he had covertly admitted as much to many of his old neighbours. Why he was not arrested, especially when so great a reward was offered for him, is inexplicable. But there was a stubborn unwillingness to believe that Bass and his company had any part in the Texas train robberies. Even after the above developments had been made and published, we find the *Denton Monitor*, in its issue of April 13th, declaring:

> There is no charge against any of this party, in Denton County, except Henry Underwood. That is for carrying a pistol, and it is not believed he can be convicted on evidence. And it is not believed here that any of this party participated in the train robbery at Eagle Ford, at Allen or at Hutchins. Certain it is that they were here on Thursday night of last week when the Eagle Ford train robbery occurred.

An explanation of this last statement will be found further on, in the sketch of Jackson's career.

The status of the band and the condition of affairs in Denton at this time, is well described by a correspondent who writes in a letter, dated Denton, April 11th:

> Reports about the railway robbers are so numerous and complicated that it would take a Philadelphia lawyer to get at the bottom facts; so, I can only give what I've heard, and leave the reader to draw his own conclusions. Sam Bass is the reported leader of the squad now. He is accused of the Nebraska train robbery and of every other one that has occurred since.
> I have seen but one man who might be a robber, and he is said since to have been Bass, and he was certainly well prepared for a fight when I met him (having a Spencer, two Colts and a knife, and well mounted), about four miles south of Denton, last Saturday morning. He approached and very politely asked me 'if I had met any armed men?' and I told him no. He then said 'some fellows had tried to steal his horse that morning and he was after them,' and rode off. I was since told that it was

Bass, and that he that day joined his party and went to the mill near Denton, and sent word to the party from Dallas, and all concerned, who were after him, that he was there and to come and take him.

The range of the Bass party in Denton and the region that abounds with their friends, I hear, lies between Pecan and Cooper creeks, running east and west across the Cross Timbers, a distance of ten miles long, between Hickory and Elm, and about four or five miles wide. It is thickly timbered, and they can go over the whole distance and camp most anywhere without being seen, except by friends. They do not confine themselves to this range, but go into the town of Denton frequently, at night, to play ten-pins, drink, and have a good time generally—actually getting the 'drop' upon an officer last Friday night and making him—no very hard job—drink with them, and leaving another friend twenty dollars in gold.

They have committed no robberies of private property in Denton County, nor do they molest travellers nor any persons they meet on the road, and are reported civil to all. They protest their innocence, but swear they will never be taken alive, and the one I saw looked as if he was 'that sort of a fellow.' A gentleman in Denton told me that either Bass or Underwood sold $1,000 in gold to a citizen not long ago, and said he knew where $8,000 more was buried. Bass is said to own a saloon in Denton. The difficulties the Dallas party have laboured under have been numerous. A few men, in a strange country, try to catch desperate men, well mounted and armed to the teeth, and knowing every inch of the ground, and with friends to warn them and furnish them the latest Dallas and other papers regularly, containing the latest movements and designs.

The good people of Denton have no sympathy with and give no aid to Bass and party, but what can they do, scattered as they are over a thinly settled country? They feel very sore over the hard things said of them by some of the Dallas papers, and would like the writers to come up and put themselves in their places awhile and have their families and then take all out upon a lonely plantation, in the timbers, often miles from a neighbour, and then see if they would like to tackle or to capture Bass and his 'horse marines.' That 'something is wrong in Denmark,' when men accused of crime can ride heavily armed over the country and into towns without being arrested, can send word where they are and soberly defy arrest no one can deny, but that does not cast a reflection upon the law-abiding citizens of Denton County, who are powerless—scattered as they are, and having among them men who will aid and comfort the robbers.

As this correspondent well says, there should be careful discrimination between the law-abiding people of Denton and the lawless characters and disreputable citizens who brought discredit upon the county.

Chapter 11
Texas Band

Although the name of each particular individual engaged in the different robberies was not fully and definitely known until after the brush at Mesquite, yet it now becomes important to the interest of the narrative to introduce the bandits to the reader without further delay.

Bass was the leader of the gang in all the robberies and was dubbed "conductor" by the squad, because he always went through the Express and mail cars, attending in person to the safes and mail bags, while to—FRANK JACKSON—was assigned the important duty of capturing the engineer and fireman. For this, reason he was called the "Engineer." Being a man of reckless daring and cool determination, he accomplished his task with remarkable success, as all the robberies well attest.

Jackson is a native of Decatur, Wise County, Texas, and for a time was considered a respectable young fellow. He lived with Dr. Ross, of Denton, a few years. Some eighteen months ago he got into a difficulty with a negro on the prairies, which gave him much notoriety. As he was alone with his victim, there is no account of the tragedy but his own story. He says that the negro stole his horse and when he demanded his return the fellow showed fight, he then shot him down. He at once reported the matter to his friends, telling them that he had "shot a n———r." After talking to them a little while he said he didn't believe that he had killed him and would go and finish the job. He returned and cut the negro's head off.

For this act he was brought before court and was acquitted it is said, on the ground of self-defence. But just what danger his life was in while sawing a badly wounded man's head off, it is difficult to see.

After this he ranged around Denton associating with wild fellows and leading a fast life. He accompanied Bass and Underwood to San Antonio last December and was believed at that time and later to have been connected with the Big Spring robbery. It was currently reported in Denton during the Spring that Bass gave him one hundred dollars per month to go with him on his exploits. But this is not well substantiated.

Jackson is believed to have assisted in all the robberies but that of Eagle Ford. At the request of Bass, he remained in Denton in company with Henry Underwood on the night of April 4th, in order to prevent suspicion and make the people believe that the gang were all at their homes. That the plan succeeded well, we have already seen.

SEABORN BARNES according to the best authority in the State, was in all the robberies. The same authority says that if there was a white feather in the gang, the plume belonged to Barnes, as his confederates stood in doubt of his courage. Barnes was a native of Tarrant County and of respectable parentage. He turned cow-boy, and then strayed off among "the wild fellows." Naturally enough, he fell in with Bass and his company.

HENRY UNDERWOOD is generally believed to have been "the brains of the crowd." He came to Denton from Missouri six or seven years ago, bringing with him his family, who lately resided in Wise County. He settled on a farm, but was wild and associated much with Bass during his career as a horse racer. He was once arrested by Tom Gerren for cattle stealing, which made him a sworn enemy of the queer Tom.

Because of his supposed resemblance to Tom Nixon, he was suspected of being the very man who numbered one of the six at Big Spring, and who fled with Berry. Learning that the officers were in pursuit of him, he fled to San Antonio, where, as we have already seen, the officers followed him, but failed to effect his capture on account of a misunderstanding among themselves. After escaping from the Alamo city, he returned across the country in company with Bass to his home in Denton, whither he was followed by Sheriff Everhart, of Sherman, and Pinkerton's detectives, and was finally captured during the last week in December.

As he was known to be a daring and desperate fellow, his capture was considered a very hazardous undertaking. But learning his exact whereabouts, the officers surrounded the house, closed in on it pistol in hand and covered their man with the deadly shooting-irons before he could make his escape or offer successful resistance. He was at once taken to Omaha where he was confronted by the detective Leech, of Ogalalla, who was with the robbers the night they divided the gold captured at Big Spring. Leech was in grave doubt about the prisoner's identity, and inclined to the belief that they had the wrong man. But Tony Waits, who seems to have engineered the matter, declared positively that Underwood was none other than the notorious Nixon. Underwood admitted that he knew Collins and Heffridge, and that he had recently been with Bass, but stoutly denied that he was Nixon, or that he had anything to do with the robbery.

He was then taken to Ogalalla for identification by several parties who knew the robbers. Their opinion being somewhat against him, he was taken to Kearney, Buffalo County, Neb., and lodged in jail.

Shortly after his incarceration there, Bass, with his usual liberality, sent him a hundred dollars. He gave seven dollars of this money to a discharged prisoner as he left the jail, with the understanding that he was to provide him some means of escape. The fellow was faithful to his promise, and returned with a file. With this and a watch spring he worked upon the hard iron for six weeks, and was at last rewarded for his long labour, by stepping out into the fresh air of night a free man. Arkansas Johnson, who was confined in the same jail, escaped with him.

The two repaired at once to the stables of the district judge, took a pair of his best horses and galloped away towards the south. When morning came they were far out of reach, and after a hard ride of sixteen days they neared Underwood's old tramping ground in Denton. Bass had by some means obtained intelligence of their escape and of their expected arrival. He mounted his horse and rode away to meet them. His search for them proved successful, and on Sunday evening, March 31st, just four days before the Eagle Ford robbery, he conducted them safely into his camp. Here the lucky Underwood was received with the wildest enthusiasm by his old companions in dissipation.

It has been strongly hinted that the capture of Underwood for Nixon was a put up job for the purpose of securing the large reward which was offered for the capture of the fated Berry's more fortunate companion. But there is not much ground for this charge, for the reason that Pinkerton's detectives are not allowed to receive rewards, but are paid *per diem*. The detectives were apparently persuaded that they had the right man. As for Sheriff Everheart, he simply effected the arrest on the papers presented. That he received a good recompense for his trouble, and justly, too, there is no doubt.

ARKANSAS JOHNSON was a stray member of the Texas band, coming in towards the last. But as he played an important part in the later history of the gang, he is placed among them.

Of his former life but little is known. According to the best information obtainable by detectives, his true name was John McKeen, his home in Johnson County, Mo. His father lives near Knob Noster, Mo. He was suspected by the detectives of being connected with the Union Pacific robbery, and search was at once instituted for him. He was discovered at Otterville, but made his escape. Afterwards he was traced to his father's house in Johnson County. In the attempt made to arrest him his sister was shot and killed, but he escaped. Afterwards he was captured and thrown into jail at Kearney. His own account of this matter, as given in Sam Bass's camp, was that he was arrested for stealing lumber.

When he first appeared in camp, he was received with ill favour by the members of the gang, even Bass himself is said to have had a very poor opinion of him. Some of the boys said he was nothing but a little "Jim Crow thief," and should never be admitted into the tony society of a band engaged in stopping the wheels of commerce and plucking plunder from rich corporations. (When Underwood, and his influence over the bold leader of the bandits was very great, assured him that he was all right, and could be trusted to play his part well.) That Underwood's usual sagacity did not fail him in his estimate of the shabby looking Missourian, was well proven afterwards. The Eagle Ford robbery occurred on the following Thursday night after his arrival in camp, and as Jackson, "the engineer," remained at home, Johnson was elected to fill his place at the engine. This he did with remarkable coolness and success, capturing the engineer and fireman and bringing them around in front the express car in a twinkling.

One of the last regrets of Bass was that he did not follow Johnson's advice in regard to two very important matters. But this belongs to a later chapter.

Briefly summoning up, we find that the Allen Station robbery was committed by Bass, the leader, Spotswood, according to the sworn testimony of the Express messenger (Thomas), Jackson and Barnes.

The Hutchins robbery was committed by Bass, Jackson and Barnes. Green Hill's name has also been mentioned in connection with this affair. But others, who were in Bass's camp, say that there were but three in the gang.

At Eagle Ford were Bass, Arkansas Johnson, Barnes, and one other who is still unknown to the authorities.

Chapter 12

Spy in Camp

At the time of the advent of Underwood and Johnson in the camp the bandits were quartered at Bob Murphy's, fourteen miles beyond Denton, on the road toward Bolivar. Here they slept in the barn at night and remained in the woods behind the field during the day, where the time was whiled away playing cards, planning future robberies or rehearsing old adventures.

On Saturday evening, the day before the arrival of Underwood, just as the sun was sinking behind the trees and the shadows were falling heavily upon the greensward, two young men entered the camp, one of whom was to prove the evil hand of destiny to the band. This was Will Scott, of Dallas, a young man highly connected in that city. The other was William Collins, a brother of the fated Joel Colins, who was killed at Buffalo Station.

Will Scott came among them as a spy, to effect the capture of Bass. As he furnished the greater part of the evidence by which some of the guilty parties were afterwards brought to justice, we give his story substantially as it was related in his sworn testimony during the late trial at Austin.

Knowing the large reward which had been offered for the capture of Bass for his connection with the Union Pacific robbery, young Scott conceived the idea of effecting his capture through strategy. In casting about for the means of effecting his purpose, it occurred to him that something might be accomplished through William Collins, because of the relationship formerly existing between Joel Collins and Bass. He at once repaired to Collins' house and there learned that some correspondence had already taken place between Collins and the Jackson's. He found, too, that Collins also had a scheme of his own in view, the gist of which was that he wanted to bring Bass and his companions down to Dallas County in order to avenge himself on some Duck Creek farmers who had prosecuted a number of the young men in the neighbourhood for disturbing a merry party of dancers, driving all the young ladies out of the house and smashing two or three of the young gentlemen's heads. The affair had acquired much notoriety, as it led to a libel suit with the Dallas Commercial.

The two at once started for Denton County, not knowing the exact whereabouts of Bass, but believing that he could be found. At Denton they obtained information which led them to believe that he was at Bob Murphy's. A letter to Murphy was secured from a Denton lawyer, and they proceeded on their journey. When they arrived at the camp, they found Bass absent in search of Underwood. But Jackson was there and they were received without disturb.

Bass returned the next evening and various plans for new enterprises were talked over between him and the new comers. Scott proposed the robbery of a Dallas bank, and a plan to rob a bank at Weatherford was also considered.

The band then left Murphy's and rode down towards Denton. While on the way some parties were seen coming from the opposite direction. Barnes at once dropped at the rear and lagged behind. "Are you not afraid to meet people in this way?" said one of the newcomers to the robber chief.

"Oh, no," replied Bass, "but Barnes back there always gets uneasy and wants to get out of the way."

The next day various plans were again discussed and finally Bass told them that when they heard of another excitement (meaning another robbery) they should return and he would go into some operation with them.

Collins and Scott left them a few miles below Denton and returned to their homes.

The next Thursday night the Eagle Ford robbery was committed, and as soon as Collins heard of it, he started for Denton. As we have already seen, Bass and his men were galloping around Denton on Saturday. Collins must have found them some place in that vicinity. On Sunday a plan for another robbery was discussed and it was finally agreed to try still another train, this time at Mesquite, a small station on the Texas & Pacific Railroad, a few miles east of Dallas.

During Monday and Monday night the party found their way to William Collins' house, situated in Dallas County, some twelve or fourteen miles east of the city of Dallas. On Tuesday young Scott set out again for a visit to Collins, to see what he was going to do, now that "the excitement" had been heard of. He found that Collins had already been to Denton and that the whole band were right there.

It was now Tuesday evening, and that night was set for the robbery. Collins had been to Mesquite that day and pronounced everything all right. Bass's party consisted of himself, Jackson, Barnes, Underwood and Arkansas Johnson. To these had been added Sam Pipes and Albert Herndon, two young men who had lived in the neighbourhood for some two weeks, working upon the farm by day and having a wild time at night. They both figured in the assault upon the dancing party.

After nightfall the party mounted their horses and set out for Mesquite, William Collins accompanying them. But as the train was late, and as they reached the station a little after the regular time for it to pass, they thought it had already gone by and returned to Collins' place. Here they concealed themselves during Wednesday. When night came, a parley ensued as to who should go, Bass objecting to so large a party. He said that the booty was likely to be small at best and would not reward a large crowd. He also said he would rather have his new friends act as outside men; that they could do more good in that capacity than by going under fire. William Collins mounted his horse, but finally yielded to the chief's persuasion and got down.

Henry Collins was all the time averse to having anything to do with the affair, and besought Pipes to the last not to go, telling him that that night would not end the matter; that a day might come when this expedition would prove a sad affair. But Pipes was "train struck" and would listen to no reason. It is said that he formerly lived in Missouri near the rendezvous of the James and Younger brothers and that evil shadows had fallen across the bright beams of childhood fancy. Be that as it may, himself and Herndon accompanied the band, making seven in all. This turn in affairs relieved Scott from all necessity of participating in the affair.

Chapter 13

Mesquite

At the close of the last chapter, we left the *banditti* mounted and ready to ride away under cover of darkness to meet the evening train. The plan of the robbery seems to have been the same as the one previously executed with so much success. But it was greatly disconcerted by the bravery of the conductor and express messenger. The near presence of a convict contraction train, surrounded by several guards armed with double-barrelled shotguns, also added much to the confusion. The last robbery really proved the only exciting one of the whole series, and had there been a few more determined men on board the train, it might have resulted very disastrously to the reckless bandits. From the reports published next day and from subsequent developments, we gather the following account of the fight:

> When the hour for the train arrived, the robbers stood under cover of darkness just behind the depot. Soon the roaring sound of the cars was heard and a few moments later the train was seen rushing in from the east. The whistle sounded and the locomotive stood at the depot. Before it had fairly ceased its puffing and snorting, the cry, 'hold up your hands! hold up your hands!' rang out upon the air.
> Captain Julius Alvord, the conductor, who was on the sleeper, had just stepped forward to the front passenger car and on to the platform. He had his lantern in his hand. He saw some parties near him who called to him to come to them, cursing him as they did so. He managed to put out his lantern as soon as possible and stepped on to the car, crossing over to the other side from the depot, he went immediately to the sleeping car and got a larger pistol. He had with him a small derringer. He put this in his coat pocket and took his larger pistol in his hand,

went to the rear of the sleeper, and opened fire on his enemies with the pistol. There were three parties firing on him, and being too much exposed he went down the steps off the platform, and at this time he was shot through the arm and a large hole shot in the back of his hat. He passed between the cars to the opposite side of the car from the robbers, with them still firing on him.

The engineer here attempted to start the train, but was stopped, only moving a short space. Conductor Alvord then took his position under the car and continued his firing. From this position he made several shots, but his wound became so painful he came out and re-entered the second-class coach. He found the passengers flat on the floor. He examined his wound by the dim light, and concluded to go to the sleeper and have it bound up. When he stepped from the second to the first-class car, several shots were fired at him. He looked to see that no one was near when he came out, but the robbers, while they were not in sight, kept shooting. Before entering the sleeper, he stuck his head out and called to them, and asked them what they wanted. They asked him who he was, and he said, 'a passenger.'

They replied, 'we want money.' They cursed him, and fired on him. He then went into the sleeper. His wound was bleeding profusely, and he took a sheet and bound up his arm and laid down. There were in the sleeper two gentlemen and their wives, going to Fort Worth. One of the gentlemen had considerable money. He had concealed it in different part of the car, thinking if they found part of it, he would still have some left. He was dressing; was very cool; he said: 'Conductor, I have a pistol, can I do anything? If you say so, I will go out and try them.'

Captain Alvord told him to remain there and shoot them if they tried to come in. There were about twenty passengers on board, and seven of them were ladies. No one else offered assistance. Captain Alvord thought he hit one of the men with his second shot, as he fell back suddenly to a pile of lumber immediately after he fired. The porter also heard them talking at the rear of the sleeper, and thought one was shot. The porter also heard them speak of Conductor Alvord, saying, 'He is a brave fellow, it would be too bad to kill him.'

Mr. D. J. Healey, at the time clerk at the Windsor Hotel, in Dallas, had quite a little experience, and his story will not be without interest: He left the city at 5:10 going east, and went up to Terrell, where he met the western-bound train. When near Mesquite he said he stepped on the platform so as to gain as much time as possible. He wanted to see the agent at Mesquite, who was a personal friend of his. He says he was the first man on the platform; that he got off before the train stopped. As he stepped down, he saw a man step on the platform a short distance off, who was soon followed by eight or ten more. He started forward and the first man made for him, while the others started for the express car.

The man who came to him presented his pistol, and told him to come on, and to throw up his hands. He took in the situation at once, and told him that he was not armed. He did not follow very rapidly, and the fellow kept cursing him. The robber went backwards, and he followed the pistol. The engineer made an attempt to start the train; Healey's guard became excited and started to assist the others to stop it, hallooing 'don't let them get away.' He took advantage of the absence and took $100 out of his vest pocket and put it in his boot. When he started to raise up from doing this the robber came on him with pistol in hand and again ordered him to follow. He started along slowly, keeping his eyes on the man in front, when someone came behind him and struck him on the side of the head with what he supposed was a pistol. It stunned him a little, and as he revived, he told the fellow he was a coward. He looked round but could not tell who struck him. He then watched his chance to get away. His guard soon gave him an opportunity by leaving him a few paces, going toward the express car.

He whirled and ran, and the robber fired; he ran east; he had run a short distance when he looked back and found he was still pursued; the robber again fired, and then returned to the train. He ran along the road until he came to the construction train where the convicts were; he hid under the train and stayed there about twenty minutes, when he approached the guards on the construction train and told them what was up. There were eleven guards on the construction train, and one went down the track and encountered a picket from the robbers' force. The robber fired and the guard returned the fire.

Healey said he wanted to get to the train but could not tell when to approach; he finally started, but before he reached the train it pulled out and he was left. While lying under the construction train he heard the sound of horses' feet, at the same time the robbers were still firing around the train. As the guards who had charge of the convicts could not leave them, they fired a number of shots from their posts, and with some effect, as we shall see hereafter.

In the meantime, one of the robbers had, as usual, taken charge of the engineer and fireman with a cocked revolver. Another subdued the station agent by the same means, but a woman who lived at the station, proved a much more refractory subject. In spite of all commands to hold up her hands, to stop, etc., she ran away to her room and locked herself in. "Conductor" Bass and two of his confederates repaired at once to the Express car to "administer" on its effects.

But Mr. Curley, the messenger, was a very determined man and faithful employee, and thought he could take much better care of the company's property than Conductor Bass or any of his trusty fellows. When commanded to open the door he positively refused to obey. The bandits told him "that if he didn't open it they would break it in." He told them to "go ahead." But as the shrewd Bass was well aware that the brave Curley and a heavily armed guard stood within with cocked revolvers in their hands, and would have nothing to do but pull the trigger the moment he showed his head, he thought it wise not to execute his threat.

He then shouted to them that if they didn't draw the bolts and swing back the door, he would set fire to the car and burn them up. They replied that they wouldn't do it. Then a can of oil, which had been hidden at a convenient place under the platform, was brought out and the car saturated with oil. Bass informed the messenger what he had done, and said he would give him just two minutes to surrender. Knowing the desperate character of the men, Mr. Curley concluded to surrender. The door was shoved back, and the robbers entered the car. After a hasty and almost fruitless search they retired. The mail car was also visited and a few registered letters were taken from the bags. The whole amount of money secured made but twenty-three dollars apiece for the seven robbers.

The bandits retreated to the horses which were hitched nearby, and mounted and rode away.

The rapid firing had awakened some of the citizens living nearby, and one or two approached and fired at the assailants, but no one thought it wise to attempt to pursue them.

Afterwards it was learned that three of the robbers were wounded in the fight. Pipes received a shot in the side, which proved a very damaging fact against him afterwards. Underwood and Barnes were both wounded in the limbs, but not seriously. The former hurried away to Denton, but the latter is said to have gone to William Collins' place, where he lay for a day or two concealed in a haystack.

Captain Alvord continued on to Dallas, where he was taken to the Windsor Hotel and at once received medical treatment. It was found that the ulna of the left arm was badly shattered. The wound proved very painful but not dangerous. On examination of his hat, it was found that a very close call had been made for his head, as a large piece had been shot out of the back part of the hat.

Captain Alvord is a single man about thirty-five years old, and was born in New York, leaving there when about seventeen years of age. Before the war he was connected with the O. & M. R. R., and also the Hannibal and St. Joe. Pie entered the army in the 30th Illinois regiment as a private, was afterwards promoted and when mustered out was Adjutant. Since the war six years of his life was spent with the M., K. & T. R. R., and for the past two years he has been on the T. & P. R. R. He is a man of great nerve, and has been much praised for his heroic defence of his train. Mr. Curley was also very highly commended for his bravery.

This was the last of the Texas train robberies, and we come now to another turn in the history.

Chapter 14

Gathering Them in

It would be impossible to describe the excitement and indignation which this fourth robbery produced.

The next morning as soon as the news spread over Dallas intense feeling was manifested and it continued to increase as the day advanced. Men walked the streets with stern faces and clenching their fists declared that this thing must be stopped if it took the whole State of Texas to do it. It was felt that local authorities had been somewhat remiss in the performance of duty or were totally unable to cope with the gigantic proportions which the evil was assuming. Loud calls were made for more determined action on the part of the Governor. That official had written not long before to the railroad officers, in answer to an inquiry from them, as follows:

> Be assured I will hereafter, as heretofore, offer in proper cases suitable rewards for the capture and conviction of all such criminals. Whatever power the law gives to the executive will be promptly exercised in aid of yourself and the civil authorities, towards providing against the recurrence to robberies of our railway trains, and to secure the speedy arrest and punishment of the felons who perpetrate them.

He was now vehemently urged by the State press to come forward with whatever aid lay in his power.

Major Jones, commander of the State police, was at once sent to Dallas to institute a vigorous search for the robbers. The city was also full of detectives, while sheriffs, constables and policemen were flying about in every direction. Every few days some poor fellow, who happened to have the smell of powder on his clothes or a wild look in the corner of his eye, was gobbled up and brought to town. But he always turned out to be the wrong man.

Major Jones proceeded to organise a small company of mounted police, or rangers, consisting of thirty picked men. These were sworn in on May 18th and placed in command of Lieutenant June Peak, formerly Recorder of Dallas.

In the meantime, the major had fallen in with Will Scott, who told him that he had been making some effort to decoy Bass into a corner where he might be captured, and that he had obtained some valuable information. This information was then imparted to him and thus the commander of the State forces was placed in possession of all the facts relating to the robberies, the identity of the guilty parties and their hiding places. These facts have already been given in the narrative.

As it was known that Pipes and Herndon were still in the county and that frequently they came to the city, steps were immediately taken to arrest them.

A plan was arranged that Scott should go out to the Collins place and reconnoitre. If the two were there he would remain overnight and Major Jones could come out and effect the capture, if not he would return to camp. As he did not return, Major Jones went out and found Scott and Henry Collins and Pipes at Mr. Collins' house.

They were all put under arrest. Scott then informed him that Albert Herndon was at Mr. T. J. Jackson's, some few miles away. A negro arrested on the outside of the house also gave the same information. Scott and Henry Collins were then turned loose, and Herndon was arrested and the two were brought to town. They very emphatically denied their guilt and seemed indifferent to proceedings. After a preliminary examination they were admitted to bail which was promptly furnished and they were turned loose again.

About this time, John and Morris Griffin, on trial for robbing the Express Company at Paris of ten thousand dollars, were found guilty, but only sentenced to two years' imprisonment.

Major Jones learning this fact concluded to change the case against Pipes and Herndon to the Federal District Court. New papers were accordingly taken out and the young men were again arrested and had a hearing before U. S. Commissioner Fearn. They were also taken to the jail and searched, as it had become known that one of them had been wounded. No marks were found upon Herndon, but a small scab was discovered on Pipes' left side. When questioned in regard to it he said that it was a little boil, then he admitted that it was a pistol shot wound which he had received from one of his comrades in the country, but he had concealed the matter to keep the man out of trouble. He became somewhat confused in his story, looked despondent and it was plain to the officers that he would be glad indeed to get his shirt back over that scab.

Commissioner Fearn, held the parties to appear before the Federal Judge at the next term of court, the bonds being fixed at $15,000 each. This they were soon prepared to give. But U. S. Marshall Russell, who had taken charge of them, received a telegram from Judge Duval, stating that he had sent a bench warrant to him and that the prisoners must be produced at Tyler. At eleven o'clock that night they, were ironed together and put aboard a special train and hurried away.

This no doubt saved some of their friends a heavy forfeiture, as they would probably have jumped their bonds, had they regained their liberty. This was April 26th, sixteen days after the Mesquite robbery.

April 29th, William Collins was attached as a witness to appear at Tyler. That afternoon he appeared in one of the newspaper offices "to get the thing right in the papers." He was interviewed at some length.

The substance of his statement will be found in the following colloquy:

Collins.—Pipes and Herndon can easily established their innocence by proving an alibi. It is true that they have been pursuing no calling for some time, but have been idle.

Reporter.—Mr. Collins, this as you know, is urged against these two young men; can you tell me anything concerning it?

Collins.—They have been idle for the reason that they were making preparations with myself to go west with me, where I intended to take a drove of cattle. Pipes, who owned land in the county has sold it, and Herndon has leased his farm.

Reporter.—Where did these young men make their homes?

Collins.—Pipes has been living for some months at my father's residence, about a mile from where I live in the White Rock neighbourhood, and Herndon has made his home at my house, staying there most of his time.

Reporter.—You say they can establish an alibi on the night of the Mesquite train robbery. Will you tell me what facts you feel justified in making known as to their whereabouts on that night and the nature of the proof they can make?

Collins.—Pipes and Hernon were both at my house that night. They went to bed about ten o'clock, and I and my wife will both establish the fact that they both staid at my house up to that hour. I saw them go to bed myself in a room above my own from which they could not have left during the night without passing through my bedroom. The next morning early, they were still in their room, and I saw them both get up. There are persons who work on my place by whom they can prove that they were at my house that night.

Reporter.—I suppose there is no doubt that Pipes has about his person a gun-shot wound received at that time?

Collins.—Oh, yes! Pipes has a wound but it was received before the Mesquite train robbery. I know all about it. It was an accident and it was made with a little old pistol which is at my house now. That matter will be satisfactorily explained and made perfectly clear at the proper time.

Reporter.—If these young men can so easily establish their innocence—in other words, if there is so little grounds for their arrest, what do you suppose has led to their being suspected and arrested?

Collins.—Well, I don't know, but suppose persons at enmity with them have put up a job on them for the purpose of injuring and harassing them.

The following description of Collins appeared with the report of this interview:

He is a young man, apparently between twenty-five and thirty years of age; is tall and well formed; has a frank, open, honest-looking face, a clear grey eye, high forehead, dark hair, and is very intelligent, conversing well and at perfect ease.

It was remarked after the handsome but unfortunate young man passed out of the room, that unless Marshall Russell and Major Jones were much less shrewd than they have credit for being Collins would soon be behind the bars with his old friends. This remark proved correct, as Collins found an indictment waiting for him at Tyler, and he was at once put under arrest.

An indictment was also found against Henry Collins, but he has not yet been captured, as he became alarmed after the arrest of his brother and joined the Bass gang.

In the meantime, Scott Mayes, a saloon keeper at Denton, and a negro named Scaggs of the same place, had also been arrested and taken to Tyler. They were charged with being accessories to the fact.

Soon after this, May 2nd, Bob Murphy, a cattle man in Denton, and Green Hill, a sporting character, were arrested at their homes in

Denton and taken directly to Tyler. They were charged with being accessories to the robberies.

On the same day Sheriff Everheart, of Grayson County, arrested Henderson Murphy, father of Bob Murphy, Jim Murphy and Monroe Hill. They were all charged with being accessories and also with harbouring Bass and his party. It was alleged that about a week before the arrest, the gang had a frolic at old man Murphy's house, where Underwood's wife was boarding; that they cut up "high jinks" and had a "high old time," practicing with their pistols and boasting what they would do with the rangers.

Just after the arrest of Pipes and Herndon, Scott determined to make another visit to Bass's camp. After consultation with Major Jones, he set out for Denton and succeeded in finding Bass at Green Hill's, about six miles below Denton. He informed him of the arrest of Pipes and Herndon, but nevertheless found Bass willing to enter into a plan to rob a Dallas bank. The exchange Bank, of Gaston and Thomas, was agreed upon as the proper one to "go through." (It is not on a record that Bass made any mention of the State Saving Bank.) The plan was partly mapped out but left in an indefinite shape, Will Scott returning to Dallas to complete the arrangements.

But in the meantime, Bill Collins had become suspicious of Scott and sent a letter to Bass by Mayes, telling him that Scott was a spy, and exhorting him to hang him to the "handiest" bush. Scott was anxious, however, to return, but Major Jones, with more mature judgment, saw the danger and forbade his going. The major was also averse to the plan to rob the bank, as he knew that the bandits were a desperate set of fellows and in the confusion of the moment some harm might be done to persons employed at the bank, and that the robbers might succeed in capturing the contents of the safe and escaping. In other words, he did not care to be held liable for damage to property with so poor a prospect of success.

CHAPTER 15

The Great Campaign against Bass

The great summer campaign against Bass which continued until the last of June, was opened about April 24th. More men were employed in this campaign, more powder burned, more bullets buried in post oaks and green hillsides, more horses rode to death, more ground galloped over, more false alarms given, more prophecies blown into thin air, more expectations blasted and fewer men captured than ever before occurred in any similar campaign in human history. Of course, we do not include in this statement the prisoners who quietly submitted to arrest at their homes, making no attempt to escape.

About the date mentioned above, Bass's old tramping ground in Denton County began to swarm with rangers, detectives, sheriffs, and the now excited citizens of the county. On that day Sheriff Eagan had a brush about a mile and a half west of Denton with the now bold, bad man, who in better days gathered with his family at his own fireside. Nothing was accomplished by the skirmish, and nothing more was attempted until early the next week. Then Sheriff Eagan again took the warpath followed by a host of deputies and all the excited citizens who could find a gun, borrow a horse or seize the steed of some unfortunate farmer who happened to be in town.

Peak also arrived in Elm Fork bottom at the same time with his company of rangers. It is said by an eye witness that there were fully 150 men on the trail. The Denton people felt the strictures which had been made upon their county and were determined to rid it of the bad gang who had so long defied arrest.

A correspondent who witnessed the scene gave the following description of it:

> They had them corralled once or twice, but Captain Bass & Co. did not seem to care for the fight much, and depended on the

run for it. Many shots were fired. The 'flying couriers,' as Bill Arp used to call them, were out in full force and made their Texas ponies' hearts sick. Every ten minutes one would come dashing up to the court house at full break neck speed to report progress. One would say 'they had sent him back because his horse was broken down;' but all agreed that 'they'd have Bass sure before nightfall.'

Your correspondent took an excursion into the 'bottoms.' Flanking the 'flying couriers' he saw some rare shooting of Winchester's and Spencers at random. He caught a glimpse of Captain Bass and his party a little distance off. Bass sat on his horse like a Comanche Indian, and didn't seem to care a continental for hurting any of the pursuing party. He and Underwood left the horses they were riding and took it afoot. Judge Hogg captured Bass's horse; but down into those everlasting, hidden bottoms went Bass & Co. In this skirmish Deputy Marshall Minor, of Denton, had a rare tumble from and with his horse. They rolled over and over and looked like fourteen gentlemen in one. Sergeant Minor returned to Denton to report a sprained ankle.

Judge Hogg, Capt. F. E. Piner and Capt. T. Daugherty were out after the *desperadoes*, as were all the prominent citizens. The saloon keepers, who were accused of harbouring and encouraging the Bass party, were also out in force, and if they could have been captured in these terrible bottoms, I believe it would have been done.

The people of Denton are as hospitable, as kind, and as law-abiding a people as I have ever met in Texas. The reason Bass gives for coming to Denton is a sensible one and a good excuse for his leaving here. Dallas, Collins, Ellis, Tarrant and other of our counties are high and rolling, with but few hiding places, but when you strike the cross timbers up here and get into Elm and Hickory bottoms, you see four or five Chickahominy swamps all boiled down into one. The foliage is dense—the vines hang in masses and the undergrowth thick, and it is not good daylight until 12, noon. Now, Bass, Underwood and company, knew these 'bottoms' thoroughly.

For nearly a year, and before that, they have made every 'hog path' a study, and they knew them as well as 'Marion and his men' knew the swamps of the Pedee in South Carolina. That they would naturally resort to such a section in their trouble, anyone who has been through them can see at a glance. The section lying between Elm, Hickory, Pecan, Copper, and Little Elm, surrounding Denton city north, southeast and west, with the Cross Timbers and the grand prairie to hide and run in, affords a place for the operations of a small force of armed and desperate horsemen, such as is not to be found elsewhere in the United States.

That no one was killed is easily accounted for. A lot of green soldiers were after men trained to the bottoms, and to hardship. Firing with Winchester rifles or Spencers from the hip, on a horse galloping through the dense timbers of the buttons, is not likely to hurt anybody much. Bass and party knew this, and though it is said Jackson's ear was shot off, the only wounded men I saw were Sergeant Minor, whose horse fell on him, and a young Mr. Hart, who placed his Winchester upon the toe of his boot and shot one of his toes off.

Of course, all engaged had wonderful stories to tell. 'How terribly they rode to the front, and all that, but the truth is, 'Captain Bass and his Horse Marines'—5 or 7 to 150, 'got away with them,' after three days riding around and firing—and as 'Charely,' of the *Denton Monitor* says, 'they're lit out and lit.' That they have gone all the good people here rejoice to know, and so will everyone be glad if they meet with their deserts. That they are bold, desperate, determined men, no one who has seen their ways can doubt. They have sworn 'to die before being taken alive,' and everyone who knows the men think they mean what they say. But let justice be done to Denton County and her good people, and hereafter, 'let him who is without sin cast the first stone.'

The correspondent was right at that time in saying that the band had fled from the country. The three days' fighting alluded to occurred April 30th and May 1st and 2nd. On Wednesday morning, May 1st, Lieutenant Peak came upon Bass while he was preparing to eat his breakfast, in the woods about four miles southeast of Denton. The bandits had barely time to escape, leaving their food on the fire. One horse was captured. They at once turned their course towards the west, closely pursued by the rangers. On Thursday they were heard of in Wise County and on Thursday night Peak arrived with his command at Decatur, the county seat of Wise. On Saturday, May 4th, a telegram was received from Decatur, saying that Peak had divided his command and was scouring West Fork bottom.

But Bass and his men being well acquainted with the country, made good their escape and nothing worse was heard of them for some days.

Sheriff Everheart, who with his usual alacrity and courage had been actively engaged in the pursuit, returned to Sherman May 17th and reported that he did not know where Bass was, though he thought he was in Denton or Wise County. He said the whole country, through Denton and Wise Counties, was alive with scouting parties out after Bass, and that his operations were greatly retarded by these bands of zealous but inexperienced robber hunters. On two different occasions his squad was charged and captured by companies of citizens. He said also that there were bands of men pretending to hunt Bass who were really his accomplices and keeping him posted in regard to the movements of the troops.

Sheriff Eagan was also heard from about the same time and reported that he was in Montague County and believed that Bass was making for the Indian Territory.

It was a general belief at that time that he was trying to reach the Territory or the Nation. Certain it was that he had vanished in the tangle wood of the western counties, and nothing more was heard from him for something over two weeks. The public began to think that the gang had surely enough escaped from the State. But suddenly the following telegram was flashed across the wires:

> Griffin, Texas, May 18.
> Sam Bass with five of his men is surrounded on Big Caddo Creek by Berry Meadows, sheriff of Stevens County. Meadows was re-enforced by ten men from Palo Pinto last night at 2 o'clock. He expected to make the attack at daylight this morning. Some fighting was done yesterday and the day before. No damage done on our side. It is not known whether any outlaws were hurt.

The manner in which they were discovered and the incidents of the attempted capture, were furnished by a correspondent of the Fort Worth Democrat as follows:

> Deputy Sheriff Freeman was informed last week by a woman of the neighbourhood, near Caddo Creek, that parties answer-

ing to the description of the train robbers were there. He, with one ranger, and Messrs. Amis and Paschall of this town, went into that section to ascertain something more definite, and learned that Bass, Underwood, Jackson, Barnes, and two others, supposed to be Welch and Collins, (Henry Colins had joined the band some time previous to this), had been camped there in the mountains for upward of two weeks. A brother-in-law of Jackson, and several other kin and friends are living near Caddo Creek, and had furnished them with supplies. They are reported to be flush with twenty dollar gold pieces, and from events developed more recently, they are found to have numerous friends in that vicinity.

Having gathered the desired information, the ranger reported to his camp in Shackelford County, and the balance repaired to Breckenridge, where Sheriff Meadows and Deputies Freeman and Hood selected several picked men, and on Sunday started for the scene of action. At midnight they sent back for reinforcements, and twenty old shot guns were collected together and the same number of volunteers. Before all of these new recruits arrived, the sheriff's posse came upon the gang near the store, thirteen miles east of here, on the Palo Pinto road, and an engagement ensued, in which about forty shots were fired by each party, and at one time three of the party dismounted and fought from behind trees.

It is thought one of their horses was wounded. They afterwards chased the robbers about two miles into the mountains. As the gang was so much better armed than the sheriff's party, and were acquainted with the locality of the mountain defiles, they then had little to fear. On Monday night they camped among the trees and thickets near Taylor's store, and the sheriff's party on the prairie one-third mile distant.

Tuesday morning, May 26th, the sheriff and his posse were gladdened by the arrival of the gallant rangers from Shackleford County, nineteen in number, armed to the teeth, and their force had also been increased by Deputy Sheriff Owen and eight picked men from Palo Pinto town. The rangers were under command of Lieut. Campbell and Sergeant Jack Smith, and the Breckenridge party of fearless Deputy Sheriff Freeman. Sergeant Smith, of the rangers, stated that if they could find them, they would capture the robbers dead or alive, if they lost half their men in the attempt. On Tuesday they followed their trail through mountains gaps and defiles, and among the hills and valleys in their winding course, but up to twelve o'clock last night had not overtaken them, though the gang had come back to near the starting point.

At McClasen's store, four miles further east, they purchased eight dollars' worth of provisions, and left word for the pursuers that they would stand their ground and give them a desperate fight, and that they did not propose to be bull-dozed, all of which is supposed to be a blind, and that they in reality were preparing to strike out for parts unknown. It was ascertained that they had been trying to swap off one of their horses. They are said to be well mounted and each armed with a Winchester rifle and a pair of six shooters. Before the arrival of the rangers the sheriff had summoned four or five citizens in that neighbourhood to secure arms and join his posse.

The Bass gang passed the same party soon after, before they had obtained arms, marched them down to the store and treated to bottle beer. It is said that parties in that vicinity have carried the Bass gang baskets of provisions and kept them informed of the movement of their pursuers. One of the gang, it is reported, is suffering from a wound received in Denton County. One of them remarked to some person at the store that they were no petty thieves, that they interfered with no private citizen, but holding out a handful of twenty-dollar gold pieces, 'that is what the sheriff and his posse want.'

They are said to have $5,000 with them and to have buried the balance. In getting volunteers from Breckenridge, it was quite manifest that a greater portion of the citizens considered it their duty to join the home guard and gallantly paraded the streets in their vigilance to find Bass whom they proposed to demolish forthwith.

The rangers from Coleman County are expected across the country, to intercept them in case of a retreat in that direction. Additional parties from Griffin passed here last night to join the forces and aid in the capture.

But all efforts to surround them proved unavailing and a few days later, May 31st, it was telegraphed from Breckenridge that the sheriff's posse and rangers had given up the chase after Sam Bass and party and that they left Bass boss of the situation in the cedar brakes and mountains, fifteen miles east of that place, where they easily eluded their pursuers.

During this "drive" after Bass the following amusing incident is reported to have occurred. We give it as told in one of the daily papers:

A gentleman from the vicinity of the late scenes of the attempted capture of the Bass and Underwood gang, tells the following unexampled story in connection with a fruitless effort on the part of four gallant farmers who were bent on heading the robbers off and taking to themselves the glory and consequent profit of their capture:

The rumour spread like wild-fire through the neighbourhood that Sam Bass and his confederates were scouring through that part of Shackleford County, brazen-faced and publicly proclaiming they did not give a continent damaged darning needle whether school kept or not.

Our gentleman informant, Mr. Nance, of Young County, says that the robbers rode up to a store located near the edge of Shackleford and Young Counties, purchased some provisions and after leaving a note stating that they were the robbers and were going on south-west to Taylor's store several miles beyond, paid for what they got and gently rode off in the direction indicated in the note. As quick as possible the alarm was given, and one of the deputy sheriffs of the county, accompanied by four farmers armed with shotguns, started in hot pursuit and overtook the Bass gang moving leisurely along the highway.

How to capture them was now indeed an enigma. They finally decided to separate, the sheriff to remain behind and intercept a possible attempt to retrace their steps, and the four shotgun heroes were to move rapidly forward in a circuit, come into the road suddenly on their side, and with cocked guns order their rich game to surrender or suffer the alternative—death. The scheme wore the aspect of a plausible one, and the four farmers started to execute it.

Putting spurs to their horses, they shot off to the right of the road and were not long in getting in an obscure position by the road-side ahead of the robbers, where they could not be seen until so desired. Apparently unconcerned and careless, the four robbers drew near, and as they got opposite, the stern demand to halt and surrender was given.

Just then a wild whoop from behind proceeded from the woods, startled the shot gun heroes, and in the disorder which ensued, the robbers getting possession of their arms, got the drop on their would-be captors and turned the table by 'taking them into the fold.'

The whooping party was one of the scouts who had been following the farmers and perpetrated the successful trick. All four of the pursuers were taken in charge, marched to Taylor's store, and in less than half an hour were boiling drunk through the hospitable treatment at the hand of their captors, who left them shortly after accomplishing their aim, in possession of a note cautioning them to make no such absurd attempt to bulldoze a gang of Sam Bass's train robbers.

CHAPTER 16

The Great Campaign against Bass Continued

After the escape of the band in the vicinity of Brackenridge, nothing more was heard of them until May 5th.

On the evening of that day a courier suddenly dashed into the little town of Elizabeth, Denton County, and as he reigned in his foaming steed, shouted out in breathless haste that Captain Sam Bass was again on his old stamping ground, having just been seen in the neighbourhood of Mr. Burnett's farm, on Denton Creek, about nine miles distant.

A posse was immediately collected and started in pursuit. But Bass was riding hard to accomplish something very different from an escape, and soon left farmer Burnet's place far to the rear.

The next morning, just as the first rays of light leaped over the eastern woods, the dashing train catcher and his band galloped down the streets of Denton past the houses still closed and silent, meeting here and there an early riser who gazed in astonishment at the dust-covered riders. Reaching the centre of town, they halted their weary steeds in front of Work's livery stable. Here they found Charles McDonald, an employee, who had just risen and begun his stable work.

He was immediately informed that they had come for the three horses captured from the band by Sheriff Eagan on the 1st of May, and that he must "bring them horses right out." At the same time Bass had drawn close to him and was flourishing a revolver in close proximity to his face. He refused to get the horses when Jackson, who had also drawn near, began to strike him over the head with his pistol. He then commanded McDonald to stand still and sent Jackson and Carter, a man who had lately joined the band, into the stable to saddle the horses and bring them out. This was soon done and the band put spurs

266

to their horses and dashed away.

Two men, heavily armed, were sleeping in the upper story of the stable at the time. They heard the noise below, one of them seized a double-barrelled shot gun, looked out of the window and saw Bass and his men starting away. He looked at them as they rode across the green into the street, but reserved his ammunition for a better opportunity.

The men engaged in this daring raid were Bass, Jackson, Underwood, Barnes, Arkansas Johnson and Carter. Carter is a reputed cattle thief, and though he had but lately joined the band, yet he had for some time been more or less connected with them. It is not known whether Henry Collins was in this raid or not.

Before the clatter of the retreating horses' hoofs had died away, the cry of "Bass," rang along the streets, and soon the whole town was in the wildest commotion. Horses were hurried from the stables, bridled and saddled and in less than half an hour a whole troop of riders dashed off in the direction taken by the bandits.

To give a full account of this pursuit of the gang across their old tramping ground, from the time that they were seen near farmer Burnett's until they disappeared near Bolivar, we introduce the details as furnished by a correspondent at the time. The letter was dated at Elizabeth and was written by a young man engaged in the pursuit.

> On Wednesday last about 4 o'clock p. m., a special courier arrived in Elizabeth bringing the message to Capt. Withers, deputy sheriff, that Bass and company had made their appearance in the neighbourhood of Mr. Burnett's, on Denton Creek, about nine miles northwest of this place. Capt. Withers immediately summoned a posse to his assistance and started in pursuit, arriving where they were last seen about dark, and scoured the bottoms, which proved fruitless, the night being too dark to strike any trail. They dispatched a man at once to Denton and the utter darkness prevented his arriving there until late the next morning.
>
> At daylight Capt. W.'s crowd struck the trail, which they followed direct to Denton. Arriving at Denton they learned that Bass and company had arrived there a little before daylight, taken from Work's livery stable the two horses which had been captured from him during his last trial, and went to the residence of Sheriff Eagan, roused him from his pleasant slumbers and told him to get up, "as the country was full of thieves," and

then rode out of Denton. Strange to say, but yet true, a man stood on the loft of the stable, with a double-barrelled shotgun and a belt of cartridges, and let Bass proceed with the horses.

Withers and command, after stopping a few seconds to hear the tale, proceed on their trail and rounded them up at Pilot Knob, about six miles south of Denton, on Saturday morning, when they had the first battle. One of the pursuers was wounded. This was George Smith, the Denton marshal, who offered to arrest Bass at the mill for the Dallas men. Bass then fled.

Runners were sent out for recruits, one going to Denton and the other starting to his place, but he was overtaken by Bass, ordered to dismount, and they took his saddle, cut his bridle into strings, turned his mule loose, and told him if they caught him again, they would kill him.

They then rode off towards the timbers. But before they reached the trees, Captain Withers was up and made a charge, but Bass was too well armed and Withers had to dismount. After he dismounted Bass and company poured about twenty-five volleys right at him, cutting the ground all around him and throwing the dirt all over him. Bass then retreated, taking a south-easterly course.

Up to this time not over seven were in close pursuit, and Bass having seven in his outfit, and armed with long-ranged rifles.

From this place Bass started in the direction of Alton, thence to Ballard's Mill, thence to Davenport's Mills, pursued closely by the command, which now had swelled to nearly forty. At Davenport's Mills Bass stopped, bought some coffee-pots and inquired for ammunition. It was discovered that one of Bass's men was shot in the side. They then took for Medlin School House, where Withers again came up within shooting distance and gave them a round, but ineffectively. They then took to the timber and rounded and came back very nearly on the same track they went down, struck out by Doe Harris' and through the timber again, when the trail was lost about ten o'clock at night.

The men being worn out, they went to camp. The next morning at daylight they were again in the saddle and on the trail. After proceeding a mile and a half they came to where Bass had camped. The trail being fresh, they made good time, and came upon Bass and company cooking their breakfast, about a mile and a half from Ballard's Mill. Bass opened the fire, shooting down two of Withers' boys' ponies. The volley was returned and one of Bass's men was shot. They then fled, putting the wounded man on his horse and one of the other getting up behind to hold him on. One of Bass's horses, his cooking utensils and provisions were captured.

Your reporter arrived at the battle-field about an hour after the battle and joined the boys, who then trailed Bass to the McKinney road, about six miles east of Denton, where the trail was lost about five o'clock Sunday afternoon, and we returned. This nearly accurately describes the whole movement.

Bass is well mounted, well-armed and has plenty of money and legions of confederates in the Cross-Timbers, and it may consume a week before he is finally either shot down or captured, as Withers and Eagan and their men are determined to follow as long as any trail can be found.

It is said one of Bass's men has fallen out.

Bass has all the advantage in the world, as he has nothing to do but to ride through the woods, while the other party have to often spend hours hunting up the trail.

Sunday evening two gallons of whiskey, some tobacco and provisions were shipped to Elm bottom from Denton, and it is thought it went to Bass, as he has runners in all directions.

He has made the remark that he intends to kill Capt. Withers before he leaves the country, as he believes Withers is the only officer in the country who is seeking to arrest him.

From what we saw of the men's performance on Sunday they are all determined to have the whole outfit or die trying.

The whole party are very much fatigued, and their horses are jaded to the last.

The people of Denton are very much aroused and are fully awaked to their duty, and are rallying to the front as fast as they can.

We left about fifty men in pursuit Sunday evening, and no doubt the crowd is doubled by this time. Courtright and two others from Fort Worth caught up with the crowd shortly after the battle Sunday morning, and took the lead with Withers at once.

The men from this place who have been and are still in pursuit, are Jack Bates, G. M. Powell, J. Goff, M. Kinser, W. H. Berbe,

A. E. Allen, and Ed. Dunning, and are as brave and true as ever breathed.

Tuesday, June 11.—The news came here late yesterday that the trail had been entirely lost in Elm bottom, and another that Bass and company had passed Bolivar with fifteen men strong. The informer said Eagan and his posse had returned to Denton, and Withers and his men were still in pursuit. We can hear most anything, but we are positive that Withers has not lost or been off Bass's trail one hour since he struck it on Wednesday last.

If they did pass Bolivar, it is almost sure that they are making for Lost Valley, where they will be joined by about thirty other outlaws, who have been traced to that point.

It may seem to your readers, Mr. Editor, that in four battles, and in the last not over fifty yards apart, that Bass surely ought to have been taken in ere this, but if you were better acquainted with some of his dodges and tricks it would appear different.

All the creeks had to be swum up to Sunday morning, which made pursuit troublesome.

In the fight at Pilot Knob, Riley Wetzel was shot through the calf of the leg by one of Eagan's men. He was conveyed back to Denton by Mr. Allen.

Later.—Bass went into Bolivar Monday, bought a sack of flour, four sacks of coffee and clothes. He was remounted and in good trim. They ate their dinner near Bolivar. The crowd cannot be far in the rear, and no doubt will run him into Lost Valley. A company of rangers will be up by this evening. One Murphy joined Bass near Bolivar.

This was Jim Murphy, a man who figures very prominently in the narrative before it closes.

In the fight at Ballard's mentioned above, John Work, a son of Captain Work, of Dallas, was wounded in the shoulder, and the firm had two horses killed.

On the evening of June 10th, the same day on which Bass was reported to have gone into Bolivar, the band was engaged by a party under Sheriff Everheart in a running fight on the prairie, in the north part of Denton County.

A farmer who witnessed the fight, says that when he saw them the Bass crowd was riding seven abreast and going at a furious gait. The sheriff's party were from three to four hundred yards behind, stringing

L. TO R. JIM MURPHY, SAM BASS SITTING, AND SEBE BARNES

out single file, and spurring their horses to their utmost capacity. Some thirty or forty shots were fired. About three or four miles farther on the Bass crowd reached a strip of timber, dismounted and disappeared.

The next seen of the gang was in Wise County, where they were discovered by Captain Peake and his command. The Rangers had followed them into the tangle wood along Salt Creek, near Cottondale, on the morning of the 12th. Most of the day was spent in searching through the dense bushes for the hidden robbers. In the afternoon they were suddenly discovered lounging under the trees on the bank of the stream, their horses having been lariated out a few rods away. The Rangers at once crossed, opened fire upon them, and the fight which ensued was the sharpest and most successful of the campaign. The bandits seemed more anxious to escape to their horses than to fight, but the Rangers crossed the stream and headed them off from the horses.

During the fight, one of the robbers exposed his person boldly to view, Sergeant Floyd, a crack shot of the Stonewall Greys, of Dallas, seeing him, dropped upon his right knee and taking deliberate aim fired, killing him instantly. The victim afterwards proved to be Arkansas Johnson. Bass was standing at his side, but escaped unhurt.

Shortly after the fall of Johnson, the robbers slipped away through the tangle wood and escaping under the bank of the creek, concealed themselves in a large excavation. While here, as was afterwards learned, one of the Rangers came very near and stood plainly in view. Jackson levelled his rifle upon him and asked Bass if he should shoot. The chief said, "no, not unless he turns this way."

Underwood, however, escaped to the horses, mounted one of them and was returning, when he was met by Captain Peak in the woods. A pistol duel at once opened, but Captain Peak shouted to his men and Underwood put spurs to his horse and fled. The heads of the robbers' horses were now seen in a clump of trees not far distant. As Captain Peake did not know where the robbers were, and fearing that they might be with the horses, he ordered his men to fire upon the horses, which they did and two of them were killed. The rest were captured.

Johnson was buried by citizens living near the place.

Thus ended the career of one of the bravest and most hardened of the gang. Though despised at first, he soon proved bold and bad enough for the worst undertakings of the band. Johnson showed more wisdom than any of his confederates in his estimate of Will Scott. As soon as he took a good look at him, he pronounced him a spy, and advised Bass to get rid of him. Bass afterwards greatly regretted that he did not follow the advice. One other piece of advice given by Johnson, was, to leave Texas and go to Arkansas and rob a bank. Bass also regretted that he did not take this advice.

During this Salt Creek fight Henry Underwood, Henry Collins and Carter disappeared. Underwood was never seen again by Bass.

The next night after the battle the robbers stole some horses in the neighbourhood and, as has since been learned, directed their course towards their old hiding places in Denton and Cooke Counties. But they were not discovered again by their pursuers.

The Salt Creek fight, which occurred June 12th, virtually ended the great campaign against Bass. It began with a light skirmish April 24th, and continued seven weeks. During that time Bass and his men were almost continually harassed by their pursuers. They were kept on the run day and night, through the woods, across prairies, over swollen streams (for unprecedented rainfalls occurred during a greater part of the time), on horseback and on foot, and they were under fire something like a score of times. But still only one of the band was killed and none captured.

If the question be asked, why the campaign proved so fruitless, it should be answered because of the forests and the tangle wood. This gave the robbers all the advantage. They could hide in a moment, and could at any time turn upon their pursuers and shoot them down. That they did not kill them can only be accounted for on the supposition that Bass was determined not to stain his hands with blood if possible, to escape without it. He said afterwards, that he frequently lay in the woods within ten feet of his pursuers, but allowed them to pass unmolested.

Had he so determined, it is easy to see that he could soon have made it so fatal to pursuing parties that but few would have had the courage to follow his trail through the dense forests.

One of the most experienced detectives in the country gives it as his opinion that the tramping ground selected by Bass, is one of the best places in the country for such purposes. In Nebraska, where the Union Pacific robbery was committed, and in Kansas where Collins was captured, the country is open, and a single horseman can be seen for many miles away. It is difficult to pass in any direction without being discovered. But in Denton and adjoining counties, parties can ride through the forests for days without being noticed.

It must also be remembered that numerous confederates in all parts of the circuit constantly afforded invaluable assistance, supplying the robbers with provisions and conveying secret intelligence at the slightest note of alarm.

The campaign proves, that in such a country a pell-mell drive after robbers, is not the best way to capture them. Brains are better than eyes. The keen, strategic mind runs further, faster and more surely than the swiftest steed. Robbers are not wise. Their abandoned course shows a perversion and obscuration of intellect as well as of morals.

Again, all robbers are traitors to human society. By the very principle and practice of their profession they are easily led to betray one another. How well these principles were established before the close of Bass's career, will be seen in the subsequent narrative.

CHAPTER 17

Pipes and Herndon

We return now to the case of Pipes and Herndon and the other prisoners who had been captured and taken to Tyler to await the sitting of the Federal court. The bonds were fixed at a very high amount and the prisoners remained in jail until May 21st, when the case was called.

Long before the hour for opening court the room was crowded with spectators eager to catch a glimpse of the men who had dared to put the brakes upon a train without going through the formality of a regular engagement with the company.

The case was numbered 1456 and was entitled, "The United States *vs*. Sam Bass, *et al*."

The Prisoners brought to the bar were Samuel Pipes and Albert Herndon.

District Attorney Evans announced ready for trial. But the defendants, Judge Barksdale and Sawnie Robertson, of Dallas, and Robertson & Robertson, of Tyler, felt persuaded that there were several good reasons for delay.

First, they presented a plea in abatement, in substance alleging that two of the grand jury which preferred the indictment were disqualified, because they gave aid and comfort to the Confederacy in the late civil strife.

Mr. Sawnie Robertson presented the motion, and in a forcible argument insisted that the bill should be quashed. Judge Evans replied on the part of the government and made a considerable State's rights speech. Judge Barksdale closed the argument for the defendant.

The motion was overruled by the Judge.

Next the defendant's counsel made a motion to transfer the case from the District Court to the Circuit Court of the United States.

This met the same fate at the hands of the Court.

Col. John C. Robertson presented additional exceptions to the indictment, alleging that the description of the offense was insufficient.

This Judge Duval also overruled.

Next the defence asked for a continuance, pleading the absence of material witnesses and moving that the continuance be granted. The Judge replied that there was but one ground in the application on which he would grant the continuance, and that was that Mrs. Shipley, a material witness, was sick and unable to attend. After careful examination the continuance was granted on this ground. The case was therefore postponed until the court met at Austin, June 24th.

The prisoners were at once taken to Austin and placed in jail to await the calling of their case.

That they did not find this prison as pleasant as the free air of North Texas where they used to scamper over the prairies and run scrub races on Sunday and raise a wild whoop along the roads by night, is easily gathered from a brief description of the place given by one of their old neighbours, who, while attending the trial, visited their prison.

Passing through a hall walled in by solid masonry, the jailer unbolted a pair of heavy iron doors and he found himself in a large room filled with rows of iron cages. It was a hot day in July, and a July day in Austin is not to be described by any figure of speech which will not stand the test of white heat. The room was dark and not very well aired. The men were stripped to the waist and the perspiration was dripping from their bodies. The cages were of solid iron bars, the floor was sheeted with iron. There were no bedsteads in the cells, a blanket or quilt answered all sleeping purposes.

From one to three occupants were in a cage. There were more than three-score prisoners in all. Among them was the notorious John Wesley Hardin, accused of twenty-seven murders, and captured in Florida last summer, by running him off in a train of cars amid a shower of bullets which laid one of his confederates stark and stiff upon the sand and frightened a score of passengers out of all recollection of themselves. John wrestled and struggled on the floor while the train ran twenty-five miles and then cried all day because he had been caught.

He was pert and saucy as ever and advanced to the front of his cage for a chat.

"This is a very bad place to come to," said he, "people better keep out of here. They say there is honour among thieves, but don't you believe it. There's not a word of truth in it. When they can't steal from anybody else, they steal from one another. (A remark which had a terrible fulfilment for Bass a few days later.) They tell lots of lies about me. They say I killed six or seven men for snoring, but it isn't true. I only killed one man for snoring."

But Pipes and Herndon did not have to remain here long, for their trial opened July 2nd, and after a few days delay got well under headway. It ended July 17th with a verdict of "guilty of robbing the United States mail and endangering life." The jury affixing the penalty at ninety-nine years in the penitentiary, but the judge sentenced them for life, the difference being somewhat immaterial.

The principal part of the evidence for the prosecution was that already given in Will Scott's statements. He testified to the facts related in earlier chapters. The defence attempted to break down his testimony by an effort to prove that he did not relate these facts to Major Jones until after the arrest of the prisoners at the bar. They also attempted to prove an alibi, somewhat according to the plan intended by William Collins. The wife of Collins was present but was not allowed to testify.

After their conviction and especially while on their way to the penitentiary, the condemned men freely admitted their guilt, charging William Collins with getting them into their troubles. They said they were present at Mesquite and assisted in the robbery. They greatly praised Curley for his heroic defence of the express car, but attributed the numerous little gun-shot wounds received that night to the buckshot fired at them by the convict guards.

Scott Mayes, Monroe Hill and Bob Murphy were immediately rearrested on another charge. Afterwards they gave bonds for their appearance and were set at liberty.

Green Hill and the negro Scaggs are still in jail at Austin.

It is a well-established fact that just previous to William Collins' arrest he received eighteen hundred dollars from Bass. It is difficult to discover whether this money was intended for use in the trials of Bass's various friends, or whether, as is claimed by parties cognisant of the transaction, it was given for the purpose of establishing a stock ranch in the West, which was to be used by Bass and his band as a rendezvous.

Collins was taken with the remainder of the prisoners to Austin, but afterwards gave bonds in the sum of $15,000. But he jumped his bonds and the unfortunate sureties have been notified of the forfeiture by the U. S. Marshal. Unless Collins is speedily produced, there will be a nice little bill to pay. Collins' whereabouts since his hasty departure are unknown.

CHAPTER 18

The Betrayal

One of the disciples was pronounced a thief and it was prophesied that he would betray his Master.

John Wesley Hardin, whose native shrewdness and bitter experience make him a good authority on the subject, says there is no honour among thieves. Bass had many friends who constantly betrayed law and justice to shield him. At last, it was found that one these friends was just as ready to betray Bass himself, when the price was offered That price was not thirty pieces of silver, but liberty—liberty to go in the sweet sunshine and walk the green fields of earth.

As we have already seen, Jim Murphy and his father Henderson were among the prisoners taken to Tyler. As the flying train hurried Murphy away to prison, he was busily ransacking his brain for a plan of escape, and even before he crossed the dark threshold of the jail, he half determined upon a sacrifice of the leader of the bandits who had so often assisted him with his stolen gold. But as no one can tell the story better than Murphy has told it himself, and in order to avoid all appearance of injustice to the parties concerned, we give as it came from his own pen. In his statement made at Austin, July 26th, an exact copy which has been furnished us, he writes as follows:

> I will give you all the true statements of the plan that was laid to catch Sam Bass:
> I, W. Murphy, was arrested May 1st, 1878, by Sheriff Everheart, of Grayson County, for harbouring Sam Bass. I was innocent of the charge, and told Everheart so. I asked him why he did not tell me long ago that he wanted Sam Bass. He gave me no answer of any satisfaction but pushed me off from my family and put me in jail at Sherman. Walter Johnson took me from the Sherman jail and put me in jail in Tyler. On the way to the

jail at Tyler I hinted the plan for capturing Sam Bass to Taylor, and he said he would send Johnson to see me soon. Johnson came to see me after I had given bond. I told him that I could plan a job to capture Sam Bass if I was foot loose. Johnson told me that he would see me again soon. So, he went off and came back with June Peak, and we talked the matter over. June says, 'I will go and see Major Jones.'. The major came and talked with me about the plan for the capture of Bass.

At this time, I made a contract with Major Jones as to what he would do for me and my father if I would catch Sam Bass. He said if I would lay the plan for the capture of Sam Bass, that he would have my case and my father's dismissed, and that he would see that I should have my part of the reward' and his part too. He said that he did not want any of the reward, and that I should have what was right. I worked this plan under three men, Jones, Peak and Johnson. Nobody else was to know anything about it. They were the men I relied on. After a short time, Sheriff Everheart worked into the secret through Johnson. The first time that Everheart came to me I gave him no satisfaction. The second time he came a man by the name of Taylor was with him. Taylor told me that whatever Everheart told me would be all right with Johnson, and I let him into the secret against my own will.

The following is the memorandum of the contract entered into with U. S. Attorney Evans:

> Whereas, James Murphy stands indicted as an accessory in robbing the United States mails, in several cases now pending in the United States District Court at Tyler, and, whereas, I believe public justice will be best subserved, hereby, I, Andrew J. Evans, United States Attorney for the Western District of Texas, bind the United States as follows:
>
> 1st. If the said Murphy should leave Tyler, I will protect him and his bondsmen at this term of the court.
>
> 2nd. If the said Murphy shall be instrumental in securing the arrest and delivery to the United States Marshal of the Western District of Texas, of all or any one of the following principals, in their order (Bass, Jackson, Underwood, Barnes and Johnson) in said indictments, then all prosecutions are to be dismissed as to said Murphy; growing out of his acts as accessory to the said

principals; to be done upon certificate of Major John B. Jones. 3rd. In case the said Murphy shall use all reasonable and possible means in his power to capture the said Bass and his above-named associates, and if Major John B. Jones will certify to such facts to the United States District Attorney, then the said Murphy is to have the relief named in section 2nd above, although he may be unsuccessful. (Signed)   A. J. Evans, May 21st, 1878.   U. S. Attorney.

This contract, as seen by the date attached, was entered into May 21st, the first day of the trial at Tyler.

In order to convince Murphy of his sincerity and his power to secure his liberation from all charges, Major Jones had the case against his father dismissed at once. With many admonitions to prove faithful and perform his task well, he was allowed to go on his mission. It was immediately given out that he had "jumped his bond," and so published in the papers. Previous to Murphy's departure it was arranged that he should report progress to Major Jones, Captain Peak or Deputy Marshal Johnson, according as it was most convenient. It was also the purpose of Major Jones to keep Captain Peak's command at Dallas, so that Murphy would know where they were and could make his calculations accordingly. If word reached Peak that he was needed by Murphy, he was to hasten to the required point.

If, however, it was more convenient to communicate with Johnson, the latter was to immediately telegraph to Captain Peak at Dallas. But on account of the pressure of public opinion—because the public didn't understand the situation—it was found very difficult to keep Captain Peak's command at Dallas. People were greatly excited and extremely nervous lest Bass should escape. They were also impatient of the delays and failures which had attended the efforts of the sheriffs and rangers in Denton and the western counties. The air was constantly full of rumours, and every straw of Bass news was eagerly caught at by the reading public. Newspaper men were constantly on the alert for the latest, the truest or the wildest report about this "greatest of modern bandits." An amusing instance of this occurred to two newspaper reports in Dallas.

Notwithstanding the fact that the grass had been green upon the grave of Bass's mother for seventeen years, yet one of these reporters was suddenly persuaded one morning that he heard her name echoed through the air on the voice of the winds. He immediately laid plans to clutch the fact and make it his own. But we leave the story to a reporter who slyly watched proceedings and told it at the time as follows:

> This morning an item reached the ears of a newspaper man which was full of promise. He was told in confidence that Sam Bass's mother was in town, and the strides he made as he struck out for her supposed stopping place, the St. Charles hotel, were a wonder to see. Here was fruit, surely and he congratulated himself as he tore along at his good luck, and he chucked at the thought of having struck the biggest thing yet. In fact, he hadn't been so happy since the Saving's bank "busted." The proprietor of the hotel named was the first man run against, and the news gatherer pressed him into service and the two proceeded to find the individual who could put them on the track of Sammy's mamma. Their search was successful, and a sable gentleman with chalk eye and gizzard foot was ushered into the reportorial presence. Interrogatories breathless and pointed were put to him, and imagine the consternation created when he said the venerable Mrs. B. had just departed for Denton.
> Knowing the utter uselessness of trying to overtake a member of the Bass family, the reporter determined to make the most out of what the darkey knew about her, and a scorching examination revealed the fact that the woman told him that she was 'some kin to Massa Bass,' and considering her elderly appearance he 'kalkelated' she was his mother; and as she went towards Denton, he 'kalkelated' that town was her destination. This put a different face on matters, indeed. The reporter looked daggers at the man, threatened to stab him through and through with a Faber, and he would have reached the office sadder and wiser if it had not been for the fact that just as he was leaving another victimized newspaper man came stealing around, having gotten wind of the bonanza. 'Misery likes company,' you know, and No. 2 was permitted to work up the case, and together the boys shared the immense water haul.

CHAPTER 19

The Betrayer with the Band

The adventures of James Murphy in the prosecution of his plan to capture Bass are of thrilling interest and are given nearly as he afterwards related. As soon as he was released at Tyler, May 21st, he returned to his home near the line between Denton and Cooke counties. At that time Bass and his gang were in the mountains and cedar brakes of Stephens County. Murphy could not reach them at the time. But about two weeks later they returned to Denton County, and on the 6th of May dashed into the town of Denton. They were hotly pursued on the 6th, 7th and 8th and on the 9th, they took refuge at Murphy's house. When he saw them coming he is reported to have bounded forward to greet them with unbounded hypocritical enthusiasm. He told them, which was true, that he had been "laying out" for two weeks, trying to get with them, but the opportunity had never offered.

About this time, he learned that Sheriff Everhart was also in the secret and he entered into a plan at his own house to betray the band to him. Murphy told him he would have two of them back of his field that night and that he could arrest them if he wanted to. But for some reason which Murphy does not know the sheriff's party did not come. Murphy then mounted a good horse and arming himself with a six-shooter, went off with the band. As we have already seen, they continued their course towards Bolivar and secretly entered the town.

From Bolivar Bass hastened west to Wise County, where the Salt Creek fight occurred. While there, Bass stole some horses and returned to the north part of Denton County. Murphy says:

> I laid a plan to bring the gang to Bolivar, and after I got the gang there I told Clay Withers and Taylor just where the gang were, and that they would go to Billy Mount's stable, in Denton, to steal his horses, and I would stay outside. The men I had

there were Sam Bass and Frank Jackson. No action was taken that night. The next night three of us, Sam, Frank, and myself, went to Mount's stable and stole a horse, there in Denton, and then went to Elm Bottom. We stole the horse about 12 o'clock at night; Sam and Frank went into the stable and got the horse. We got to Elm Bottom about daylight and slept some fifteen or twenty minutes there. Then we went across Big Elm at Rock Crossing. We camped on this (east) side of Elm Bottom and stopped there for breakfast; laid there until noon; then Sam noticed a good many men on the road and directed us to saddle; then we went along the bottom to near Hilltown, where we camped again; stole some corn and had dinner. We then travelled through a big pasture and got kind of lost. We stopped at the house of a man named Burton, I think, some ten miles from Dallas, all night. Next day we went to W. O. Collins' and stopped there about two hours. Sam went there but could not get anything. We did not go to the house. We then went northeast to a church and met Seaborn Barnes.

While here Henry Collins, in company with a stranger, brought the news from Fort Worth that Jim was a traitor in the camp; that he was in collusion with the Rangers. Upon this Jim was notified that he would have to die, and they asked him what he had to say. Jim replied that it was all true what Collins said, but that he had entered into an agreement to get away from the officers of the law, inasmuch as he was indicted and would have to go to the penitentiary. His intention then as now, was to give them the "slip," and that if they would let him live and remain with them, he would take the lead in all they undertook.

Jackson plead for Murphy also. He said he had known him from a boy, and didn't believe that Murphy would betray them. They let the matter rest there. But Bass and Barnes were not convinced that all was right and were sullen all that night. The talk was a long and earnest one, and there is no doubt that the party were on the point of riddling Murphy with bullets. After that Bass kept a strict watch over him, and he found it almost impossible to communicate with anyone.

Murphy resumes his narrative of this and succeeding events as follows:

> It was this meeting with Barnes that nearly cost me my life, as on that night the rest of the crowd got the information that I was a spy. There was a stranger with Barnes when we met him.

We talked a long time there, and I convinced Frank Jackson that I had sold out to Major Jones to fool him and get out of a bad scrape myself. He stuck to me or I should have been killed that night, and I owe my life to him. After talking a long time, we started together and kept on towards Rockwall. The next night we stopped all night near Rockwall. The camp was near the edge of town, and while there, Bass looked up and saw the gallows on which a man had recently been hung.

He said, 'Boys, if I had seen that I would not have stopped here. It makes me feel bad to look at it. How I would hate to die on that.' (*Many readers will remember that this gallows was erected for the execution of Garner, the murderer of the sheriff. But the night before his execution, his wife went into the cell with poison upon her person, intending to die with him. The poison not proving sufficient, Garner hung his wife to the prison wall with the bale of a bucket, and then choked himself to death by filling his mouth and nostrils with strips of cloth torn from his clothes. When the jailor visited the cell at the dawn of day he had just expired. No greater prison horror has ever occurred in the country.*) We then struck out towards Terrell, and got there late in the evening and struck camp just south of the town about 8 p. m.

Next morning Bass and Jackson went into Terrell and viewed the bank, and came back and said they did not believe we could make it. I proposed viewing some other banks and taking the easiest. We then struck out for Kaufman, and Barnes and me went into Kaufman and bought a suit of clothes, and left my old clothes in the store, as a guide to Everheart and others who might bs on the hunt for us. We found no suitable bank there and passed on down to Ennis. I could not leave them a moment to telegraph, and had to stay with them. We stopped a day and night at Ennis. Sam and me examined the bank, and thought it unsafe to tackle it, as it was too high for us.

We then struck for Waco; reached there about 1 p. m., and camped on the north side of town. Frank and me went into town, looked around, put our horses into a livery stable, got shaved, got dinner in a restaurant, then got a $5 bill changed in the bank and saw lots of money, and we returned and reported to Bass, and I suggested that he (Bass) better go and see it as Frank Jackson was excited. Next morning, we were on the south side of town, and Bass and Jackson went and looked at it, and decided to rob the Waco bank. So that evening we all moved our camp up on the west side of the Bosque River, to look out a place to retreat to. Sam then proposed that Frank Jackson and me should go in and see where to hitch our horses and get some bacon, lard and coffee, and arrange for retreat if we robbed the bank.

On the way I worked upon Frank as to the dangers of it, so that he decided not to rob it, but I did not know what conclusion they had arrived at until next morning at breakfast. Up to this time I had no word from anybody, and was anxious to get someone on the trail. Bass said. 'Jim, we'll go where you say.' We then went south of town again, and that night, before leaving Waco, Seaborn Barnes went and stole a fine pacing mare, with two white hind feet, the one he had when he was killed.

At Belton I sold Seaborn Barnes' horse and gave a bill of sale in my name, to leave a clue. I also wrote a letter to Johnson and Everheart a few lines only—for God's sake come at once, as we are bound for Round Rock to rob the bank there. I slipped it in the post office. After we left Belton, we went to Georgetown. There I wrote to Major Jones, at Austin, that we were at Georgetown, and on our way to Round Rock to rob the railroad bank, or to be killed, and to prevent it for God's sake. I just got that letter in as Bass came in. He asked me what I was doing in there so long. I said I was trying to talk this man out of his paper. The man took the hint, threw down the paper, and said he would loan but said he could not sell it. Bass said 'that's all right,' and I read it to him one side. Then we went on to Round Rock and camped out about a quarter of a mile west of old Round Rock town, on the San Saba road, and bought feed and grub there from May & Black; also bought some in the town. This was on Sunday night. We fooled around until Friday. Some matters of local interest are not given in the above narrative.

At Terrell, Hall & Company's bank was thought the best one to rob, but they didn't think it safe to try the job. Their appearance in this town as afterwards described was as follows:

One drizzly day, some weeks ago, there rode down Moore Avenue five mounted men, with a shotgun each thrown across their saddles in front of them. The leader was a devil-may-care looking fellow, with a saucy cock of his *sombrero* on the side of his head, and an eye like an eagle. The balance of the cavalcade were rowdyish enough, wearing slop-shop clothes and rakish hats. They disappeared at the east end of the avenue and finally turned up on Bread Street on foot.

They were seen to enter Messrs. Holt Bevins & Cooley's bank, come out and walk up and down the Star Block, and then go in the direction of Uncle Jim Harris' livery stable. Back of this, it appears, they had hitched their horses, and springing into their saddles they rode leisurely in a north-easterly direction. It now turns out that these men were the famous bandits—Sam Bass and his reckless followers—as the description since minutely given of them, corresponds to a dot to the noted and chivalric brigand and his devoted men.

At Kaufman, they strolled around town during the afternoon, and went into camp in the woods nearby. The next morning Bass, Jackson and Murphy went back to the town, got their horses shod, Sam and Frank got shaved, went and got their horses after they were shod, put them in the livery stable and had them fed; and then went to the hotel and got their dinners. Then they went over to the east side of town and entered the largest store there was in town. The object was to find a safe to rob that night.

Sam Bass threw a twenty-dollar bill on the counter and asked the old man of the store to change it. He took the bill and went to the safe. When he opened the safe, Sam Bass took a good look into it, and afterwards said there was scarcely money enough in it to change the bill. They then returned to camp and started out for Ennis where they camped a mile from town. Bass and Murphy rode into Ennis and took a look at the bank. They put their horses in a livery stable, took dinner at a hotel, and took a second look at the Ennis bank and concluded that it was fixed too well to rob.

While at Waco, Bass went to the Ranche saloon, and after taking a drink threw a twenty-dollar gold piece on the counter. This was the last of the money obtained in the Union Pacific robbery, and he remarked afterwards, "It is all gone, now, and that is all the good it has done me."

Chapter 20

The Last Fight

As we have seen, according to Murphy's statement, the gang reached the vicinity of Round Rock Sunday evening, July 14th, and there went into camp. The next night they moved their camp nearer new Round Rock, south of the grave-yard, near some negro quarters. Here they remained, resting their horses and visiting the town, going into the bank and taking a good look at the situation. Bass and Murphy both had $5 bills changed at the bank. Murphy delayed the robbers as long as he could, in order to give Major Jones time to arrive. Finally, when their horses were fully rested and the bank and all its surroundings had been thoroughly examined, Bass fixed upon the following plan of robbery:

They were all to go to the bank on foot, leaving their horses hitched in an alley near the bank. Barnes was to give the cashier a $5 bill to change—the last they had, so it is said—and while he was doing this Bass was to go behind the counter and level his pistol at the cashier and make him hold up his hands, when Barnes would jump over the counter, take the money and put it in a sack. In the meantime, Jackson and Murphy were to stand in the door of the bank to keep anybody from coming in. After getting the money they were to move out the San Saba road a short distance, then turn to the right, go up west of Georgetown and make their way up to Denton, where they proposed to kill Deputy Sheriffs McGing and Wetzell, of Denton County.

They swore death to Billy Scott, the witness, if they had to ride to Dallas for him. Saturday, July 20th, was the day fixed upon for the robbery. It was to be in the afternoon just as the bank was to be closed, at which time they expected all the business men would have deposited their money.

In the meantime, Major Jones had received Murphy's letter from Belton and Georgetown at Austin. As soon as the letter reached him, he immediately sent to Lieutenant Reynolds, in command of a squad of rangers at Lampasas, to meet him at Round Rock the next morning. Three men were also sent to Round Rock early on the morning of the 18th, and the major himself followed on the first train. He took with him Maurice Moore, deputy sheriff of Travis County, whom he happened to meet on the street as he was going to the depot. Moore was formerly a sergeant in his command.

Arriving at Round Rock he went to the post office, expecting a letter from Murphy, but found none. He then warned the banker that the robbers were in the vicinity, and would probably attempt to rob them. He called on Deputy Sheriff Grimes, who was once a member of his command, and took him and Mr. Albert Highsmith into his confidence. They sent spies out to search the country round for the robbers' camp. At nightfall, having heard nothing of the robbers, and not knowing but what they had passed on to Austin, or concluded to strike the train at some other point, Major Jones notified Captain Hall and the sheriff and United States Marshal to look out for them in Austin, and telegraphed the railroad officers at Hearne and Austin to have the trains guarded.

That night he had his men concealed at the depot to protect the train, and also had the town thoroughly patrolled. Next morning his spies were out by daylight, searching the country for the camp. His men were instructed particularly to keep a lookout about the bank. About noon, having learned' that Lieutenant Reynolds had removed from Lampasas to San Saba, and fearing that he would not arrive in time, he telegraphed to Austin for Captain Hall, who arrived at 2 o'clock p. m. After consultation they telegraphed to Austin for Lieutenant Armstrong and some of Hall's men, as it was supposed the robbers numbered seven or eight men.

The critical hour was not at hand. But we turn back for a moment to follow the movements of the robbers as they approached the scene of deadly conflict.

Murphy says:

> Friday morning, the 19th, Frank Jackson and me went into town to look for rangers, as Sam Bass said he saw two rangers who looked like cowboys. So, we went to see, and we could not find any, and at eleven o'clock we left town and reported to Bass. We then smoked awhile, and agreed that all should go to town after some tobacco and things, as we should rob the

bank next day. When we arrived at the old town I suggested remaining there to see if I could learn anything of the rangers. They agreed to this, and Bass, Barnes and Jackson went into the new town.

Murphy's work was now accomplished. What immediately follows is best told by Deputy Sheriff Maurice Moore:

> About 4 p. m., I was standing in front of Smith's livery stable, and three men passed up the street. Smith remarked to me, 'There go three strangers.' I noticed them carefully and thought one of them had a six-shooter under his coat. The others were carrying saddle-bags. They looked at me rather hard and went across the street into a store. I walked up the street to where Grimes, the Deputy Sheriff of Williamson County was standing, and remarked to him, 'I think one of those men has a six-shooter on.' Grimes remarked to me, 'Let me go over and see.' We walked across the street and went into the store. Not wishing to let them know I was watching them, I stood up inside the store door with my hands in my pockets, whistling. Grimes approached them carelessly and asked one if he had got a six-shooter. They all three replied, 'Yes,' and at the same instant two of them shot Grimes and one shot me.
>
> After I had fired my first shot, I could not see the men on account of the smoke. They continued shooting and so did I, until I fired five shots; as they passed out, I saw one man bleeding from the arm and side; I then leaned against the store door, feeling faint and sick, and recovering myself, I started on and fired the remaining shot at one of the men.
>
> Having lent one of my pistols to another man the day before, I stopped and reloaded my pistol, went into the stable and got my Winchester and started in pursuit of them, and was stopped by Dr. Morris, who said, 'Hold on; don't go any further, for if you get over-heated your wound may kill you;' I stopped and gave my Winchester to another man; went with the doctor and Judge Schultz to the hotel; Grimes did not have time to draw his pistol; six bullet holes were put through his body.

Sheriff Moore was shot through the left lung.

In the meantime, the three rangers had come from where they were stationed and fired on the robbers as they retreated across the street. Major Jones, who was coming from the telegraph office when the firing began, ran to the Robinson corner, when seeing the situation, he called on his men, drew his pistol, ran up the street, and when within fifty yards of the robbers, commenced firing upon them. One of the robbers turned as he reached the corner around which they are retreating and fired deliberately at Major Jones, the ball passing over his head and entering the wall of a building in his rear. At this time the excitement in the town was fearful to witness.

Men were running in every direction, some to get out of range of the whistling bullets and take shelter behind a friendly corner, tree or post; others to get such arms as they could lay their hands on and join in the fight; women and children were screaming and flying from the houses between and around which the robbers were retreating. All this presented a scene which beggars description. The robbers retreated across the street, half way up the square and down the alley, at the lower end of which their horses were hitched, closely pursued and constantly fired at by rangers and citizens, but taking shelter and firing back at their pursuers at every convenient place. When half way down the alley, Bass received his second wound, the one which caused his death.

This fatal shot which ended the wild career of the robber chieftain, was fired by George Harrell, a ranger.

Just as the robbers reached their horses, R. C. Ware, one of the rangers, took deliberate aim at one of them and shot him through the head, killing him instantly. As the other two mounted and ran off, Major Jones, Ware, and J. F. Tubbs, a one-armed citizen who had taken Grimes' pistol and joined in the fight, fired several shots at them but without effect. F. L. Jordan fired at the robbers from the back door of his store as they ran down the alley. Albert Highsmith shot at them from the back yard of his stable, and might have killed one of them had not a cartridge shell hung in his Winchester.

Captain Hall was at the hotel lying down when the fight started, but was quickly on the spot with Winchester and pistol in hand, mounted a horse which happened to be 'near and, accompanied by the three rangers, one of whom rode the dead robber's (Barnes) horse, gave chase to the flying robbers. Several citizens who had horses at hand went with him. As soon as Major Jones could get a horse, he, accompanied by Major Dick Mangrum and several other citizens, went in pursuit of the robbers also, but they did not go more than two or three miles before the old plug which the major had gotten from the livery stable played out and the party returned.

Capt. Hall pursued the robbers until the trail was lost in the brush and then returned to town, as it was too near night and his horses were too nearly broken down to follow further.

When the flying robbers passed through old Round Rock, Jim Murphy was still there and saw them as they dashed by. He says:

> I was sitting in a door at old Round Rock as they came by, and Frank was holding Bass on his horse. Bass looked pale and sickly, and his hand was bleeding, and he seemed to be working cartridges into his pistol. Jackson looked at me as much as to say, Jim, save yourself if you can. Barnes had been killed instantly. I then saw Major Jones go by, and hallooed to him, but he did not hear me. I then went into the new town; there was a good deal of excitement, and someone asked who the dead man was. I said if it is the Bass gang, it must be Seaborn Barnes. Someone asked how they would know. I said he has got four bullet holes in his legs—three in his right and one in his left leg, which he got at Mesquite. They found the wounds, and was going to arrest me, when Major Jones came up, and shortly after recognised me, and I went down with him and identified the dead body as that of Seaborn Barnes."

About two hours after the fight, Lieutenant Reynolds arrived with ten men, having ridden from San Saba, a distance of one hundred miles since seven o'clock the evening before. He left his men a mile or two out of town and came in to report to Major Jones secretly before bringing his men in.

Later in the evening Lieutenant Armstrong's party from Austin arrived.

Chapter 21

Capture and Death

It was fully known that one of the robbers who had escaped was badly wounded, as he made two attempts before he was able to mount his saddle. He was also seen holding up his hand as he dashed away, and apparently maintained his seat with great difficulty. As we have already seen, Murphy was very positive that this was Bass.

Major Jones was therefore greatly elated with the prospect of his capture early the next morning. As soon as it was light, Sergeant Nevill of Lieutenant Reynold's company, with eight men was sent out to look for the trail and continue the pursuit. Deputy Sheriff Tucker, of Georgetown, was sent along as guide, as he was thoroughly acquainted with the country. The party proceeded to the point where the trail was lost the evening before. This was about four miles from town. Soon after arriving there, a man was noticed lying under a tree, not far from the new railroad, but as there were some mules grazing nearby and as the railroad hands were not far distant Sheriff Tucker said it must be one of the hands and no further attention was paid to him.

The lost trail was found and followed until it divided. After wandering about for some time Sergeant Nevill again emerged upon the prairie, and meeting one of the railroad hands asked him if he had seen a wounded man in the vicinity. He replied that there was a man lying under "that tree out there," pointing to the man seen before, "who was hurt, and who said that he was a cattle man from one of the lower counties, and had been in Round Rock the day before and getting into a little difficulty, had been shot." Sergeant Nevill at once approached the tree and when within about twenty feet of it the wounded man held up his hand and said: "Don't shoot; I am unarmed and helpless; I am the man you are looking for; I am Sam Bass!"

He had parted with Jackson the evening before after giving him his rifle, pistol and pocket-book, feeling convinced that he would never need them again. During the long, weary hours of the night he lay in the silent woods alone, his body wracked by pain and his mind harassed with the hopelessness of escape.

In the morning he dragged himself out in the hope of obtaining help. Soon after a negro came by with a team and he tried to hire him to haul him away and secrete him, but failed.

Major Jones was notified, and in company with Dr. Cochran, a physician of Round Rock, went out with an ambulance to bring the prisoner in. After an examination of his wounds, the doctor pronounced them fatal and assured the bold bandit that his last hour was close at hand. Bass was fully persuaded of the truth of the doctor's opinion and expressed no hope of recovery.

He was placed in the ambulance and taken to Round Rock, and at once it was telegraphed abroad that he was dying. The fatal bullet had entered the small of the back and come out in front. Much attention was shown him by Major Jones and all present, and nothing was left undone to soothe his pains, in hope of gaining his confidence and softening his fixed determination to reveal nothing against his confederates who were still at large.

He continued in a sinking condition during Saturday, but Sunday morning seemed much better and at once began to entertain a hope of recovery. His physician besought him to make a confession, as he must soon die and appear before the Great Judge. But the wounded robber turned and looking coolly up at the doctor, said, "don't you be too sure of that."

Major Jones tried every inducement to secure important statements from him, and someone was constantly present with paper and pencil in hand, to write down his utterances, but nothing valuable in the way of evidence, escaped from his lips. His self-control and resolute purpose to remain faithful to his friends were wonderful. Though surrounded by a number of shrewd men and though constantly interrogated by one whose long experience in the capture of outlaws had given him a keen insight into their disposition and made him an adept in handling them, and though the death damp was gathering upon his brow, and final dissolution was wrenching body and spirit apart, yet his wonderful shrewdness and sagacity of instinct remained intact. Had he been seated at a camp fire in his old fastness, surrounded by his pals and sound in health and limb, he could not more successfully have parried the interrogatives put to him and thwarted the purpose of his captor. Major Jones said:

I tried every conceivable plan to obtain some information from him, but to no purpose. About noon on Sunday, he began to suffer greatly and sent for me to know if I could not give him some relief. I did everything I could for him. Thinking this an excellent opportunity, I said to him, 'Bass, you have done much wrong in this world, you now have an opportunity to do some good before you die by giving some information which will lead to the vindication of that justice which you have so often defied and the law which you have constantly violated.' He replied, 'No, I won't tell.' 'Why won't you?' said I. 'Because it is agin my profession to blow on my pals. If a man knows anything he ought to die with it in him.' He positively refused to converse on religion and in reply to some remark made, he said 'I am going to Hell, anyhow.'

I made a particular effort to obtain some information from him in regard to William Collins. I asked him if he was ever at Collins' house. He said no. I then put the question in a different form, saying 'where did you first see Will Scott?' He replied at Bob Murphy's. I then said, 'You saw him at Green Hill's too, didn't you?' He replied, 'yes.' These answers were not of any consequence, but I then said, 'when did you see him at William Collins?' He said, 'I don't remember, as I never paid attention to dates, being always on the scout, I only saw him these three times.' This answer was important, as it fixed the fact that Bass was at Collins' house. But this was the only statement of any importance which he made. All his other statements were of facts well known or concerning individuals beyond the reach of future justice.

Among these statements he said:

I am twenty-seven years old, have brothers John and Denton, at Mitchell, Indiana. Have been in the robbing business a long time. Had done much business of that kind before the U. P. robbery last fall.

Q.—How came you to commence this kind of life?

A.—Started out sporting on horses.

Q.—Why did you get worse than horse racing?

A.—Because they robbed me of my first $300.

Q.—After they robbed you, what did you do next?

A.—Went to robbing stages in the Black Hills—robbed seven. Got very little money. Jack Davis, Nixon and myself were all that were in the Black Hills stage robberies. Joel Collins, Bill Heffrige, Tom Nixon, Jack Davis, Jim Berry and me were in the Union Pacific robbery. Tom Nixon is in Canada. Have not seen him since that robbery. Jack Davis was in New Orleans from the time of the Union Pacific robbery till he went to Denton to get me to go in with him and buy a ship. This was the last of April, 1878. Gardner, living in Atascosa County, is my friend. Was at his house last fall. Went to Kansas with him once. Will not tell who was in the Eagle Ford robbery besides myself and Barnes. When we were in the store at Round Rock, Grimes asked me if I had a pistol, I said yes; then all three of us drew our pistols and shot him. If I killed Grimes, it was the first man I ever killed. Henry Collins was with me in the Salt Creek fight four or five weeks ago. Arkansas Johnson was killed in that fight. Don't know whether Underwood was wounded or not at Salt Creek fight. 'Sebe' Barnes, Frank Jackson and Charles Carter were there. We were all set afoot in that fight, but stole horses enough to remount ourselves in three hours, or as soon as dark came; after which we went back to Denton. Stayed there until we came to Round Rock.

Q.—Where is Jackson now?

A.—I don't know.

Q.—How do you usually meet after being scattered?

A.—Generally told by friends.

Q.—Who are these friends?

A. I will not tell.

This was his usual reply to questions which he did not wish to answer, and was in the most deliberate manner possible.

Even in the midst of his intense agony on Sunday afternoon he clung to the delusion that he would recover. But about twenty minutes before his death, when warned by his physician that dissolution was near at hand, he calmly replied, 'let me go.'

A few minutes later he said to his nurse, "the world is bobbing around me." His pains had ceased and he rested at ease. There were a few gasps and he was dead. This was at 4 p. m., Sunday, June 21st.

The next day the body was interred at Round Rock. And thus, the earth gathered back to her bosom one who had lived to harass and torment his kind.

What is known in regard to the rest of the band is easily told. Jackson made good his escape, reaching Denton County two hundred miles distant after a three days ride. But his capture may occur at any time. Underwood had not been seen since the Salt Creek fight, and his whereabouts are unknown. Carter, who joined Bass towards the last, is said to have been sent out of the country by his father. The two Collins, under indictment by the grand jury, are still in concealment. Jim Murphy received his reward, and is now at his home near Rosston in Denton County.

Chapter 22

Notes and Comments

It is now evident that there was some remissness in not making a more prompt and determined effort to hunt down the train robbers before they had so successfully repeated their outrages. It must also be admitted that the great campaign against Bass in Denton and Wise counties was not a success. But after all the State of Texas has reason to congratulate herself on what has been accomplished. The first robbery was committed February 22nd, and before that date in July the leader of the gang and two of his leading accomplices had been laid in bloody graves, three others had been convicted and sent to the penitentiary, one other is still in jail, five others have been indicted and arrested as accessories, and are now out on bond, two others under arrest were allowed their liberty for services rendered the State. Only two principal members of the band, Jackson and Underwood have made their escape.

This makes an excellent showing for our authorities, and speaks well for the determined and efficient manner in which the band has been hunted down amid wild woods and a sparsely populated country. It was thought that much was accomplished by the pursuers of the Union Pacific robbers and yet only three out of six of the robbers were captured. But in the case of the Texas train robbers, six out of eight of the principals in the crimes have been killed or convicted. If we number Green Hill and William Collins among the principals, the former is safe in jail at Austin, and the appearance of the latter before court is secured by a $15,000 bond.

In regard to the failure of the campaign against Bass, justice requires that Captain Peak should be set right before public opinion. For all that occurred between April 24th and May 21st he is responsible to the just expectations of the public. But it must be remembered that on May 21st the contract was entered into with James Murphy to betray Bass, and in furtherance of this purpose it was arranged that Captain Peak should hold his force at or near Dallas.

The agreement with Murphy being necessarily concealed from the public some unjust criticism was indulged in against Captain Peak for his inaction. But now that the whole plan has been uncovered, it is plain that he was fully justified in holding his command stationary at a convenient point whore Murphy could readily reach him with his communications. But on account of the pressure of public opinion he was compelled to continue more actively in the pursuit of the gang than was deemed desirable. This led to the pursuit of the band into Wise County and the fight at Salt Creek the only fight in the long pursuit which was attended by a good result.

In regard to the action of sheriffs and local authorities there is also need of a word of explanation and justification. The laws of the State make no provision for the expenses of a sheriff's posse engaged in a prolonged pursuit of outlaws. It matters not how far or how long a sheriff may ride, or how many armed and mounted men he may employ to assist him, or how much money he may spend on the trip, he is only allowed one dollar each for the criminals he may capture, and that after conviction. The Sheriff of Dallas County declared that he could not pursue that gang who robbed the trains in the county, because he could not afford it.

It will be a very important question for our next Legislature to consider, whether the laws should not be amended in this respect, and our local authorities strengthened and made far more efficient by a proper provision for necessary expenses in cases of emergency.

Another very important question which should also be considered, is whether it would not be well for the State to employ a regular force of detectives to ferret out and secure the arrest of criminals.

It is well known that there are many outlaws and fugitives from justice in the State. A list of four thousand was published not long since, and this did not include reports from a large number of counties. Many criminals have also escaped from other States and fled to Texas for refuge. Against these outlaws the State police is performing very efficient service. But their efforts should be supplemented by detectives, working secretly among the outlaws, discovering them in their hiding places and securing the proper chain of evidence for their conviction.

There has been too much of a tendency heretofore to rely upon revolvers and bold riders. But it should be remembered that the pell-mell drive after Bass accomplished little, while to a spy and to a betrayer we are primarily indebted for the capture of leading members and final overthrow of the band. The method pursued for the breaking up of the Molly Maguires is very instructive in this connection. This was, perhaps, the worst combination of outlaws ever known in this country. When Franklin B. Gowan, president of the Beading railroad, determined to break it up, he employed the ablest of Pinkerton's detectives to accomplish the task. They went into the counties infested by the members of the organisation, and continued their efforts until they arrested and convicted more than sixty of the outlaws, many of whom were hung. Similar service against the, thousands of criminals who infest the State, would undoubtedly be attended with most important results.

But back of all considerations of the best method of pursuing criminals, lies a still more important question not only for the State Government but for society, and that is how to prevent men from becoming criminals. The occasional case of Sam Bass's criminal career is easily stated. He, himself, and his employees, and neighbours say, that it was the purchase of the race mare. Horseracing soon led him into a career of idleness and dissipation, and from that the descent to open outlawry was easy.

That the influence of horse-racing and gaming was ruinous in this instance, is a plain fact, testified to in the dying confession of a slain outlaw. That it is almost invariably demoralising must be admitted by all. It should not, therefore, be encouraged by the laws of the State or voluntary organisation of the people. When our fair associations devote the larger part of their premiums to horse-racing, and when they admit all forms of light gaming to a place among their exhibitions, they do more to demoralise the young and to impair the moral integrity of a community than they do to promote its industrial and agricultural interests.

Again, it should not be forgotten that Sam Bass was uneducated. For this Texas was not responsible, for he was a young ignoramus thrust upon us by Indiana. But ignorance is a fruitful source of crime and costs the State infinitely more than education. We can never prevent crime until we go back to the sources of intellectual and moral life. The work must bs begun near the cradle, and pursued with never wearying vigilance until the character is fully matured and the mind thoroughly imbued with the highest and noblest principles.

In conclusion, one word to the young. The history of these robbers is an appalling argument against such a life. Their career was very short. They were driven from the face of their fellowmen. Their ill-gotten gains did them no good. Vengeance came swift and terrible, and in a few days, or at most a few short months, they were in bloody graves, or imprisoned at hard labour and forever disgraced. Mankind rejoiced at their fall. For those who lift their hands against law and order, the world has only condemnation disgrace and death.

To mark the grave of that restless man a simple monument stands in the little town of Round Rock bearing the inscription

Samuel Bass
Born July 21st, 1851
Died July 21st, 1878
A Brave Man Reposes in Death Here. Why Was He Not True?

Sam Bass was true to his friends and his convictions, but what of Jim Murphy? That man, hated of all men, despised even by the rangers whom he had served, returned to Denton. Words cannot express the supreme contempt and hatred for the man (used for classification only) who, like a rattlesnake, turned and bit the one who befriended him. A guilty conscience weighing heavily upon him caused him to seek protection from the sheriff when his distorted imagination led him to believe Frank Jackson was lying around in the Elm Bottoms waiting for a chance to kill him. The sheriff granted him permission to take up his abode in the jail. However, his stay in his jail home was of short duration, as in a few weeks his ignominious career was brought to a close by suicide.

ALSO FROM LEONAUR
AVAILABLE IN SOFTCOVER OR HARDCOVER WITH DUST JACKET

THE FALL OF THE MOGHUL EMPIRE OF HINDUSTAN *by H. G. Keene*—By the beginning of the nineteenth century, as British and Indian armies under Lake and Wellesley dominated the scene, a little over half a century of conflict brought the Moghul Empire to its knees.

LADY SALE'S AFGHANISTAN *by Florentia Sale*—An Indomitable Victorian Lady's Account of the Retreat from Kabul During the First Afghan War.

THE CAMPAIGN OF MAGENTA AND SOLFERINO 1859 *by Harold Carmichael Wylly*—The Decisive Conflict for the Unification of Italy.

FRENCH'S CAVALRY CAMPAIGN *by J. G. Maydon*—A Special Correspondent's View of British Army Mounted Troops During the Boer War.

CAVALRY AT WATERLOO *by Sir Evelyn Wood*—British Mounted Troops During the Campaign of 1815.

THE SUBALTERN *by George Robert Gleig*—The Experiences of an Officer of the 85th Light Infantry During the Peninsular War.

NAPOLEON AT BAY, 1814 *by F. Loraine Petre*—The Campaigns to the Fall of the First Empire.

NAPOLEON AND THE CAMPAIGN OF 1806 *by Colonel Vachée*—The Napoleonic Method of Organisation and Command to the Battles of Jena & Auerstädt.

THE COMPLETE ADVENTURES IN THE CONNAUGHT RANGERS *by William Grattan*—The 88th Regiment during the Napoleonic Wars by a Serving Officer.

BUGLER AND OFFICER OF THE RIFLES *by William Green & Harry Smith*—With the 95th (Rifles) during the Peninsular & Waterloo Campaigns of the Napoleonic Wars.

NAPOLEONIC WAR STORIES *by Sir Arthur Quiller-Couch*—Tales of soldiers, spies, battles & sieges from the Peninsular & Waterloo campaingns.

CAPTAIN OF THE 95TH (RIFLES) *by Jonathan Leach*—An officer of Wellington's sharpshooters during the Peninsular, South of France and Waterloo campaigns of the Napoleonic wars.

RIFLEMAN COSTELLO *by Edward Costello*—The adventures of a soldier of the 95th (Rifles) in the Peninsular & Waterloo Campaigns of the Napoleonic wars.

AVAILABLE ONLINE AT www.leonaur.com
AND FROM ALL GOOD BOOK STORES

ALSO FROM LEONAUR
AVAILABLE IN SOFTCOVER OR HARDCOVER WITH DUST JACKET

OFFICERS & GENTLEMEN by *Peter Hawker & William Graham*—Two Accounts of British Officers During the Peninsula War: Officer of Light Dragoons by Peter Hawker & Campaign in Portugal and Spain by William Graham .

THE WALCHEREN EXPEDITION by *Anonymous*—The Experiences of a British Officer of the 81st Regt. During the Campaign in the Low Countries of 1809.

LADIES OF WATERLOO by *Charlotte A. Eaton, Magdalene de Lancey & Juana Smith*—The Experiences of Three Women During the Campaign of 1815: Waterloo Days by Charlotte A. Eaton, A Week at Waterloo by Magdalene de Lancey & Juana's Story by Juana Smith.

JOURNAL OF AN OFFICER IN THE KING'S GERMAN LEGION by *John Frederick Hering*—Recollections of Campaigning During the Napoleonic Wars.

JOURNAL OF AN ARMY SURGEON IN THE PENINSULAR WAR by *Charles Boutflower*—The Recollections of a British Army Medical Man on Campaign During the Napoleonic Wars.

ON CAMPAIGN WITH MOORE AND WELLINGTON by *Anthony Hamilton*—The Experiences of a Soldier of the 43rd Regiment During the Peninsular War.

THE ROAD TO AUSTERLITZ by *R. G. Burton*—Napoleon's Campaign of 1805.

SOLDIERS OF NAPOLEON by *A. J. Doisy De Villargennes & Arthur Chuquet*—The Experiences of the Men of the French First Empire: Under the Eagles by A. J. Doisy De Villargennes & Voices of 1812 by Arthur Chuquet .

INVASION OF FRANCE, 1814 by *F. W. O. Maycock*—The Final Battles of the Napoleonic First Empire.

LEIPZIG—A CONFLICT OF TITANS by *Frederic Shoberl*—A Personal Experience of the 'Battle of the Nations' During the Napoleonic Wars, October 14th-19th, 1813.

SLASHERS by *Charles Cadell*—The Campaigns of the 28th Regiment of Foot During the Napoleonic Wars by a Serving Officer.

BATTLE IMPERIAL by *Charles William Vane*—The Campaigns in Germany & France for the Defeat of Napoleon 1813-1814.

SWIFT & BOLD by *Gibbes Rigaud*—The 60th Rifles During the Peninsula War.

AVAILABLE ONLINE AT www.leonaur.com
AND FROM ALL GOOD BOOK STORES

www.ingramcontent.com/pod-product-compliance
Lightning Source LLC
Chambersburg PA
CBHW031618160426
43196CB00006B/179